HANSARD SOCIETY SERIES IN POLITICS
AND GOVERNMENT

Edited by F.F. Ridley

HANSARD SOCIETY SERIES IN POLITICS AND GOVERNMENT

Edited by F.F. Ridley

The Quango Debate, edited with David Wilson

British Government and Politics since 1945: Changes in Perspectives, edited with Michael Rush

Sleaze: Politicians, Private Interests and Public Reaction, edited with Alan Doig

Women in Politics, edited with Joni Lovenduski and Pippa Norris

Under the Scott-Light: British Government seen Through the Scott Report, edited with Brain Thompson

Britain Votes 1997, edited with Pippa Norris and Neil T. Gavin

Protest Politics: Cause Groups and Campaigns, edited with Grant Jordan

Parliament in the Age of the Internet, edited by Stephen Coleman, John Taylor and Wim van de Donk

Democracy and Cultural Diversity, edited by Michael O'Neill and Dennis Austin

Britain Votes 2001, edited by Pippa Norris

Women, Politics, and Change, edited by Karen Ross

Britain Votes 2005, edited by Pippa Norris and Christopher Wlezien

The Hansard Society Series in Politics and Government brings to the wider public the debates and analyses of important issues first discussed in the pages of its journal, Parliamentary Affairs

Britain Votes 2005

Edited by Pippa Norris and Christopher Wlezien

OXFORD JOURNALS
OXFORD UNIVERSITY PRESS

in association with

HANSARD SOCIETY SERIES IN POLITICS
AND GOVERNMENT

OXFORD

UNIVERSITY PRESS

Great Clarendon Street, Oxford OX2 6DP

Oxford University Press is a department of the University of Oxford.
It furthers the University's objective of excellence in research, scholarship,
and education by publishing worldwide in

Oxford New York

Athens Auckland Bangkok Bagota Buenos Aires Calcutta
Cape Town Dar es Salaam Delhi Florence Hong Kong Istanbul
Karachi Kuala Lumpur Madrid Melbourne Mexico City Mumbai
Nairobi Paris São Paulo Shanghai Singapore Taipei Tokyo Toronto Warsaw
and associated companies in
Berlin Ibadan

Oxford is a registered trade mark of Oxford University Press
in the UK and in certain other countries

Published in the United states
by Oxford University Press Inc., New York

A catalogue for this book is available from the British Library

Library of Congress Cataloging in Publication Data

ISBN 019 856940 8

Typeset by Integra Software Services Pvt. Ltd, Pondicherry
Printed in Great Britain by Bell & Bain Ltd, Glasgow
on acid-free paper

Contents

Contributors

Robert Andersen is Senator William McMaster Chair in Political Sociology at McMaster University

John Bartle is Senior Lecturer in the Department of Government, Essex University

Rosie Campbell is a Lecturer in research methods at Birkbeck College, University of London

Harold D. Clarke is Ashbel Smith Distinguished professor, School of Social Sciences, University of Texas at Dallas and Adjunct professor, Department of Government, University of Essex. He is co-director of the 2005 British Election Study

Ivor Crewe is Professor of Government and Vice Chancellor of Essex University

John Curtice is Professor of Politics and Director of the Social Statistics Laboratory at Strathclyde University and Deputy Director of the Centre for Research into Elections and Social Trends

Patrick Dunleavy is Professor of Political Science and Public Policy, LSE Public Policy Group, London School of Economics and Political Science

Geoffrey Evans is Official Fellow in Politics, Nuffield College, and Professor of the Sociology of Politics, Oxford University

Ron Johnston is Professor in the School of Geographical Sciences at the University of Bristol

Joni Lovenduski is the Anniversary Professor of Politics, Birkbeck College, University of London

Charles Pattie is a Professor in the Department of Geography at the University of Sheffield

Peter Snowdon is a freelance writer whose books include *The Conservative Party: An Illustrated History*, 2004.

Marianne C. Stewart is Professor and Executive Dean, School of the Social Sciences, University of Texas at Dallas and Adjunct Professor, Department of Government, university of Essex. She is co-director of the 2005 British Election Study

Helen Margetts is Professor of Society and Internet, Oxford Internet Institute, Oxford University

Pippa Norris is the McGuire Lecturer in Comparative Politics, John F. Kennedy School of Government and the Government Department, Harvard University

David Rossiter is a Senior Research Fellow in the Department of Geography at the University of Leeds

Andrew Russell is Senior Lecturer, Department of Government, International Relations, and Philosophy, University of Manchester

David Sanders is Professor and Head of the Department of Government at Essex University. He is co-director of the 2005 British Election Study

Anthony Seldon is Headmaster of Brighton College and co-founding Director of the Institute for Contemporary British History

Paul Webb is Professor of Politics, Department of International Relations and Politics, University of Sussex

Paul Whiteley is a Professor in the Department of Government at Essex University. He is co-director of the 2005 British Election Study

Christopher Wlezien is Professor of Political Science at Temple University and he was Reader in Comparative Government and Fellow of Nuffield College at Oxford University

Dominic Wring is Senior Lecturer in Communications and Media Studies, Department of Social Sciences, Loughborough University

Preface and Acknowledgments

This book and special issue of *Parliamentary Affairs* is the third in the series published after each election since 1992 by Oxford University Press. The study, as ever, owes multiple debts to many friends and colleagues. The volume received encouragement in conversations over the years with many colleagues and we are most grateful to all those who went out of their way to share datasets and to provide feedback on draft chapters. Amongst others, particular thanks are due to Jim Alt, David Butler, John Curtice, Jim Cronin, David Denver, Steve Fisher, Mark Franklin, Jane Green, Peter Hall, Ron Johnston, Peter Kellner, Colin Rallings, James Tilley, and Michael Thrasher.

The book could not have been written without the evidence collected by collaboration amongst many colleagues. The study owes a large debt of gratitude to all who conducted the British Election Study 2005 surveys, and who assembled and released the initial Campaign Rolling Panel Survey and the Pre-Election Survey datasets in such timely fashion, especially the principal investigators Harold Clarke, David Sanders, Marianne Stewart and Paul Whiteley, the BES research officer Kristi Winters, as well as ESRC which generously supported the BES survey. We also greatly appreciate the support of Clare Ettinghausen and Declan McHugh at the Hansard Society and the assistance of Howard Goodman, James Garmston, and Chris Mead at the Press Association for release of the constituency results for the 2005 election. *The British Parliamentary Constituency Dataset 1992–2005*, assembled for this volume with the election results and the census data, is available for downloading from www.pippanorris.com. We would like to thank Richard Cracknell and his team at the House of Commons Library for kind permission to reproduce the maps included in chapter 1. We also appreciate the help of Nick Sparrow who generously supplied the pooled ICM survey dataset from the election. The annual conference of the Elections, Parties and Public Opinion (EPOP) section of the PSA has also provided invaluable feedback on British elections and voting behavior over the years.

The support of Oxford University Press has been invaluable, particularly the efficient assistance and continuous enthusiasm of our editors, Martin Green and Gill Mitchell. We also appreciate the research assistance of Andrew Vogt at Harvard. Lastly, this book would not have been possible without the encouragement and stimulation provided by many colleagues and students at the John F. Kennedy School of Government and the Department of Government, Harvard University, as well as at Nuffield College, the University of Oxford and Temple University.

Pippa Norris and Christopher Wlezien

PIPPA NORRIS AND CHRISTOPHER WLEZIEN

Introduction

The Third Blair Victory: How and Why?

The results of the 5 May 2005 UK general election produced mixed signals for all the main parties, whether the outcome was judged by the criteria of power, seats, or votes. The 1997 general election first swept Tony Blair triumphantly into Downing Street with a massive landslide of seats. The 2001 contest consolidated new Labour's ascendancy at Westminster, leaving their majority almost untouched.[1] The regular swing of the pendulum in postwar British politics usually brings a rotation of the parties in power. The election on 5 May 2005 broke records, however, by returning a third successive Labour government, the first time in British history that the party had ever achieved a consecutive hat trick. The closest postwar parallel was Mrs. Thatcher's hegemony from 1979 to 1987. The contest elected 356 Labour members, generating a solid 66-seat parliamentary majority for the Blair government, albeit one more vulnerable to backbench rebellions.

This book seeks to tell the story of how and why Labour won a historic victory on 5 May. Should the outcome be seen as public endorsement of the performance of the Labour government in delivering a healthy British economy and better public services during their eight years in power? Rather than issues, was the result due to the personal popularity of Tony Blair and public perceptions of the effectiveness and competence of the Labour leadership team, compared with evaluations of Michael Howard and the Conservative shadow cabinet? Did party activities, media coverage, and opinion polls published during the official campaign play a vital role by shaping the public's issues agenda and influencing party images? Or was the outcome determined far earlier than this, due to partisan bias towards Labour in the electoral system used for Westminster? These are just some of the questions considered

© Oxford University Press 2005
doi: 10.1093/pa/gsi060

here as we examine the campaign and analyse the outcome of the 5 May contest.

To set the stage, this introduction focuses on exploring the key highlights and main features of the UK election by analysing the national and constituency levels results. We consider (i) the vote and seat share won by each of the main parties, understood in historical perspective; (ii) the reasons for constituency variations in the national swing of the vote; (iii) the role of the electoral system and how the translation of votes into seats contributed towards Labour's parliamentary majority; (iv) why electoral turnout remains low in Britain; (v) the performance of the minor parties; and lastly, (vi) the outcome for the new parliament. We then present the plan of the book. The concluding chapter summarises the main findings and reflects upon some of the broader implications for understanding the process of electoral change and the dynamics of party support during the campaign.

The vote and seat share for the main parties in historical perspective

Despite their historic return to power, Labour's mood on election night felt flat and subdued, even despondent. With about 9.5 million ballots, the government won 35.2% of the UK vote (see Table 1), and one fifth (22%) of the electorate, in both cases the lowest share for any ruling party in modern times.[2] The party lost almost four-dozen MPs on election night (see Table 2), with notable Conservative victories over Stephen Twigg in Enfield Southgate and Chris Pond in Gravesham. Against the odds, the Liberal Democrats snatched Hornsey and Wood Green and Manchester Withington (both of which should have been safe for Labour), as well as hitting more predictable bulls-eyes, such as Cardiff Central. Independents also drew blood with by-election sized upsets in two of Labour's safest seats, Oona King's defeat at the hands of Respect's George Galloway in Bethnal Green and Bow, and the loss of Blaenau Gwent following a candidate selection dispute over the use

1. The Share of the UK Vote, 2001–05

	Share of the UK Vote (%)			
	2001	2005	Change	Number of Votes, 2005
Labour	40.7	35.2	−5.5	9,563,097
Conservative	31.7	32.3	+0.6	8,769,755
Liberal Democrat	18.3	22.0	+3.7	5,981,874
Scottish National	1.8	1.5	−0.3	412,267
Plaid Cymru	0.7	0.6	−0.1	174,838
UK Independence Party	1.5	2.3	+0.8	602,746
Green	0.6	1.0	+0.4	282,978
British National Party	0.2	0.7	+0.5	192,746
Other	4.5	4.4	−0.1	1,152,026
Turnout	59.4	60.9	+1.5	27,132,327
Lab to Con swing			3.3	

Source: The British Parliamentary Constituency Database, 1992–2005.

2. The Distribution of UK Seats, 2001–05

	2001 General Election (i)	2001 Notional (ii)	2005 General Election (iii)	Net Change (ii) to (iii)	Number of Candidates, 2005
Labour	412	402	355	−47	627
Conservative	166	165	197	+32	630
Liberal Democrat	52	51	62	+11	626
Scottish National	5	4	6	+2	59
Plaid Cymru	4	4	3	−1	40
UK Independence Party	0	0	0	0	495
Green	0	0	0	0	202
BNP	0	0	0	0	119
Others	19	19	22	+3	758
Speaker	1	1	1	0	
Total	659	646	646	−13	3552
Lab majority	165	158	66	−92	

(i) The actual results in June 2001. (ii) The 'notional' results of the June 2001 election when calculated under the new Scottish boundaries. Sources: The British Parliamentary Constituency Database, 1992–2005; D. Denver, C. Rallings and M. Thrasher (eds), *Media Guide to the New Scottish Westminster Parliamentary Constituencies*, BBC/ITN/PA/Sky, University of Plymouth, 2004.

3. Projections of Seat Change by Uniform Vote Swing in the Next General Election

Swing	% UK Vote			Number of Seats				Government	Parl. Maj.
	Con	Lab	Lib Dem	Con	Lab	Lib Dem	Other		
−1.0	31.3	36.2	22.0	186	368	63	29	Lab	90
0.0	32.3	35.2	22.0	197	356	62	31	Lab	66
1.0	33.3	34.2	22.0	216	341	59	30	Lab	36
2.0	34.3	33.2	22.0	231	326	58	31	Lab	6
2.3	34.6	32.9	22.0	235	323	57	31	–	–
3.0	35.3	32.2	22.0	249	309	57	31	–	–
4.0	36.3	31.2	22.0	263	294	58	31	–	–
4.8	37.1	30.4	22.0	281	278	57	30	–	–
5.0	37.3	30.2	22.0	284	275	57	30	–	–
6.0	38.3	29.2	22.0	302	258	56	30	–	–
7.0	39.3	28.2	22.0	313	248	55	30	–	–
7.6	39.9	27.6	22.0	326	235	55	30	Con	6
8.0	40.3	27.2	22.0	332	229	55	30	Con	18
9.0	41.3	26.2	22.0	350	214	53	29	Con	54

Note: The estimates assume a Con–Lab uniform national swing across the UK with no change in the share of the vote for the other parties. Source: The British Parliamentary Constituency Database, 1992–2005.

of all-women shortlists. When the Prime Minister's Jaguar returned to Downing Street, it was back to business as usual with a sober speech and a cabinet reshuffle; there was no repeat of the flag-waving cheering crowds of party faithful.

One of the most striking features of 5 May was the fall in the Labour share of the UK vote, which plummeted from 40.7% to 35.2%. The pattern was evident across all major regions from the toe of St Ives to the tip of the Na h-Eileanan an Iar (see Figure 1). The results of the 2005 election can be interpreted as a negative backlash against the government but, in an era of multiparty competition, without generating a positive flow of support towards any single contender. As discussed

1. General Election 2005 Change in Share of Vote, 2001–05: Labour

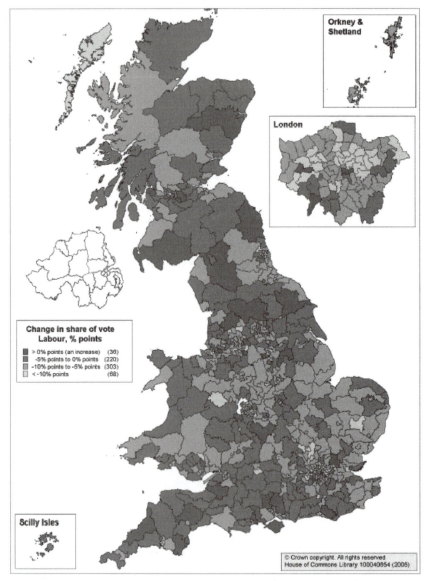

Source: A. Mellows-Facer, R. Young and R. Cracknell, *General Election 2005*, House of Commons Research Paper 05/33, 17 May 2005, www.parliament.uk. Crown Copyright Ordnance Survey. All rights reserved.

further in chapter 9, Greater London proved the worst region for Labour, with a Lab–Con swing of 5.4%. The government lost eleven seats in the London suburbs, including Hammersmith and Fulham, Croydon Central, Wimbledon, and Ilford North, all regained by the Conservatives. The 4.6% Lab–Con swing in the South East caused the loss of another eight Labour MPs. The government maintained their support best in Scotland, where the Labour vote dipped by just 3.4%.

Judged by seat gains, however, under Michael Howard's leadership, victory laurels went to the Conservatives. The party celebrated 53 new Conservative MPs. Three dozen challengers defeated Labour and Liberal Democrat members, while the remainder inherited seats from retiring Conservative incumbents. This influx swelled the Conservative benches to 197 MPs in total, or about a third of the House of Commons, closely reflecting their share of the vote. There was much media hoo-ha surrounding Justine Greening's victory in Putney, symbolising success for a younger generation of Conservative women. Shailesh Vara was returned in Cambridgeshire North West to replace retiring Conservative MP, Brian Mawhinney, while Adam Afryie was elected in the safe Conservative seat of Windsor, both representing the first ethnic minority MPs in the Conservative party since 1992. Despite these victories, as discussed in chapter 12, the parliamentary party struggled with the issue of diversity, compared with the social profile of the Labour members. The influx of new blood into the parliamentary party was seen by many Conservatives as a sign that the party was resurgent, bringing in a fresh generation of talent. Optimists hoped that 'one more heave' in the next general election could be sufficient to return them to power. After all, it would just take a further 2.3% Lab–Con uniform national total swing in the next general election to deprive the government of its overall parliamentary majority. Moreover the Conservatives knew that they would not have to face Tony Blair again in the next contest, after he announced that he would not fight another general election as prime minister.

The government's vote eroded, but rather than accumulating in the Conservative column, ex-Labour supporters scattered into opposing camps. As a result, the champagne at Conservative Central Office lost its fizz once it became clear that they had made only painfully modest progress in boosting their share of popular support: winning 30.7% of the UK vote in 1997, 31.7% in 2001, and 32.3% in 2005 (representing an anemic 0.2% growth per annum). Indeed their performance in vote share was highly uneven across the nation, actually falling further in some of their weakest regions, such as Scotland and the North of England, while recovering best in the leafy suburbs and shires of England, especially in the South East and Greater London (see Figure 2). The Conservatives won the endorsement of just one fifth of the total electorate. The party has only one MP in the whole of Scotland, just three in Wales, and none in the major urban cities of England: Birmingham, Newcastle, Leeds, Sheffield, Liverpool, and Manchester.

Michael Howard's campaign focused attention upon the issues of asylum and immigration, adopting a more rightwing stance on these issues than the party's position under William Hague in 2001. Such a strategy consolidated their voting support most successfully among the

2. General Election 2005 Share of Vote: Conservative

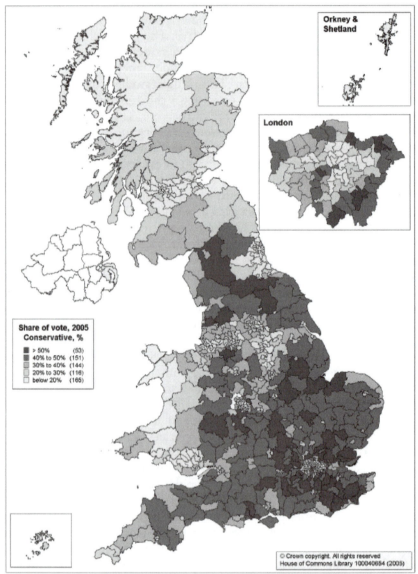

Source: A. Mellows-Facer, R. Young and R. Cracknell, *General Election 2005*, House of Commons
Research Paper 05/33, 17 May 2005, www.parliament.uk. Crown Copyright Ordnance Survey. All
rights reserved.

Tory faithful in their own seats, and perhaps converted a few BNP supporters. What Michael Howard failed to do, however, was to attract
sufficient waverers and deserters from other parties to make substantial
progress. In Labour constituencies, far from making any advances by
capturing floating or undecided voters, the Conservative share of the

vote actually fell slightly (−0.21%). The Conservative campaign reinforced their core base, but failed to reach beyond it.

The hurdles facing the Conservatives remain formidable. It would still take a 4.8% uniform national total swing in the next general election to make the Conservatives the largest party in a hung parliament. It would require a substantial 7.6% swing to propel the Conservatives back into No.10 with an overall parliamentary majority. This has occurred before; the closest historical parallel would be Tony Blair's triumph over John Major in 1997, which generated a 10.2% total vote swing. But, although not unprecedented, such a large swing remains extremely rare in postwar British general elections. Immediately after the election, Michael Howard announced that the party was back on the road to recovery but he would stand down in the autumn once the party had reformed the selection rules and decided upon his successor. The Conservative party immediately started squabbling about the most suitable internal reforms, absorbed for many months in complex leadership machinations and plots, giving the government an easy ride from the official opposition.

Yet if the election result was evaluated instead against each party's improvement in popularity, the Liberal Democrats could claim that they had made the most substantial progress. The Liberal Democrat campaign tried to fight a war on two fronts, against the Conservatives and Labour, but during the campaign they focused most attention upon center-left policies such as favoring higher public spending and opposing the Iraq war. This campaign strategy can be expected to prove most successful when making inroads into traditional areas of Labour support, and indeed it seems to have paid dividends. In Labour seats, the government's vote fell most strongly (by 6.8%) and the Liberal Democrats were the main beneficiaries who picked up votes (+5.2%). By contrast, the Liberal Democrats had far less success against the Conservatives.

The party won almost six million ballots, representing 22% of the UK vote, up 3.7% from 2001. As discussed in chapter 6, their share of the vote strengthened in every region, especially in Scotland and the North where they made inroads into traditional areas of Labour support (see Figure 3). After the election, the Liberal Democrats were in a promising position to make further advances in subsequent contests, placed second in more than one hundred Labour seats, twice as many as before. But under Charles Kennedy, on 5 May the party still failed to make a decisive breakthrough at Westminster, gaining only eleven more MPs (compared with the 'notional' 2001 results) to swell their parliamentary ranks to 62. This represents their largest parliamentary representation for eighty years but nevertheless the party President, Simon Hughes, had dreamed of more than double this number of seat gains. In particular, while taking a dozen seats from Labour, they missed many of their key Conservative targets, exemplified by Orpington, Surrey

3. General Election 2005 Change in Share of Vote,
2001–05: Liberal Democrat

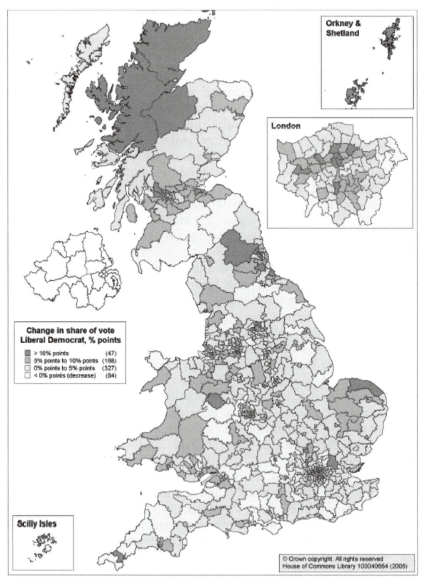

Source: A. Mellows-Facer, R. Young and R. Cracknell, *General Election 2005*, House of Commons
Research Paper 05/33, 17 May 2005, www.parliament.uk. Crown Copyright Ordnance Survey. All
rights reserved.

South West, and Dorset West. Overall they lost more seats to the Conservatives than they gained, with a string of defeats in Newbury, Guildford,
Ludlow, and Devon West and Torridge. If the Westminster election had
been held under a proportional representation party list electoral system,

where the distribution of seats reflected the proportion of votes cast, Dunleavy and Margetts estimate that the Liberal Democrats would have been returned with 140 MPs, not 62. Under a number of different electoral scenarios, discussed further in chapter 13, Liberal Democrat fortunes would have been transformed into the 'king-maker' third party in a hung parliament. In the aftermath, Charles Kennedy announced an internal inquiry into their performance, including considering whether they should continue to locate themselves on the left of the Labour party, on issues such as taxation and public spending, or whether they should return towards the classical liberalism of the center ground on issues such as identity cards, to attract disaffected Conservatives.

Mixed indicators could also be observed for interpreting the performance of the minor parties. Voting support for the Scottish Nationalists and for Plaid Cymru eroded slightly, although the SNP still made two seat gains. Much media attention surrounded the British National Party, but in fact their electoral performance was very comparable to that achieved by the UKIP and the Greens. Overall 61.2% of the electorate in Great Britain cast a ballot, representing an extremely modest improvement (+2.1%) compared with 2001. The rise occurred across the UK, with the exception of Northern Ireland, but this still left many significant variations among constituencies, ranging from low participation where around four out of ten electors cast a ballot in some of Labour's safest seats, such as Liverpool Riverside, Salford, and Manchester Central, to over seven out of ten electors in more hotly contested constituencies, such as Richmond Park, Norfolk North, and Dorset West (see Figure 4). As discussed further in chapter 8, the level of turnout on 5 May was nowhere near the patterns common during the 1990s despite recent attempts to facilitate voter participation, such as the easier availability of postal voting, and an election result expected by many commentators to be closer than in 2001. Out of a total of over 43 million eligible electors in Britain, almost 17 million abstained, opting for 'none of the above' on polling day.

Therefore, all the main parties had some cause to celebrate after election night, but none could claim a decisive outright victory which fulfilled all their hopes. Each remains delicately balanced in an uncertain position to make further advances in subsequent contests, or else to suffer significant setbacks.

Constituency variations in the national swing of the vote

The mean national vote swing from Labour to the Conservatives was 3.3% across Britain. If uniform across the whole country, this should have returned another Labour government with a comfortable parliamentary majority of over 100. In fact, the national vote swing was far from uniform, producing a 66-seat majority for Blair. This phenomenon raises an important puzzle: why did the Conservatives and Liberal Democrats snatch some Labour seats from well down their target lists,

4.   General Election 2005 Turnout by Constituency *expressed as*
valid votes as % the electorate

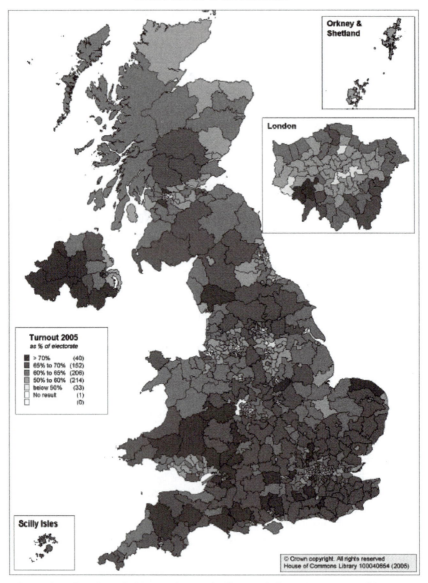

Turnout 2005
as % of electorate

> 70%   (40)
65% to 70%   (152)
60% to 65%   (206)
50% to 60%   (214)
below 50%   (33)
No result   (1)
             (0)

Source: A. Mellows-Facer, R. Young and R. Cracknell, *General Election 2005*, House of Commons
Research Paper 05/33, 17 May 2005, www.parliament.uk. Crown Copyright Ordnance Survey. All
rights reserved.

while they failed to win more vulnerable Labour marginals that should
have been within their sights? The explanation rests with local patterns
of party competition, the socioeconomic character of constituencies, the
impact of specific issues, and the effect of any tactical voting.

Local party competition

Local party competition could plausibly influence constituency variations in Labour support. This includes the vote share won by each of
the other main parties and rivalry from UKIP, Green, and BNP candidates, and any differential changes in voter turnout, for example if
Labour proves less effective at mobilising through get-out-the-vote
drives. Table 4 shows the simple correlations of the vote changes. The
results confirm that Labour vote losses were strongly related with Liberal Democrats gains, as observed earlier, and they were more weakly
linked with the change in Conservative support. It might be expected
that the Conservatives would have been most damaged by any rise in
BNP rivals threatening their far right flank, but in fact the Labour vote
share appears to have been most affected, suggesting that the BNP may
have appealed most strongly to disaffected working class ex-Labour
voters. The change in UKIP performance (up, on average, by less than
300 votes per candidate) was insufficient to have a significant impact
upon changes in support for the main parties; this was nowhere near
the UKIP support achieved in the 2004 European elections. Labour also
performed more poorly than average in seats where turnout fell.

Socio-economic characteristics

The socioeconomic characteristics of an area could also prove important through compositional effects. As chapter 9 discusses in detail,
regions in Britain vary in their patterns of party voting largely because
of the geographies of class and prosperity which have characterised different areas for many decades. Similar variations can be expected at
constituency level. Since the early-1990s, the Labour party has shifted
towards the center-right in its policies and image, in the attempt to
widen its appeal to middle-England. This strategy did not start with
Blair, but it was reinforced under his leadership. This shift is expected
to have gradually boosted Labour's support in areas with many professional middle classes residents, such as constituencies with above-aver-
age proportions of teachers, doctors, and local government officials

4. Correlations with Changes in the Vote Share for the Main Parties, GB

	Change in the % Share of the Vote for Each Main Party, 2001–05			
	Lab	Con	Lib Dem	N. cases
% Change in Labour vote 2001–05		.11	−.48	627
% Change in Conservative vote 2001–05	.11		−.40	626
% Change in Lib-Dem vote 2001–05	−.48	−.40		625
% Change in BNP vote 2001–05	−.60	−.32	−.17	22
% Change in UKIP vote 2001–05	−.01	−.05	.01	365
% Change in turnout 2001–05	−.19	.04	−.01	568

Note: The figures represent simple correlations with the percentage change in the share of the vote for each
party since 2001, without any prior controls. Figures in bold indicate that the correlation is significant at
the 0.01 level (2-tailed). Source: The British Parliamentary Constituency Database, 1992–2005.

working in the public sector. Moreover, it might also be expected that in the May 2005 election, Labour may have lost most ground among core working-class communities in 'old' Labour urban areas, such as in Newcastle, Liverpool, and Glasgow, characterised by multiple indicators of social deprivation.

Yet the correlation analysis in Table 5 indicates that, contrary to this hypothesis, although social class continues to predict party support at constituency level, the *change* in Labour votes was not confined to working class areas; instead there were weak and mixed correlations across different socioeconomic groups, perhaps reflecting the cross-class appeal of the Blair government. By contrast, the Conservative party consistently reinforced its support among the most middle classes constituencies, while reducing its share of the vote among the more working class communities. Social dealignment has therefore weakened the traditional working class basis of Labour party support, reinforcing its catch-all or bridging appeal among different social sectors. By contrast, in this election the Conservative party became more dependent upon its core professional and managerial middle class base.

Issue voting

The local impact of specific issues could also count. In particular, government support could have fallen following a backlash against unpopular policies which affected certain communities more strongly than others. Potential candidates include the issue of academic 'top up' fees, one of the most controversial policies during Blair's second term, with an impact that could be most evident among students and academics living in university constituencies. Equally controversial, debate about the Iraq war formed a backdrop to much of the campaign debate, especially accusations that Blair had lied about the reasons for the military intervention. If there was a popular backlash against this action, its effect might be expected to be most evident in seats with many Muslims.

5. Socio-Economic Status of Constituencies and Changes in the Vote Share
for the Main Parties, England and Wales

| | Change in the % Share of the Vote for Each Main Party, 2001–05 | | | |
	Lab	Con	LibDem	N. Cases
% Large employers or managers	.04	**.34**	−.13	534
% Higher professionals	−.10	**.26**	.06	534
% Lower managerial and professionals	.04	**.37**	−.11	534
% Intermediate occupations	−.05	**.27**	−.10	534
% Small employers & petit bourgeoisie	**.37**	.15	**−.34**	534
% Lower supervisory and technical	.13	−.15	−.13	534
% Semi-routine workers	.05	**−.23**	−.05	534
% Routine workers	−.01	**−.28**	.04	534

Note: The figures represent simple correlations with the percentage change in the share of the vote for each party since 2001, without any prior controls. **Figures in bold** indicate that the correlation is significant at the 0.01 level (2-tailed). The occupational class classifications by SEG are derived from the 2001 Census for England and Wales. Source: The British Parliamentary Constituency Database, 1992–2005.

6. The Social Characteristics of Constituencies and the Change in the Vote for the Main Parties, 2001–05, England and Wales

		Change in the % Share of the Vote for Each Main Party, 2001–05			
		Lab	Con	LibDem	N. Seats
% FT students	Low (<.6.9)	−5.16	+0.50	+2.92	392
	High (>7.0)	−7.45	+0.12	+5.09	140
	Diff	*−2.29*	*−0.38*	*+2.17*	*531*
	Eta	**.283*****	.054	**.243*****	
% Muslim pop.	Low (<4.9)	−5.19	+0.59	+2.99	449
	High (>5.0)	−8.83	−0.64	+6.19	83
	Diff	*−3.64*	*−1.23*	*+3.20*	*531*
	Eta	**.371*****	**.145*****	**.295*****	
% Non-white pop.	Low (<4.9)	−4.80	+0.39	+2.89	349
	High (>5.0)	−7.75	+0.16	+5.03	214
	Diff	*−2.95*	*−0.23*	*+2.14*	*562*
	Eta	**.386*****	.036	**.247*****	

Note: The figures represent the mean percentage change in the share of the vote for each party since 2001, without any prior controls. The significance of the mean difference between seats is tested through ANOVA. Figures in bold indicate that the difference is significant at the 0.01 level (2-tailed). The social characteristics of constituencies are derived from the 2001 Census for England and Wales. The proportion of full time students (SEG_11) is classified as low (less than 6.9%) or high (7.0% or more). Source: The British Parliamentary Constituency Database, 1992–2005.

Given their policy stance to the left of Labour on both these issues, the Liberal Democrats could be expected to be the main beneficiaries of any loss of Labour support. Meanwhile, Michael Howard's calls to restrict the influx of immigrants and asylum seekers may have reduced the Conservative share of the vote in ethnic minority constituencies.

A comparison of the mean change in the share of the vote in Table 6 confirms that Labour did indeed lose more ground in university constituencies with a high student and academic population, down by about two percentage points more than average, while the Liberal Democrats gained, as discussed further in chapter 6. Labour support also fell more than three percentage points more than average in seats with many Muslim residents, where again the Liberal Democrats proved the main beneficiaries. This evidence is suggestive that these issues mattered at local level. It remains more difficult to establish from the constituency-level results that the Conservative policies on race and immigration hurt them among minority communities; Conservative support was slightly lower than average in ethnically diverse constituencies, but this difference was not significant. The constituency results suggest that both the issue of university top fees and the Iraq war may have damaged Labour popularity in certain areas, contributing towards the improvements in the Liberal Democrat vote, although this needs confirming using individual-level survey analysis to have full confidence in the results.

Tactical voting

The local political context could also matter; in particular, the impact of any *tactical* ('strategic' or 'insincere') voting. This phenomenon is most likely to occur where supporters of the party ranked third in a constituency decide to switch to their second preference party instead, in order to defeat the party holding the seat. Two distinct types of tactical voting shift might be evident in the May 2005 general election—directed against either the Conservatives or Labour.

First, the results might display the traditional form of anti-Conservative tactical voting, found in a series of general elections during the Thatcher/Major years. The closure of the ideological gap between the Labour and Liberal Democratic parties during the late-1980s made it easier for their supporters to transfer on tactical grounds, switching to whichever party was most advantageously placed to defeat Conservative MPs.[3] If this traditional pattern persisted in the 2005 general election, then in Con–Lab seats, Liberal Democrat supporters can be expected to switch disproportionately towards Labour. And in Con–LD seats, Labour supporters can be expected to switch towards the Liberal Democrats. Figure 1 illustrates the changes in party vote since 2001 by the type of contest in each seat. The results suggest little evidence of any new anti-Conservative tactical voting in this election. In the Con–Lab constituencies, for example, few Liberal Democrat supporters appear to have switched towards Labour on tactical grounds; the Labour vote fell by 6.1%, about the national average. In Con–LibDem seats, as well, there appears to be no evidence of a systematic tactical shift among Labour supporters towards the Liberal Democrats; the Liberal Democrats share of the vote rose by 0.5%, far less than the national average. The traditional form of anti-Tory tactical voting appears to have dissipated in recent years, perhaps because any past antipathy towards the Conservative government has faded during their eight years in opposition. Indeed the fact that the Conservatives did better in their own seats than in the nation as a whole may suggest some indications of a tactical unravel, where past anti-Conservative tactical voting from 1997 to 2001 subsequently faded away.

Yet this is not the end of the story because a newer pattern of tactical voting appears to have emerged in this general election, where Conservative and Liberal Democratic supporters living in Labour seats decided to vote tactically against the Blair government, casting a ballot for their second preference party. During the campaign, the public's lack of trust in Tony Blair's leadership was widely reported in many opinion polls, as discussed in chapter 11. Many polls also registered that a public backlash was evident against Britain's involvement in the Iraq war, including the way that the cause for intervention in Iraq had been presented in parliament. The question is whether any antipathy directed towards Blair personally, or towards the government, was sufficient to encourage new tactical voting against Labour. If this is the case, in Lab–Con seats Liberal Democrat supporters would be expected to vote for the Conservative candidate. In Lab–LD seats, in a reciprocal pattern,

Conservatives would be expected to switch to support the Liberal Democrat candidate, as the challenger best placed to defeat the Labour MP. At the same time, any tactical vote along these lines may well be limited due to the extensive ideological distance between the Conservative and Liberal Democratic parties on many issues. It was easier for Liberal Democrat and Labour supporters to switch votes during the late 1980s and early 1990s, because these parties are so similar in their center-left political orientations, and the Liberal Democrats were traditionally the middle-of-the-road party. By contrast, after 1997 the Liberal Democrats have positioned themselves slightly left of Labour on many issues, such as taxation and public spending, after Blair moved Labour towards the center ground.[4] As such, it would be more difficult for Conservatives and Liberal Democrats to switch all the way across the ideological spectrum, if they are seeking to defeat Labour MPs.

The results in Figure 5 demonstrate how the Labour vote fell most sharply (7.0%) in their own seats, with the Liberal Democrats the primary beneficiaries in these constituencies, as observed earlier. Most importantly, this pattern was especially evident in the 53 Lab–LD seats, which is consistent with the idea that in these constituencies some Conservatives may have decided to switch towards the Liberal Democrats on tactical grounds. If so, this represents a new and distinctive form of tactical voting which is directed against the Labour government in an attempt to reduce Blair's majority. The number of Conservative supporters who switched tactically probably remains modest, although the

5. Change in the Vote since 2001, by Type of Seat, GB

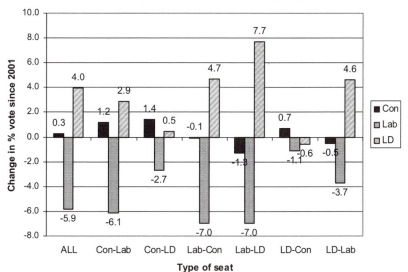

Note: The change in the vote share for each party since 2001 by the type of seat, defined by the main party in first and second place in each constituency in 2001. Source: The British Parliamentary Constituency Database, 1992–2005.

extra votes may have helped the Liberal Democrats gain a few Labour seats, such as Dunbartonshire East, Falmouth and Camborne, Leeds North West, Cambridge, and Rochdale. From the analysis of the election results, however, it does not appear that there was a reciprocal move by Liberal Democrats shifting tactically towards the Conservatives in Lab–Con seats. So the results appear to indicate some grounds for anti-Labour tactical voting among Conservatives but not, apparently, among Liberal Democrats.[5]

The role of the electoral system

How far did Labour's parliamentary majority depend upon the workings of the electoral system and what factors contributed towards electoral bias in this contest? As chapter 13 discusses in detail, majoritarian electoral systems, including the single member plurality system of First-Past-the-Post used for Westminster contests, generate a 'manufactured majority' for the party in first place. This type of electoral system aims to turn even a close result in the popular vote, such as Harold Wilson's wafer-thin victory in 1964, into a solid working parliamentary majority for the party in government. It is intended to facilitate a decisive outcome where the party with the largest share of the vote forms a single-party cabinet, producing 'strong' government, clear accountability, and transparent decision-making.[6] Such a system allows the winning party to implement their manifesto policies and to take difficult decisions during their term in office, when assured of the support of their backbenchers, without the need for post-election negotiations and compromise with coalition partners. Proponents of majoritarian systems argue that the bias is also intended to reduce the representation of minor parties, especially those such as the BNP and the Greens with voting support widely dispersed across constituencies. The effective vote threshold facing fringe parties and independent candidates reduces parliamentary fragmentation and penalises extremist factions such as the National Front. But the disproportionality in the UK electoral system does not necessarily operate equitably for the main parties: since the 1950s, it has been characterised by systematic bias towards the Labour party.[7] This disproportionality is a product of the regional distribution of the party strength, malapportionment (differences in the size of electorate within parliamentary constituencies), patterns of differential turnout, and any anti-Conservative tactical voting, where votes are exchanged among Liberal Democrat and Labour supporters.

The Scottish Boundary Commission's revision of the constituencies north of the border sought to address some of the causes of malapportionment. In the past, in recognition of their distinctive interests and concerns, Scotland and Wales were over-represented at Westminster in terms of the size of their population, primarily benefiting Labour as the strongest party in these regions. Following the introduction of the Scottish Parliament and Welsh Assembly, the government decided to reduce the number of MPs at Westminster drawn from these regions. The Scottish Boundary Commission was required to use the electoral quota in England (69,934 electors) to determine the number of Scottish constituencies in the House of Commons. The new boundaries, which came into effect just before the UK general election, reduced the number of Scottish seats from 72 to 59. The average size of the constituency electorates in the region rose from 55,337 in 2001 under the old boundaries to 67,720. Based on calculating the 'notional' results of the 2001 election, the net impact of the introduction of the new boundaries was estimated by Denver, Rallings and Thrasher to cut the number of Scottish Labour MPs automatically by ten, while simultaneously reducing the number of Scottish MPs at Westminster for the Liberal Democrats, SNP and Conservatives by one each.[8]

Despite these boundary revisions, Figure 6 shows that in fact, rather than diminishing, the disproportional votes-to-seats ratio for Labour increased again slightly in 2005. The votes–seats ratio for the government was commonly fairly modest during the 1950s and 1960s, at the height of two-party politics. A majoritarian electoral system can be fairly proportional in its outcome where there are only two main parties, for example in the United States House of Representatives. The government's votes-to-seats ratio rose greatly in 1983, when voting support for the Liberal-Social Democratic Alliance surged and Labour reached its modern nadir. But the ratio sharply increased to 1.46 with Blair's victory in 1997, then rose again slightly in 2001 and in 2005,

6. **The Votes–Seats Ratio for the Governing Party, UK, 1945–2005**

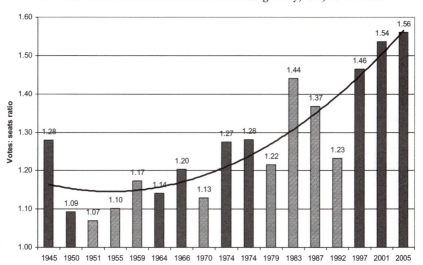

Note: The votes-seats ratio is calculated as the percentage of UK seats divided into the percentage of UK votes for the governing party. A ratio of 1.0 would indicate no electoral bias for the government. Source: Calculated from C. Rallings and M. Thrasher (eds), *British Electoral Facts 1832–1999*, Parliamentary Research Services/Ashgate, 2000; The British Parliamentary Constituency Database, 1992–2005.

when it reached 1.56. This represents the greatest disproportionality in the government's votes-to-seats ratio in Britain during the postwar era.

The projections of seat change by a uniform total vote swing also illustrate the bias in the electoral system. If the Conservative and Labour parties gain about the same share of the vote in the next general election, 33.5%, then Labour remains in power with an overall parliamentary majority. By contrast, as Figure 7 shows, the Conservative share of the vote needs to rise above 40% for them to gain an overall parliamentary majority, with the Labour vote share squeezed down to around 28%. The constituency boundary revisions due to go into effect in Wales and England before the next general election will alter these calculations, to compensate for population changes since the 1992

7.   The Impact of a Uniform National Vote Swing in the Next
UK General Election

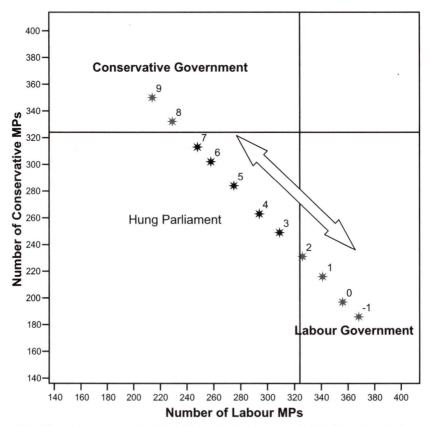

Note: The estimates assume a Con-Lab uniform national swing across the UK with no change in the share of the vote for the other parties. A positive swing indicates a fall in the Labour party, and increase in the Conservative party, share of the total vote. A negative denotes the opposite. The 'winning post' necessary to assure an overall parliamentary majority for one party is half the 646 MPs ie 324. Source: Table 3.

revisions. It is estimated that these changes will probably reduce the number of Labour seats by about ten, while reducing the Conservative seats by about six. But this will not compensate for all the sources of electoral bias existing in the British system, about which more is discussed in chapter 13.

Continuing low turnout but some modest recovery

Another reason for the disparity is differential turnout, since voting participation is usually lower in Labour constituencies. There was considerable concern that turnout, already severely anemic in 2001, would plummet still further on 5 May. Chapter 8 analyses how about 26 million people voted in the 2001 general election (59.1% of the total eligible electorate in Great Britain), down from 31 million in 1997. This was the lowest British turnout since the khaki election of 1918. Equally remarkable, it was also the lowest turnout recorded in any postwar general election in any EU state. Many believe that this situation reflected (at best) widespread public disinterest in the campaign and citizen apathy with public affairs. Or even (at worst) lack of trust in the government and alienation with representative democracy. There were many attempts to boost civic engagement, notably parliamentary initiatives to make postal ballots widely available upon application, to use a rolling register, and the Electoral Commission's public information campaigns among target groups such as the young.

In the event, levels of turnout recovered in 2005, but extremely modestly: up to 61.2% of the eligible electorate in Great Britain (see Figures 4 and 8). Participation levels rose in nearly every major region. The important exception to this pattern was Northern Ireland, where turnout fell by 5.1%, perhaps because turnout rose more than average in 2001 and there may have been some subsequent disillusionment with the Good Friday agreement and slow progress with the peace process. The modest rise in British turnout was regarded as encouraging, although seen in longer-term perspective the level was nowhere near the usual rate of electoral participation common in Britain during the postwar era, or even the three-quarters of the electorate who usually voted during the 1990s. As discussed further in chapter 8, many factors commonly associated with electoral participation could have contributed towards the slight improvement in turnout in this election.[9] In terms of incentives, public interest could have been stimulated by strongly emotional issues debated during the campaign, such as the anti-Iraq war movement mobilising the left, or concern about asylum-seekers and immigration energising the right. The context of party competition could also have played a role; compared with 2001, a closer Labour vote lead was widely predicted by the campaign opinion polls and discussed in media commentary.[10] Turnout could also have been helped by local party mobilisation efforts and targeted get-out-the-vote drives in the most contested marginals. The rise in turnout could also reflect the

8.　UK Turnout 1832–2005

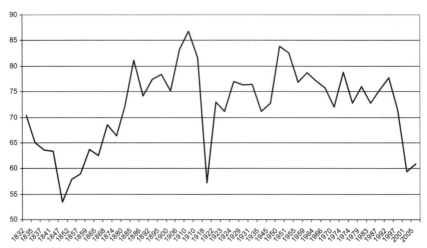

Note: The number of valid votes cast as a proportion of the eligible UK electorate. Source: C. Rallings and M. Thrasher (eds), 2000. *British Electoral Facts 1832–1999*, Parliamentary Research Services/ Ashgate; The British Parliamentary Constituency Database, 1992–2005.

administrative reforms piloted by the Electoral Commission and introduced by parliament, notably the adoption of the Rolling Register and also the easier access to postal ballots, which were issued to an estimated 12% of the electorate.

Chapter 8 considers further the role of some of these contributing factors. In this chapter, the analysis of levels of turnout, and changes in turnout since 2001, provide indicators which are consistent with the incentive thesis: in marginal seats (with a majority of less than 5% in 2001) voter turnout was nine points higher than in the safest seats (with a majority of 20% or more). Party also mattered: turnout remained well above average in safe Conservative seats. In safe Labour seats, however, turnout was particularly low or increased less than average since 2001. As other studies have found, the closer the anticipated outcome in any election, the greater the rational incentive for electors to cast a ballot and for parties to mobilise their support.[11] By contrast, chapter 8 suggests that any impact on turnout from the easier availability of postal voting was, at best, very small.

Minor parties and independents

So far we have focused upon explaining shifts in support for the main parties in Britain but, as discussed in detail in chapter 7, one of the most important characteristics of this election concerns the performance of the minor parties and independent candidates. Table 7 summarises the share of the vote won by these parties in Britain and the change in the share of the vote since 2001. In total there were 3,552 candidates across

7. **Minor Party Candidates and Votes, 2005**

			2005 Mean				Change 2001–05 Mean	
	PPC	%Vote	Votes/PPC	Total vote UK	PPC	% Vote	Votes/PPC	Total Vote UK
SNP	59	18.0	6,987	412,267	−13	−2.3	−882	−52,047
PC	40	13.2	4,371	174,838	−1	−1.3	−425	−21,812
BNP	119	4.3	1,619	192,746	+85	+0.5	+231	47,200
UKIP	495	2.8	1,217	602,746	+81	+0.6	+282	215,612
Green	202	3.4	1,400	282,978	+61	+0.6	+265	122,919

Source: The British Parliamentary Constituency Database, 1992–2005.

646 constituencies from 114 different parties, 176 independent candidates and the Speaker. In Scotland, the SNP won 18% of the vote in the region, but this was a fall since 2001, and they were overtaken by the Liberal Democrats in second place behind Labour. Despite this setback, the Scottish National Party increased its number of seats to six, with gains in the Western Isles and Dundee East. In Wales, Plaid Cymru also saw its share of the vote erode slightly. The party failed to take its number one target of Ynys Mon from Labour, and they also lost Ceredigion to the Liberal Democrats. Blaenau Gwent delivered by far the biggest shock in Wales when an independent candidate received 20,505 votes, or 58% of the total. Peter Law had been the local Welsh assembly member for Labour until he left the party in protest at the use of all-women shortlists. The Labour party's candidate, Maggie Jones, won 11,384 votes, or 32%, which was 40% down on Labour's 2001 result. The number of independents at Westminster has usually been negligible, given the substantial hurdles of the electoral system. But the number has increased after the entry of Martin Bell in 1997. Richard Taylor was returned again for Wyre Forest as the Independent Kidderminster Hospital and Health Concern, along with George Galloway as the Respect candidate for Bethnal Green and Bow, and Peter Law, making a total of three independent MPs in the current House of Commons.

The BNP, UKIP and the Greens all increased the number of candidates they fielded in this election. The greatest media publicity surrounded the British National Party, led by Nick Griffin on a radical anti-immigrant platform. The party increased its total number of parliamentary candidates from 33 to 119, but in the end the party lost its £500 deposit in 84 seats, leaving it with a bill of about £42,000 overall. Its average share of its vote rose by only a few hundred per candidate to about 1,619, with the best BNP result in Barking, with 16.9% of the vote. The Greens, who contested 202 of the 646 seats, won 1.07% of the vote or about 1,400 per seat. They lost their deposit in 177 seats. Their best result was in Brighton Pavilion with 22% of votes, where the Labour incumbent won but the Green candidate in third place polled 9,530—up 13% on 2001's result. In Lewisham, the Greens won 11.5% of the vote and they performed relatively well in Norwich South. The party got 282,978 votes in total, up by 122,919 votes since 2001.

Among the minor parties, the well-financed UKIP fielded the greatest number of candidates—495. The party was buoyed by taking 16.1% of the vote in the 2004 European elections but at the start of the general election campaign the party suffered internal splits. UKIP, shorn of its most high-profile campaigner Robert Kilroy-Silk, subsequently lost its deposits in at least 451 seats—costing it about £225,500. Even the UKIP leader, the former Tory MP Roger Knapman, could only poll 3,914 votes (7.74%) in Totnes, Devon. Kilroy-Silk suffered an even more ignominious defeat under the 'Veritas' banner, taking just 3,000 votes in Erewash.

The adoption of alternative electoral systems for non-Westminster elections has encouraged the fragmentation of the British two-party system in the House of Commons. Parties such as UKIP, the BNP, and the Greens can build their organisational base and achieve a more credible performance under the PR party list system used for European contests, as well as the AMS system used for the Scottish Parliament and Welsh Assembly. This has consequences for general elections, where smaller parties can become more competitive by gaining their share of the vote, even if failing to gain MPs.

In Northern Ireland, the complex politics of the province produced some dramatic results, most notably the defeat of David Trimble, leader of the Ulster Unionists, in Upper Bann, as well as the loss of four other UUP members. The result was the resurgence of the Democratic Unionist party (DUP), led by Ian Paisley, the more hard-line wing of the republican community, to take the largest share of the vote and nine seats in the province. While David Trimble had sought to work with the nationalists, the DUP has strongly opposed the Good Friday Agreement and refused to work with Sinn Fein in any power sharing arrangement. The nationalist community remains more politically divided between the five seats for Sinn Fein (with one net gain and 24% of the vote in the province), led by Gerry Adams, and three for the SDLP (with 17% of the vote). Sinn Fein has made steady progress in expanding its share of the vote at successive general elections since 1997, and the party's support did not appear to be hurt by its policy of abstention from taking its seats at Westminster, nor by its association with the million-pound Northern Bank raid in December 2004 and the killing of Robert McCartney in January 2005. The outcome of the election is one which makes it harder to make progress on the peace settlement, further polarising the community, despite the real achievements in security and prosperity which have transformed Northern Ireland in recent years.

The outcome for the new Parliament

What are the consequences of the election for the new parliament? One of the most striking developments in modern Britain is growing multicultural diversity, by race and religion, as well as growing demand for equal opportunities for women and minority groups in elected office.

Women have made considerable strides in Westminster, doubling from 60 in 1992 to 120 MPs in 1997, an advance which was largely sustained in 2001 (see chapter 12). The proportion of women at Westminster rose slightly to 128 (19.8%) after polling day. Overall 721 out of 3,552 candidates were women (20.3%) but their situation varied a great deal across parties. As discussed further in chapter 12, the proportion of women candidates did increase to 19.5% in the Conservative party, but very few inherited safe seats, and most challengers faced unpromising contests. As a result, while the number of Conservative women MPs rose to 17, this was only 8% of the parliamentary party, far less than in the Liberal Democrats or Labour party. Women remain the grassroots of the Conservative party at constituency level, and Theresa May had attempted to introduce reforms into the Conservative selection process to encourage more women. The party leadership has also spoken of the need for greater diversity within their parliamentary ranks but the party's unwillingness to adopt any guaranteed equality strategies means that they continue to lag behind their main rivals. The Labour party more or less maintained the status quo that they established in 1997; women were 26.5% of their candidates and 27% of their MPs. The Liberal Democrats saw the greatest advance in this election, fielding 145 women candidates (23.2%) and doubling their number of women MPs to ten (16%).

By contrast, Westminster has always included few ethnic minority MPs. The results of this election suggest that any achievement here, while real, remains very limited and slow. The basic numbers are shown in Table 8. The previous parliament included only 13 black or Asian MPs (a dozen Labour and one Liberal Democrat). The main parties selected more ethnic minority candidates in this contest, including 113 black or Asian candidates (41 Conservative, 32 Labour, and 40 Liberal Democrat). Yet few get winnable seats. In the Conservative party, the two ethnic minority candidates who inherited safe Conservative seats were returned. Shailesh Vara was selected for Cambridgeshire North West to replace retiring Conservative MP, Brian Mawhinney, who had

8. Ethnic Minority Candidates and MPs for the Main Parties, 1979–2005

	Conservative		Labour		Lib Dem		Total in Main Parties	
	PPC	MPs	PPC	MPs	PPC	MPs	PPC	MPs
1979	2	0	1	0	2	0	5	0
1983	4	0	6	0	8	0	18	0
1987	6	0	14	4	9	0	29	4
1992	8	1	9	5	5	0	22	6
1997	9	0	13	9	17	0	39	9
2001	16	0	20	12	28	0	64	12
2005	41	2	32	13	40	0	113	15

Note: The Liberal Democrat MP, Parmjit Singh Gill, was elected for Leicester South in a by-election in 2004, but lost the seat in May 2005. Sources: C. Rallings and M. Thrasher (eds), *British Electoral Facts 1832–1999*, Ashgate, 2000; Operation Black Vote www.obv.org.uk; and The British Parliamentary Constituency Database, 1992–2005.

a majority of 18.4% in 2001. Vara is well-connected in the party, as a Vice Chairman, and he worked in the City. The Conservatives also selected Adam Afryie, a millionaire businessman, as the candidate for Windsor to replace their retiring MP, Michael Trend. The other ethnic minority Conservative challengers, facing difficult contests, failed to break through.

Eleven ethnic minority Labour MPs restood, following the retirement of Paul Boateng. In addition, Labour selected five black or Asian inheritors for safe Labour seats, including Shahid Malik in Dewsbury to replace Ann Taylor and Sadiq Khan to replace Tom Cox in Tooting. The remaining 17 minority Labour challengers fought Conservative or Liberal Democrat incumbents with majorities of 10% or more. The Liberal Democrats picked 40 ethnic minority candidates, but most were in seats where they started in third or fourth place, or they faced daunting majorities. Parmjit Singh Gill, elected for Leicester South in the 2004 by-election, was defeated by 3,000 votes as Labour retook the seat.

The number of ethnic minority MPs at Westminster rose from 13 in 2004 to 15 after polling day. This represents modest progress but the UK Census estimates that the minority ethnic population was 4.6 million in 2001 or 7.9% of the total population. If the House of Commons reflected the UK population, it would contain 51 ethnic minority MPs (not 15). And there would be 149 candidates for the main parties (not 113). If parties are committed to speeding the pace of change, in subsequent elections they could consider following some of the measures which have proved effective at boosting the number of women in office, exemplified by the implementation of all-women shortlists for many of Labour's target seats. Parties could adopt similar all-minority candidate shortlists in certain constituencies, but whether parties are genuinely committed to bringing more minority representatives into parliament remains to be seen.

The plan of the book

Therefore this election was one where each of the main parties achieved some of their core objectives, yet they each failed to gain as much as they had hoped. The real advance of the Conservatives in gaining seats might have been expected to lead to celebrations at Central Office but instead the next day Michael Howard announced his retirement and the party was plunged into yet another interminable and debilitating leadership contest. The Liberal Democrats also had some victories to their credit—advancing their share of the vote during the campaign and expanding their parliamentary party. Charles Kennedy was seen by many to have run a positive and largely successful campaign. Yet they too were disappointed by their failure to mount a substantial break through at Westminster and the party has launched an internal inquiry into their party strategy. Lastly, after an eight year period when the government seemed impervious to the usual tug of political gravity in the opinion polls, Labour lost seats and votes, shaking their sense of invulnerability. Blair immediately set about business as usual, with an extremely ambitious agenda at home and abroad, despite the reduced majority, as if determined to stamp his mark upon history during his last term in power. But despite breaking all historical records, Labour's third successive electoral success was subdued rather than celebratory.

To consider these themes further, Part I of this book seeks to outline the context of the election campaign then Part II goes on to analyse the results thematically in greater depth. Chapter 2 by Ivor Crewe considers the record of the opinion polls published during April, in particular how far changes in methodology since 2001 allowed the final polls to generate more accurate vote estimates, compared with previous general elections. In chapter 3, John Bartle then considers the role that newspapers, television and the Internet played in communicating the party messages. The study concludes that a continuing process of partisan dealignment has influenced political reporting in the press, which has changed from intense partisanship towards more grudging support. Subsequent chapters by Dominic Wring, Anthony Seldon and Daniel Collins, and by Andrew Russell explore the campaign mounted by each of the main parties, including the national and ground war, the major themes and the strategies followed by each camp. The Labour campaign described in chapter 4 reflected the way that the Blair government has successfully straddled the middle of the British political spectrum for eight years. Tribal Labour remains instinctively on the center-left on a range of social policies, exemplified by spending upon health care, education, and family policy, as well as investment in overseas aid and African debt relief. Under Blair's leadership the government has also adopted a more center-right hard-line stance on issues such as law and order, university tuition fees, private-public partnerships, and military intervention with America in the Iraq war.[12] By contrast, as discussed in chapter 5, the Conservative campaign veered uncertainly between the center-right pledges to match Labour's expenditure on public services, and a more hard right appeal on immigration and asylum-seekers. A largely one-man show, Michael Howard's personal appeal proved insufficiently attractive to boost Conservative support. And chapter 6 emphasises that the Liberal Democrats campaigned generally from the left of Labour, exemplified by proposing higher levels of public expenditure on education, abolishing tuition fees, promising that the council tax should be replaced by a local income tax, as well as by taking the clearest and most consistent pacifist stance among the major parties against the Afghanistan and Iraq wars. In chapter 7, Paul Webb focuses on the elections fought by the minor parties and evaluates their success. Contributors examine how each party sought to highlight the particular issues it decided to prioritise, as well as discussing innovations in electioneering, and then judge the impact of each campaign.

On this basis, *Part II* then turns to analysing the results. Chapter 8 by John Curtice focuses on explaining levels of voter turnout and the reasons why participation rose slightly in this election, including the impact of marginality and postal ballots. In chapter 9, Ron Johnston, Charles Pattie and David Rossiter examine the regional pattern of results from 1992 to 2005, suggesting that the composition of each area continues to play a major role in patterns of party votes and seats. Chapter 10 by the team responsible for the British Election Study in 2001 and 2005, Paul Whiteley, Marianne C. Stewart, David Sanders and Harold D. Clarke, uses the campaign panel survey data to consider the impact of the issue agenda on voting choice. The analysis concludes that valance issues concerning economic performance and public service delivery were important influences on Labour and Conservative voting in 2005, along with leadership images and partisanship. Issues were not sufficient for Labour's victory, by any means, but Blair was returned in part because the public gave the government positive grades for its performance on matters such as the economy, health and education. Chapter 11 by Geoffrey Evans and Robert Andersen continues to examine the impact of leadership upon voting choice, concluding that appraisals of Blair, Howard and Kennedy were strongly related to voting behavior. Blair's loss of popularity cost Labour some support although Howard's appeal was insufficient to allow the Conservatives to capitalise upon this. Chapter 12, by Rosie Campbell and Joni Lovenduski, turns to the role of women in this election, both as candidates and as voters. The study examines the strategies used by each of the main parties when recruiting women candidates and explores the reasons for the relative success of the Labour party in getting women elected, compared with their rivals. Chapter 13 by Patrick Dunleavy and Helen Margetts analyses the impact of the electoral systems used in the UK on partisan bias and then develops models for the outcome of the election played under different electoral rules. Lastly, the conclusion recapitulates some of the main themes to emerge from the book, examines the dynamics of the election campaign, and then summarises some of the broader implications which emerge for understanding British politics and for the study of voting behavior and elections.

---

1 For details, see P. Norris (ed.), *Britain Votes 2001*, Oxford University Press, 2001.

2 For a detailed summary of the results, see A. Mellows-Facer, R. Young and R. Cracknell, *General Election 2005*, House of Commons Research Paper 05/33, 17 May 2005, www.parliament.uk.

3 H. Kim and R.C. Fording. 'Does Tactical Voting Matter? The Political Impact of Tactical Voting in Recent British elections', *Comparative Political Studies* 34(3), 2001, 294–311.

4 I. Budge. 'Party Policy and Ideology: Still New Labour?' in P. Norris (ed.), *Britain Votes 2001*, Oxford University Press, 2001.

5 Although the observed results are suggestive, caution should be noted about this interpretation. Any analysis based only on the constituency results necessarily remains limited. To have full confidence that Conservative shifts towards the Liberal Democrats were actually the result of tactical or strategic voting calculations, or whether they were due to other factors, awaits confirmation from the further research using individual-level survey data of voter preferences.

6 P. Norris, *Electoral Engineering*, Cambridge University Press, 2004.

7 R.J. Johnston, C.J. Pattie, D.F.L. Dorling and D.J. Rossiter, *From Votes to Seats: The Operation of the UK Electoral System since 1945*, Manchester University Press, 2001.

8 For details, see D. Denver, C. Rallings and M. Thrasher (eds), *Media Guide to the new Scottish Westminster Parliamentary Constituencies*, BBC/ITN/PA/Sky, University of Plymouth, 2004.

9 For a discussion, see P. Norris, *Democratic Phoenix: Reinventing Political Activism*, Cambridge University Press, 2003; M. Franklin, *Voter Turnout and the Dynamics of Electoral Competition in Established Democracies since 1945*, Cambridge University Press, 2004.

10 A. Heath and B. Taylor, 'New Sources of Abstention?' in G. Evans and P. Norris (eds), *Critical Elections: British Parties and Voters in Long-Term Perspective*, Sage, 1999.

11 Norris, *Democratic Phoenix*, op. cit.; Franklin, op. cit.

12 For discussions and evaluations of the Labour government's policies and record see P. Toynbee and D. Walker, *Better or Worse? Has Labour Delivered?*, Bloomsbury, 2005; A. Seldon and D. Kavanagh, *The Blair Effect II*, Cambridge University Press, 2005.

IVOR CREWE

The Opinion Polls: The Election They Got (Almost) Right

In the game of elections, opinion polls merely attempt to keep the score. By doing so publicly, as discussed in the book's conclusion, they frequently influence the way the game is played and occasionally the outcome. The drumbeat of polls, amplified and sometimes distorted by the media, affects the timing of the election, the morale of party workers, the tactics of the parties' campaign planners and media advisers, the issues chosen by the leaders, and the anticipation of the final outcome by the voters themselves—with consequences for turnout and, in a close-run contest, arguably the result itself. The accuracy of the polls is therefore a matter of legitimate public concern, as well as critical to the credibility and commercial prospects of the polling organisations and the market research industry. The polling organisations go to considerable trouble to forecast the result correctly and precisely—and to defend errors—because a great deal is at stake.

The British polling industry is haunted by its 1992 debacle.[1] The polls showed the Conservative and Labour parties level pegging throughout the campaign, and the four final polls, when averaged, placed Labour less than 1% ahead. All the indications were of a hung parliament and a coalition Government. In the event, Labour ran 7.6% behind the Conservatives in the popular vote, and the Conservatives were re-elected for five more years with a reduced but clear overall majority of 21. The polls had miscalculated the gap between the two parties by more than eight percentage points, in Labour's favour.

The polls' record in the 1997 and 2001 election was more creditable, but the polls were not put to the test of forecasting a close-run contest. At both elections the polls consistently recorded large double-digit Labour percentage leads in the vote, which led the media to forecast the Labour landslides, which duly occurred. Closer scrutiny revealed that despite the measures taken by some polling organisations to minimise a repeat of the 1992 errors, there remained an inherent pro-Labour bias

© Oxford University Press 2005
doi: 10.1093/pa/gsi074

in their estimates. Polling accuracy is measured by the mean percentage point discrepancy between the final forecast polls and the parties' share of the vote in the actual election result. In 1997 this discrepancy was the third largest since 1945. Five of the seven final polls and both exit polls underestimated the Conservative vote and eight of the nine final or exit polls over-estimated the Labour vote. Labour's lead over the Conservatives was exaggerated by an average of 4 percentage points.

There was a similar story in 2001. Throughout the campaign, the polls were reporting Labour leads in the 16–18% range; the five final polls put Labour 14% ahead and the two exit polls 12.5% ahead; in the event the Labour lead in the actual popular vote was 9.3%. Once again, the polls were inflating Labour's true lead by four to five percentage points.

This degree of error can be ignored in elections with runaway winners. But in seven of the sixteen post-war elections the winning party's margin of victory in the popular vote has been less than 5%. Moreover, inaccuracy to the tune of four or five points can make the difference in voters' eyes between a runaway winner and a neck-and-neck contest to the finish, and thus between voting or abstaining, and between casting a tactical or first-preference vote.

The field in 2005

In 1997 and 2001 the opinion polls took a low profile during the campaign. The number of published national polls fell from 57 in 1992—a postwar peak—to 44 in 1997 and dropped again to 36 in 2001 (see Table 1). The most probable reason is that the polls were consistently

1. The Fluctuating Intensity of Opinion Polls in General Election Campaigns, 1945–2005

Election Year	Number of National Polls in Campaign	Number of Different Agencies Conducting Polls	Number of Different Newspaper/TV Programmes Commissioning Polls
1945	1	1	1
1950	11	2	2
1951	n/a	3	3
1955	n/a	2	2
1959	20	2	4
1964	23	4	4
1966	26	4	8
1970	25	5	6
Feb. 74	25	6	9
Oct. 74	27	6	11
1979	26	5	8
1983	46	6	14
1987	54	7	15
1992	57	7	18
1997	44	5	13
2001	36	5	11
2005	52	8	14

Note: The number of polls excludes daily rolling polls, election-day surveys and private polling by the parties, as well as regional and local surveys. Source: Author's opinion poll database.

pointing to a foregone conclusion and thus gave the media little incentive to spend money on additional surveys.

In 2005 the media's interest in commissioning polls recovered to the level of 1987 and 1992: seven different newspapers and television companies published 52 national polls.[2] The number of polling organisations entering the field (eight) was a post-war record. In addition there were two daily 'rolling polls', as well as polls of Scotland, marginal constituencies, and occupational groups (e.g. of directors, doctors, teachers, academics and students). It was noticeable, however, that the imaginative profusion of polling topics that characterised the 1987 and 1992 elections was lacking in 2005: the national survey of vote intentions, with (typically) up to ten additional questions on the party leaders and campaign issues, constituted the bulk of the commissioned polls. A noticeable contrast with the elections of the 1980s and 1990s was the paucity of panel surveys, and the failure of the media to make much use of the panel data that did exist in, for example, the YouGov polls. The greater prominence of polls in the 2005 campaign probably reflected the media's anticipation of more potential excitement in the outcome. Very few commentators or members of the public expected anything other than the re-election of Labour for a third term, but most assumed that Labour's majority would be cut, perhaps significantly, with side-effects for the survival of Tony Blair as prime minister and for the balance of power between the Blairites and Brownites within the parliamentary Labour party. Almost all the polls in the 2001–05 parliament placed Labour ahead, but from the first quarter of 2003 the Labour lead (measured as the average over a quarter) was in single digits, never more than six percentage points. From June 2003 to September 2004, when politics was dominated by the fallout of the Iraq invasion, Labour was barely in front, its lead reduced to between one and three points (see Figure 1). In September 2003 and July 2004 it lost the safe seats of Brent East and Leicester South in by-elections. Although Labour's lead widened to five and six percentage points over the autumn and winter of 2004–05, it was not fanciful to imagine that this modest lead would be whittled away during the campaign, and would anyway be exaggerated by the polls, just as Labour's lead had drifted downwards and been inflated by poll bias in 1997 and 2001.

A rather different set of polling organisations entered the lists in 2005 compared with 2001. Gallup, the longest established polling company of them all, associated for four decades with the *Daily Telegraph*, retired from the field altogether. It was replaced by YouGov, founded in 2000 by among others the political commentator Peter Kellner, to use the internet to gather formation about vote intentions. After 2001 it soon established itself as the most prolific polling organisation of them all, conducting polls also for the *Sunday Times* and the *Mail on Sunday*. During the campaign it published bi-weekly polls for the *Daily Telegraph* but also weekly polls for the *Sunday Times* and *SkyTV*.

1. National Opinion Polls, July 2001–March 2005

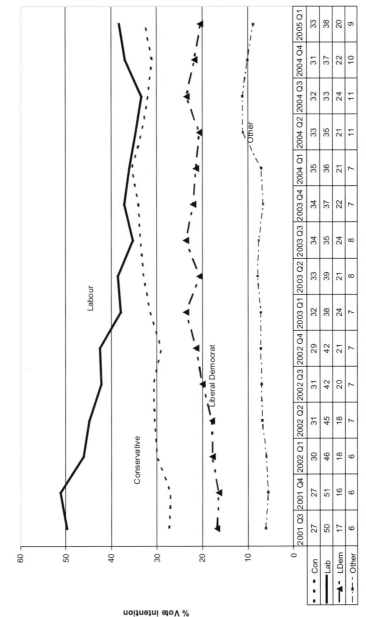

Source: Author's opinion poll database.

There were two other newcomers to the market. Populus, founded by two former staff members of Conservative Central Office, began to poll regularly for *The Times*, replacing MORI. Much of its polling for *The Times* during the campaign consisted of a cumulative 'rolling poll' in which a small subsample of its initial sample was replaced each day by a new subsample. Communicate Research, founded in 2003 by a former executive at Harris, conducted polls for the *Independent on Sunday*, replacing Rasmussen, a US company which burst upon the scene in 2001 only to disappear.

Of the veteran polling companies, MORI, abandoned by *The Times* after its erratic performance in 2001, continued to publish largely uncommissioned polls. During the campaign it produced weekly polls for the *Financial Times* as well as occasional polls for the *Observer*, *Sunday Mirror*, *Sun* and *Evening Standard*. NOP conducted no polls during the 2001–05 parliament but it was taken on by the *Independent* for the election. ICM, the company that pioneered important methodological innovations after the 1992 election, with considerable success in 1997 and 2001, stayed with its regular outlet, the *Guardian*. Harris, a prominent UK polling company in election campaigns until 1997, published a couple of internet-based polls on the eve of the election from its website. Finally, BPIX, the polling arm of the British Election Study at the University of Essex, published four polls in the *Mail on Sunday*, and the British Election Study website presented the results of its own daily rolling poll (which used YouGov to do the fieldwork).

Methods

The various polling organisations used one or more of three different methods to cope with potential pro-Labour bias (see Table 2). Firstly, all but YouGov either filtered or weighted by respondents' self-declared probability of voting. The decline in turnout in 2001 to 59%, and the numerous indications in the polls that the turnout level would be similar in 2005, meant that many respondents who declared a voting intention in the poll would not, in fact, cast a vote—with potentially differential impact on the parties. Labour sympathisers are concentrated in those social groups with a historical record of relatively low turnout; moreover, all the polls reported that Labour supporters' self-reported intention to vote was weaker than that of Conservatives', who by 2005, after two heavy defeats, appeared particularly determined to vote. The precise filtering and weighting methods varied between the polling companies but all had the effect of reducing the 'raw' Labour lead, particularly in the first half of the campaign.[3]

Secondly, ICM, Populus, YouGov and NOP (sometimes) weighted their results by respondents' recall of their vote at the previous general election. ICM adopted this measure after the 1992 election to counteract the risk of drawing a pro-Labour sample. The method is risky, however, because respondents' electoral recall is notoriously unreliable, and

2. The Design of the Different Polls

Polling Organisation	Data Collection Method	Typical Sample Size	Weighting	Weight by Past Vote?	Filter by Turnout?	Reallocate DKs and Refusers?
Communicate Research	Telephone: quasi random. Random selection of telephone numbers; 1 added to number to catch ex-directory numbers; quota used to select from within household.	1,000	Age, sex, class + likelihood to vote	No	Yes: excludes Rs scoring themselves 4 or below on probability of voting; weight remainder by score (1.0, for score of 10, 0.9 for 9 etc)	No—but uses extra 'squeeze' question on DKs.
HI Europe (Harris)	By internet	3,700	Age, sex, education, income and location + 'propensity score weights' which take account of the unrepresentative attitudes and behaviours of an online sample	No	Yes: limit forecast to respondents saying they are 'absolutely certain' to vote	No
ICM	Telephone: quasi random. Random selection of telephone numbers; 1 added to number to catch ex-directory numbers; quota used to select from within household.	1,500	Age, sex, class, region + probability of voting	Yes: to mid-point between actual result and average recalled past vote over 20 most recent polls	No	Yes: 50% allocated to party recalled voting for at previous election.
MORI	Face to face and telephone	1,000	Age, sex, class, region	No	Yes: only includes (*not excludes*) Rs giving themselves a score of 10/10 on a 10-point scale from 'absolutely certain not to vote' to 'absolutely certain to vote'.	No

2. The Design of the Different Polls *continued*

Polling Organisation	Data Collection Method	Typical Sample Size	Weighting	Weight by Past Vote?	Filter by Turnout?	Reallocate DKs and Refusers?
NOP	Telephone: quasi random. Random selection of telephone numbers; 1 added to number to catch ex-directory numbers; quota used to select from within household.	950	Age, sex, class, region	Only if recalled vote falls outside target range	No	Only if recalled vote of DKs/refusers is significantly out of line with rest of sample
Populus	Telephone: quasi random. Random selection of telephone numbers; 1 added to number to catch ex-directory numbers; quota used to select from within household.	1500	Age, sex, class, region + probability of voting	Yes: to benchmark of 'normal forgetfulness'	Yes until 11/2004; then ceased.	Yes: 60% allocated to party recalled voting for at previous election.
You Gov	By internet from sample drawn from pre-selected panel of 50,000	varies but usually over 2000	Age, sex, class, region + newspaper	Yes	No	No

Source: Author's opinion poll database.

in non-random ways: people have a tendency to confuse a recent local election with a more distant general election, to project current voting intentions onto their past behaviour, and to forget if they voted for the Liberal Democrats or a minor party.[4] At a time when the Labour Government's popularity had lost much of its shine it was unclear whether weighting by past vote would reduce or increase a pro-Labour bias.

Thirdly, ICM and Populus reallocated a proportion of their 'don't knows' and 'refusers' to the party respondents recalled voting for at the previous election. ICM adopted this method after 1992 to deal with the alleged 'closet Tories' who were reluctant to acknowledge that they supported an apparently unpopular or unfashionable party. By 2005 the political atmosphere was very different and it appeared that this adjustment slightly boosted Labour's standing in the polls.

A more significant innovation than any of these adjustments, however, was the adoption by YouGov of the internet as the medium for collecting information about vote intentions. YouGov established a large panel of 50,000 volunteers, designed to be a cross-section of the electorate, who were paid 50p a time to complete polls. Representative subsamples of the panel were randomly generated by computer and weighted by the normal demographics, newspaper readership and past vote.

YouGov's methods were fiercely criticised by some prominent members of the polling industry, mainly on the grounds that self-selected internet users were inevitably more interested in politics than the typical voter, that they were socially unrepresentative of the electorate even when their responses were weighted to align with the electorate's social characteristics, and that the absence of an interviewer meant there no way of ensuring that the respondent's answers were genuine.[5] In response YouGov argued that the lack of an interviewer had the advantage of eliminating social biases in responses and the flexibility of the internet—leaving it to the respondent to answer when convenient— increased the response rate. It did not filter by probability of voting or reallocate 'don't knows' because, it claimed, an anonymous computer screen encouraged more honest answers from respondents than an interviewer would have done. Moreover, YouGov could flourish a trump card: its record of predicting the 2001 general election, the Scottish Parliament election, the Conservative leadership election and even the Pop Idol contest was impressively accurate.

Whatever the strengths and weaknesses of YouGov's new fangled methods, they did appear to make a systematic difference. As Table 3 shows, YouGov tended to report a smaller Labour lead (a mean of only 0.5% in the period January 2003–March 2005) than Populus (2.8%), MORI (4.7%) and ICM (5.8%); in particular it consistently gave the Conservatives a higher share of the vote than the other organisations did. In the 2001–05 parliament only 19 of the 243 national polls put the Conservatives ahead, and 13 of these were YouGov polls.

3. The Monthly Polls by ICM, MORI, Populus and YouGov Jan 2003–March 2005

Polling Organisation	No. of Polls	Labour Lead	Cons	Labour	Lib Dem	Other
ICM	26	5.8	32.0	37.8	21.8	8.1
MORI	27	4.7	32.6	37.3	21.6	8.4
Populus	26	2.8	32.4	35.3	22.6	9.7
YouGov	27	0.5	34.8	35.3	21.7	8.3

Source: Author's opinion poll database.

This pattern was more or less repeated during the campaign itself. Four of the polling companies—Communications Research, ICM, NOP and Populus—put Labour ahead by, on average, 6 percentage points, whereas YouGov consistently gave Labour smaller leads of 2 to 3 points. Its main divergence from other polls was in the low share of the vote it reported for Labour, mainly to the advantage of the Liberal Democrats. Thus the election result was anticipated to be a critical test of the validity of internet polling compared with the more tried and tested methods of face-to-face and telephone interviewing.

Change and continuity during the campaign

A first impression from the polls is that the campaign made not the slightest difference to the result. As Table 4 shows, in each of the three months before the campaign, Labour was between five and six percentage

4. The Opinion Polls and the 2005 Election

			Labour Lead	Con	Lab	Lib Dem	Other
Pre-Campaign Polls							
Jan 2005 (9)			5.7	31.8	37.4	21.4	9.3
Feb 2005 (7)			5.7	33.1	38.9	19.4	8.6
March 2005 (7)			5.4	33.1	38.6	20.1	8.3
Campaign Polls							
Week 1 (9) April 1–7			1.7	35.1	36.8	20.4	7.7
Week 2 (10) April 8–13			4.5	33.6	38.1	21.3	7.0
Week 3 (11) April 15–21			5.8	32.8	38.6	21.3	7.0
Week 4 plus (15) April 22-May 1			5.2	32.4	37.6	22.3	7.8
Final Forecast Polls							
1–3 May	ICM	*Guardian*	6	32	38	22	8
1–3 May	NOP	*Independent*	3	33	36	23	9
1–4 May	Harris	HI Europe website	5	33	38	22	7
2–3 May	Populus	*The Times*	6	32	38	21	9
3–4 May	YouGov	*Daily Telegraph*	5	32	37	24	7
3–4 May	MORI	*Evening Standard*	5	33	38	23	5
Exit Poll							
5 May	NOP/MORI	BBC/ITN	4.0	33.0	37.0	22.0	8.0
Forecast poll mean (6)			5.0	32.5	37.5	22.5	7.5
Actual result (GB)			2.9	33.1	36.0	22.6	8.3

Note: Excludes the Populus/*Times* and BES rolling polls. Fieldwork dates in the week-by-week comparisons refer to the first day of fieldwork. Source: Author's opinion poll database.

points ahead; it enjoyed the same lead in the final half of the campaign; and on the eve of election the six forecast polls put Labour in front by an average of exactly 5.0%. The electorate's opinion on the issues and leaders displayed the same stability. For example, in the eight YouGov/ *Daily Telegraph* polls conducted between 5–6 April and 29 April–1 May the proportions saying that Tony Blair 'would make the best prime minister' only fluctuated within the range of 34–38% and the proportions saying Michael Howard remained within the even narrower band of 24 to 26%. The proportions choosing Labour as the party 'more likely to run Britain's economy well' varied between 44 and 49% and the proportions choosing the Conservatives were stuck at between 27 and 29%. Respondents' views on which issues were most important to them and which party they preferred on each issue showed equally little movement. The analysis of the ICM/*Guardian* polls over the same period (see chapter 13) reaches similar conclusions. Apart from a modest across-the-board improvement in Labour's standing after the first week of the campaign, there was little change in the distribution of the public's evaluation of the parties for the rest of the campaign. All the hullabaloo of the campaign—the leaders' speeches, the party election broadcasts, the studio debates, the advertising hoardings, and the daily diet of election news—appeared at first sight to leave the electorate entirely unmoved. It was as if politicians and voters occupied parallel universes.

In reality opinion and voting intentions did shift a little during the campaign (see Table 4). The announcement of the election was immediately followed by an apparent swing to the Conservatives. For example, four polls based on interviews conducted on 1–3 April all recorded sharp falls of up to nine percentage points in the Labour lead from the previous month, suggesting a sudden swing to the Conservatives and a wide open contest.[6] Labour's average lead across all the polls fell from 5.4 percentage points in March 2005 to 1.7 points in the first week of the campaign (1–7 April). MORI actually reported a five point lead for the Conservatives (based on those 'absolutely certain' to vote), enough to elect it to office. What the sudden drop in the Labour lead reflected was almost certainly not a switch of vote intentions from Labour to Conservative but the much stronger determination of Conservatives than Labour sympathisers to vote—and to tell the pollsters.[7] As the campaign progressed, so the Government succeeded in mobilising some of its natural supporters who had told the pollsters at the beginning of the campaign that they didn't know whether or how they would vote. As the differential determination to vote between Labour and Conservative supporters narrowed, so Labour's lead recovered. As the final chapter shows, there was some social class polarisation during the campaign, and women appeared to edge towards Labour at the expense of the Conservatives. The Conservatives' share of the vote—strictly speaking their share of those declaring a vote intention—steadily drifted down from 35.1% in week 1 to 32.4% in week 4 of the campaign, while Labour's share of vote intentions crept up, only to fall back in the last week, to the apparent benefit of the Liberal Democrats.

The rolling polls

The polls that set out to measure change during the campaign were the 'rolling polls' conducted by YouGov on behalf of the British Election Study (BES) at the University of Essex (and published on its website) and by Populus for *The Times*. YouGov replaced 230 respondents each day over a cycle of six days and Populus replaced 350 respondents over a cycle of four days. The idea was that the daily replenishment would help to detect the immediate impact of important events during the campaign, while the continuity from day to day (five-sixths in the case of the BES and three quarters in the case of Populus) would iron out apparent changes caused by sampling fluctuations and would identify longer-term trends.

In fact the rolling polls cast little light on the impact of campaign events. Populus reported an accelerating Labour lead from 6 percentage points in mid-April to 14 points by the end of the month, which was markedly out of line with all the other polls. *The Times'* covered their tracks by arguing that a rolling poll 'measures trends and momentum rather than predicting election results' and by using a fresh Populus poll of over 2,000 respondents for its election forecast, claiming it would 'not be affected by day to day fluctuations and will take account of factors such as postal voting'.[8] But rolling polls are no different from a daily succession of normal polls, each conducted evenly over four (or more) days, and therefore no better or worse at forecasting election results. Populus speculated that what they acknowledged to be an improbable result reflected the problems of interviewing over the long Bank Holiday weekend, but this would have affected the other polling organisations in the field too and seems an unlikely explanation.[9] The YouGov/BES rolling poll was much more in line with other polls but its fluctuations did not correlate with those of the Populus/*The Times* poll, nor with the conventional polls. For example, YouGov/BES reported a sharp fall in the Labour lead on the basis of its 20 April addition (and 14 April subtraction) whereas Populus recorded no change of lead at all. It proved impossible to disentangle the impact of sampling error (which is large on a sample of 230 or 350 respondents) from that of a campaign development and, in addition, to distinguish between the effect of adding a new subsample from the effect of subtracting an old subsample. It seems unlikely that rolling polls can add reliably to our knowledge of campaign effects and trends unless the subsamples are themselves the size of normal samples and analysed and presented as such.

The performance of the polls

The final opinion polls proved remarkably accurate in 2005 (see Table 4). Six polling organisations published forecast polls on election day. The mean of the share of the vote in Great Britain that they forecast for each of the main parties was impressively close to the actual share that the parties won—32.5% for the Conservatives (actual: 33.1%), 37.5% for Labour (actual: 36.0%), 22.5% for the Liberal Democrats (actual: 22.6%) and 7.5% for the others (actual 8.3%). The BBC/ITN exit poll was even more accurate as was the BBC close-of-polls prediction of a Labour majority of 66 which, remarkably, was spot on. By the standard measure of the polls' overall accuracy—the mean of the deviation between the average forecast for each party's vote share and actual vote share—the forecast polls in 2005 were the third most accurate in the seventeen since the war. They were on average within 1 percentage point of the actual result for three of the parties and only 1.5 points out for Labour (see Table 5).

Have the opinion polls finally cracked the problem of a pro-Labour bias? Not quite. Five of the six forecast polls over-estimated the Labour vote, although never by more than 2 percentage points. As a result, the same five polls exaggerated Labour's actual lead, putting it at between 5 and 6 percentage points when in fact it was 2.9 points. Had the main parties obtained the vote shares predicted by the six forecast polls, Labour's majority would have been 88 rather than 66—close to the media's expectations.[10] Most of the pro-Labour bias was squeezed out of the polls in 2005, but not all of it.

5. Accuracy of the Final Forecast Polls in General Elections, 1945–2005

Year	Outgoing Government	Number of Forecast Polls	Deviation of Mean Estimate from Share of Vote (GB) for:				Mean Error per Party	Mean Error on Gap between Con and Lab
			Con	Lab	Lib	Others		
1945	Coalition	1	2	−2	1	−1	1.5	Con: +4
1950	Labour	2	1	−2	2	0	1.3	Con: +3
1951	Labour	3	2	−4	1	1	2.3	Con: +6
1955	Conservative	2	1	1	−1	−1	1.0	0
1959	Conservative	3	0	−1	0	0	0.3	Con: +1
1964	Conservative	4	1	1	−1	0	1.0	0
1966	Labour	3	−1	3	−1	0	1.3	Lab: +4
1970	Labour	5	−2	4	−1	−1	2.0	Lab: +6
Feb-74	Conservative	6	0	−2	2	0	1.0	Con: +2
Oct-74	Labour	5	−2	3	0	−1	1.5	Lab: +5
1979	Labour	5	0	1	0	0	0.3	Con: +1
1983	Conservative	7	3	−2	0	−1	1.5	Con: +5
1987	Conservative	7	−1	2	−2	0	1.3	Lab: +3
1992	Conservative	4	−4	4	1	−1	3.0	Lab: +9
1997	Conservative	6	−1	3	−1	−1	2.0	Lab: +4
2001	Labour	5	−2	3	−2	0	1.8	Lab: +5
2005	Labour	6	−1	2	0	0	0.8	Lab: +2

Note: A 'final forecast' poll is defined for 1959–97 as any published on polling day and for earlier elections as any described as such. From February 1974 onwards interviews were generally conducted on the Tuesday and Wednesday immediately before election day. Source: Author's opinion poll database.

The relative accuracy of the final polls frustratingly failed to resolve any of the issues of design and method which divided the polling industry and fascinated the technical experts. The prize for the most accurate forecast went to NOP, whose poll in the *Independent* was precisely right for each party (rounded to whole numbers). However, it would be generous to attribute NOP's success wholly to the methods it adopted, because all of the other polls' forecasts were well within the 3% margin of error. Moreover, throughout the campaign NOP had reported Labour leads at the higher end of the range, including a 10 point lead in its previous poll conducted on 22–24 April. As it would be very fanciful to assume a 7-point fall in Labour's lead in the final week,[11] part of NOP's accuracy must have been the product of luck rather than skill.

The polling organisation whose methods were most under the spotlight, YouGov, did very creditably but stumbled slightly at the last hurdle. Throughout the campaign it reported a smaller Labour lead than the other polls did: as Table 6 shows, its 13 campaign polls were on average very close to the actual result. But its final poll, which put Labour five points ahead, was less accurate than NOP's, with chance rather than design being the explanation. The forecast of the Harris internet poll was close to the forecasts of the conventional polls and it was the closest of the final Scottish polls to the actual result in Scotland.[12] YouGov and Harris confirmed, if further confirmation were needed, that internet polling is as reliable as polling by conventional means. But they could not quite clinch the superiority of internet polling over more traditional methods.

The performance of the polls in 2005 may well not get the credit it deserves. Polls are conducted in order to give their readership a sense of the likely result. What commentators and the public wish to know is which party will form the government and if it will have a landslide, comfortable or narrow majority. The number of seats matters more than the share of the vote. But polls forecast vote shares, not the seats that they are converted into by an un-proportionate and unpredictable electoral system. On election day the front pages of the newspapers that published polls, under headlines suggesting a 'historic third term' for

6. Comparison of the Vote Intention Figures between the Different Polling Organisations: The Campaign Polls, 2005

Polling Organisation (No. of Polls)	Outlet	Labour Lead	Con	Lab	Lib Dem	Other
Populus (5)	*The Times*	6.6	32.6	39.2	20.4	7.8
Communications Research (3)	*Independent on Sunday*	6.3	33.3	39.7	20.3	6.7
ICM (11)	*Guardian, Sunday Telegraph, Daily Mirror*	6.3	32.7	39.0	21.2	7.1
NOP (4)	*Independent*	6.0	31.8	37.8	21.0	9.5
MORI (6)	*FT, Observer/Sunday Mirror*	4.2	33.3	37.5	21.3	7.8
YouGov (13)	*Daily Telegraph, Sunday Times*	2.7	33.8	36.5	22.5	7.1
Actual result (GB)		2.9	33.1	36.0	22.6	8.3

Source: Author's opinion poll database.

Labour' predicted majorities ranging from 90 to 130, with some adding cautionary words about the possibility of Labour doing worse than average in its marginal seats.[13] Most of the media therefore treated Labour's much lower than forecast majority of 66 as a surprise 'bloody nose' for Labour, and in particular for Tony Blair, whose authority as party leader and prime minister had been fatally holed.

The lower than expected majority cannot, however, be attributed to the polls' slight exaggeration of Labour's true lead in the popular vote. The actual swings of 3.2% from Labour to Conservative and 4.9% from Labour to the Liberal Democrats would have delivered a Labour majority of 105, not 66, on a uniform national swing. The swings suggested by the final forecast polls—of 2.4% from Labour to Conservative and 4.1% from Labour to the Liberal Democrats—would have delivered, on a uniform national swing, a Labour majority of 122. Thus the mild inaccuracy of the forecast polls can only account for a small part of Labour's lower than anticipated majority; the constituency and regional variations in swing, at Labour's expense, account for the rest, as explained in chapter 13. The performance of an opinion poll should be judged on the accuracy of its forecast of the parties' share of the votes, not on the seats forecast based on those shares.[14] But if constituency swings should again prove to be so varied at the next election, sceptical questions may come to be asked about the point of national polls.

Conclusion

The opinion polls play a larger role in some elections than others. In 1992 their inaccuracy probably influenced the outcome, and in both 1997 and 2001 their unremitting signal of a Labour landslide probably helped to depress turnout. In 2005 they were thicker on the ground but played a minor role, partly because they consistently pointed to the re-election of a Labour government but with a reduced majority, and partly because they proved more accurate than at any time since 1979. Had they been perfectly accurate they would probably have indicated smaller Labour leads during the campaign. Were the current electoral system not so heavily skewed in Labour's favour (see chapter 13), the expectation of a close contest and a genuine choice between a Labour government led by Tony Blair and a Conservative government led by Michael Howard might have led to greater interest, higher turnout and different party choices among the voters. The potential influence of polls over the character, course, and consequences of a campaign is always present, which makes their accuracy and design matters of public importance. The 2005 election was a good election for the polling organisations but did not resolve the question of whether they have at last conquered the multiple and changing sources of bias in the polls they conduct.

1   See I. Crewe, 'A Nation of Liars? Opinion Polls and the 1992 Election', *Parliamentary Affairs*, 1992/4, pp. 475–95 and Market Research Society, *The Opinion Polls and the 1992 General Election*, July 1994.

2   An invaluable source of information about the polling companies' methods—and about UK opinion polls in general—is the excellent UK Polling Report website (http://pollingreport.co.uk). The measured comments by 'Anthony' in the Commentary section are always worth reading.

3   For example, in the MORI/*Financial Times* poll conducted on 1–3 April, 74% of Conservatives said they were 'absolutely certain' to vote, compared with 57% of Labour supporters. As a result Labour led the Conservatives by 38% to 33% among all respondents but trailed by 34% to 39% among the 'absolutely certains'—a ten point difference. In its final poll for the *Financial Times*, 81% of Conservatives reported that they were 'absolutely certain' to vote compared with 70% of Labour supporters. As a result, a 15% Labour lead among all respondents was reduced to a 10% lead among the 'absolutely certains'—a five point difference. See MORI's very informative 2005 general election website: http://www.mori.com/election2005.

4   See Market Research Society, *The Opinion Polls and the 1992 General Election*, pp. 48–53.

5   See, for example, MORI, 'Polling on the internet' (http://www.mori.com/mrr/2002/c020712.shtml) and, in defence of internet polling, P. Kellner, 'For the record', *Guardian*, 12.2.03 (Politics Special Report: http://politics.guardian.co.uk/polls/comment/0,11030,893890,00.html.

6   Labour's lead fell from 12 to 3 points in the NOP/*Independent* poll, 8 to 3 points in the ICM/*Guardian* poll; 7 to 2 points in the Populus/*The Times* poll and from 0% to a 5% Conservative lead in the MORI/*Financial Times* poll.

7   See endnote 3.

8   P. Riddell, 'Conservative support reaches a record low', *The Times*, 4.5.05, p. 26.

9   'Andrew Cooper Q&A', *Times on Line*, 6.5.05.

10 On the pattern of constituency swings in 2005, Labour would have retained eleven of the seats it lost to the Conservatives (and possibly Dundee East, lost to the SNP) if the actual share of the vote had been the same as the average final poll forecast.

11 ICM, YouGov and the British Election Study recorded little change over the same period, and MORI reported an increase in Labour's lead from 2% to 10%.

12 The Harris poll (based on fieldwork between 1 May and 4 May), with the actual result in parentheses, reported Conservative 15% (16%), Labour 39% (39%), Liberal Democrat 22% (23%), SNP 20% (18%), Others 4% (4%), a mean error of 0.8%.

13 The *Daily Telegraph* predicted a Labour majority of 130; the *Guardian* one of 90–110; *The Times* one of 'well above 100 and possibly up to 130', and the *Independent*, which published the highly accurate NOP poll, a majority of 90, but under the headline 'ONE QUARTER OF VOTERS UNCERTAIN AS LABOUR SAG AT THE FINAL POST'.

14 Which makes it surprising that the Chair of MORI, Sir Robert Worcester, who has frequently made this point in the past, could not resist the temptation of trumpeting the BBC/ITN's forecast of a 66 majority as a triumph for the exit poll, which MORI coconducted with NOP. (See 'Worcester's Weblog', MORI website, 6.5.05.) It wasn't really. It owed more to the skill—and good luck!—of the forecasters.

JOHN BARTLE

The Press, Television, and the Internet

In the 1997 and 2001 general elections, New Labour triumphed at the polls and in the media. In 1997 it had received the endorsements of six out of eleven national daily newspapers and been given largely sympathetic coverage in the broadcast media. In 2001 it made even more progress among the print media, with the endorsement of seven out of the eleven. By 2001, however, its relationship with the media had became progressively more difficult. The party found it difficult to adjust from opposition to government and it quickly gained an unenviable reputation for spinning. Those at the centre, such as Alastair Campbell, the Prime Minister's Press Secretary, became increasingly sensitive to criticism. Their relationship with the BBC, in particular, became increasingly strained. A *Panorama* investigation into the NHS, broadcast shortly before the 2001 election, caused particular resentment. As early as June 2001, the Deputy Head of BBC News was quoted as saying, 'I can't remember a more fragile state of affairs between the BBC and the Labour Party'.[1]

Things changed for the worse in the next four years. Some of Labour's new friends in the press simply abandoned the party. Others remained 'on board' but were increasingly critical or demanded concessions that antagonised Labour's old friends. This latter group became increasingly disillusioned with both Labour and Blair. By 2005, therefore, Labour had few allies in the press and the Conservatives had begun to rebuild some support.

Labour's relationship with the broadcasters also became strained. From 2003 to 2004, it found itself virtually at war with the BBC over allegations broadcast on Radio 4's *Today Programme*. These allegations, about the government's case for the Iraq war, ultimately led to the death of Dr David Kelly, the Hutton inquiry, and the resignations of Andrew Gilligan, the reporter who had made the allegations, Greg Dyke, the BBC's Director General, and Gavyn Davies, the Chairman of the BBC's Board of Governors. On the day that Dyke resigned, BBC workers protested about government interference. Many felt that Gilligan

© Oxford University Press 2005
doi: 10.1093/pa/gsi059

had been broadly correct and that the Corporation had not been given a fair hearing by Hutton. They were particularly irked that the government had got off scot-free. Although the BBC announced reforms to make sure that mistakes would not be repeated, the affair inevitably soured relations. The tension lifted when Tessa Jowell, the Culture Secretary, announced that the BBC would be awarded a new charter. This guaranteed the BBC's independence and financial position for a further ten years. Some in government, however, remained worried that the BBC and other broadcasters would be out for revenge. Others worried that the BBC would not be sufficiently robust in its examination of the government's record. In the event, the BBC—like all the broadcasters—walked the tight-rope with consummate skill.

The media is important for elections because it is assumed to influence the attitudes and opinions of voters. If the press and broadcasters have any influence on voters, moreover, it is via the steady drip-drip of information rather than through either their election coverage or formal endorsements.[2] In order to consider the possible effect of the media, therefore, it is necessary to consider the general tenor and tone of its reporting and commentary over extended periods of time as well as during the May 2005 general election campaign.

The national daily press

The parties continued to view the press as significant political actors, to be listened to, flattered, and actively courted. Labour and Conservative politicians, in particular, lavished attention on editors and proprietors. In 2004, for example, Michael Howard attended a *News International* Conference in Cancun, Mexico, and Tony Blair reportedly had conversations with Rupert Murdoch about a referendum on the proposed EU constitution. It still appears that the media are 'not separate limbs or membranes in the anatomy [of Britain] so much as part of the lifeblood or nervous system'.[3]

The parties have continued to court the press despite evidence that the newspapers are a declining influence on public opinion. Sales of the dailies, for example, have continued to fall; from around 13.1 million in 2001 to 12.3 million in 2005. These figures, furthermore, understate the true extent of the decline, since they include the free copies distributed in hotels and airports.[4] Intense competition for sales has reduced profits and made newspapers increasingly sensitive to sales. Newspapers are just as weak as politicians in the face of changes in consumer sentiment.

The press has responded to the changing market in various ways. The *Times* and *Independent* have both moved to a 'compact' format and have witnessed a growth in sales. The *Guardian* will shortly follow suit, leaving the *Daily Telegraph* and *Financial Times* as the only daily broadsheet on the market. Smaller format publications are more dominated by headlines and images, so this change has increased the importance of the scoop. This has affected political reporting. The *Independent* has sought to appeal to younger readers by campaigning on issues such as Iraq. Others have also sought to capture the new spirit of scepticism by adopting a more critical tone of reporting and focussing on the failures of politicians. Thus, even those newspapers that still think of themselves as involved in party politics have become less positive about the party they back, even if they remain hostile to another party. 'Negative partisanship', consisting of 'entrenched and intense hostility to the rival party' is *de rigour*, but outright advocacy of a party is unusual.[5] This change mirrors the shift in party competition from ideological disagreement to debates about competence. The press can hardly claim that the party they support is the only way to achieve a good society when the debates are technical and managerial. The intense partisanship of the 1980s has given way to shoulder-shrugging or grudging support.

Partisan dealignment in the press, thirteen years on

Press partisanship has varied over time. In the immediate post-war period, the Conservatives enjoyed a substantial advantage over Labour. This was sharply accentuated in the 1970s, as the industrial conflicts between labour and capital, and the political conflicts between left and right, intensified. The ideological approach and personal style of Margaret Thatcher appealed to newspaper proprietors and brought the Conservatives the enthusiastic support of the press from 1979 to 1987. Relations between the Tories and the press soured after her ejection from office, but most continued to support John Major. Indeed, Neil Kinnock attributed his defeat in 1992 to the devastating and highly entertaining attacks launched by tabloid newspapers such as the *Sun*, *Mail* and *Express*. The 'Tory press', like their readers, however, were badly burned by the ERM crisis, tax raises, and 'sleaze' that surrounded the Major government 1992–97. Yet, as disillusioned as they were, few showed interest in supporting John Smith's 'Old Labour'. Blair's emergence as Labour leader was the turning point. He persuaded people that he could marry commitments to the market with social justice, profitability with workers' rights, and pro-European policies with the national interest. Such 'triangulation' created a highly successful coalition, but one that contained the seeds of its own destruction.

The point is illustrated by considering the *Sun*, Britain's best-selling daily newspaper. This publication had been one of Thatcher's strongest supporters in the 1980s. Rupert Murdoch, the owner of *News International*, was a strong supporter of free markets, trade union legislation, the Atlantic alliance, and a firm opponent of European integration. The *Sun*'s political sympathies reflected Murdoch's own beliefs, combining working class patriotism and populism. Its conversion to Labour in 1997 was thought to be one of the 'defining moments' of that campaign. In spite of this conversion, however, the *Sun* retained distinctive attitudes and priorities. In Labour's first two terms it continually harried the government on the issues of crime, immigration and Europe. The columnist, Richard Littlejohn, attacked both Labour's 'political correctness' and the Prime Minister's wife (whom he labelled the 'wicked witch'). From 2003 onwards the *Sun* began to warn darkly that it might switch back to the Conservatives. Murdoch was particularly worried about Blair's opposition to a referendum on the EU constitution.[6] The Prime Minister's about turn in 2004, therefore, provided him with reassurance, but the *Sun* still gave no commitments to Labour. In one week in January 2005 it ran no less than three leading articles devoted to immigration, alleging that Labour had failed its readers. In March it devoted thirteen pages over three days to attacking John Prescott over his policy towards travellers (Roma). At the start of the campaign, it noted 'the Conservatives in many ways speak our language'.[7]

In the end, the *Sun* declared for Labour, 'Give them one last chance' it said ominously.[8] Even this support was hedged with qualifications. It recognised Labour's economic achievements but emphasised the need to 'liberate British workers and business to compete'. It felt the NHS had got better but argued that 'billions have been squandered by public-sector managers not fit to run a corner shop'. It declared immigration a 'disgrace'. The government was criticised for its failure to get a grip on violent crime. The *Sun* condemned Labour for its commitment to the 'disastrous European constitution' but accepted Labour's reassurance that there would be a referendum. It even appeared to hanker for a return to the old Thatcherite certainties: 'When the Tories start acting like Conservatives they might deserve our support'. It backed Labour for two reasons: 'Standing firm on Iraq and the lack of a real alternative'. Littlejohn remained unconvinced 'I'd rather eat my own toenail clippings than vote for Labour' (*Sun*, 5.5.05).

The *Sun*'s 'support' for Labour was the result of cold, hard calculation. In 1997 it had followed rather than led its readers. In 2005 Murdoch realised that Labour enjoyed a lead among *Sun* readers that could not be reversed by a last minute switch. Labour would win without the *Sun*'s support. It was vital, however, to maintain the myth of 'It's the *Sun* wot won it' and provide its proprietor with leverage in his dealings with government. The day after the election, the *Sun*'s headline 'Kicked in the ballots' seemed to gloat at Labour's losses.[9] The *Sun* warned: 'Blair and Chancellor Gordon Brown have made a cast-iron promise that National Insurance will not be going up to fund the NHS. We don't want to see other taxes rising instead by stealth'.[10] As Joe Haines might have said, 'the *Sun* supports Labour as the hangman does a hanged man'.[11]

The *Mirror* was Labour's oldest ally. It had even supported Labour in the dark days of the 1980s. In 1994 it had welcomed Blair's leadership and enthusiastically supported Labour in 1997 and 2001. Its support was tempered, however, by growing resentment about Labour's relationship with the *Sun*. A particular source of grievance was the way in which Labour granted the *Sun* scoops (including getting Bill Clinton to write for the paper, and the story of the birth of Leo Blair in 2000).[12] The greatest pressure on the relationship, however, was that the *Mirror's* sales were in steep decline. This made it vital to recruit younger readers and to gain advertising revenue. Given the cynicism among the young towards politicians, it made little sense to nail the *Mirror's* colours to the government's mast. In 2000 it provided a warning shot by endorsing Steven Norris, the Conservative candidate for London Mayor. From 2001 onwards Piers Morgan, the editor, became increasingly critical of Labour. The *Mirror* criticised proposals for foundation hospitals and the failure to join the Euro. The greatest source of tension, however, was Blair's policy on Iraq. On 14 March 2003 it published a front page headline, 'Prime Monster?' which warned 'Drag us into this war without the U.N. Tony and that's how history will judge you. For God's sake man, DON'T DO IT'.[13] The *Mirror* supplied anti-war demonstrators with placards, providing a highly visible illustration of the gulf between paper and party. Iraq continued to drive a wedge between the old friends. Relations only improved when Morgan was forced to resign after he had published photographs of British soldiers attacking Iraqi prisoners. These were later revealed to be fakes. Morgan's bid to attract new readers had failed, and the *Mirror* lost many loyal Labour readers.

Following Morgan's resignation, the *Mirror* reverted to being Labour's most partisan supporter. On 6 April 2005, the day after the election was announced, it published a handwritten note from Blair admitting to 'disagreements', but urging *Mirror* readers to support Labour. He said that their votes would be 'vital in deciding whether this country keeps going forward with Labour or goes back with the Tories'. The *Mirror* gave both David Blunkett and Gordon Brown space to state the Labour case. Throughout the campaign it emphasised that the NHS was improving and sought to nail the 'Tory lies' about waste. When it came to the formal endorsement, however, it realised that it would be vain 'to argue that this government has been perfect' and recognised that it had major differences with Blair over the 'illegal' Iraq war.[14] It praised Labour for its management of the economy, improvements in the NHS and providing assistance to pensioners. The clinching argument, however, was negative. The 'simple truth is that in most seats a vote that is not for Labour is a vote for Michael Howard's Tories and all that would mean for Britain'. The *Mirror's* words did not quite amount to an appeal to vote for the 'least worst' alternative, but they fell short of its usual strong support.

The *Sun* and the *Mirror* are, in many ways, the most interesting cases because they were the largest components in the New Labour coalition. The growing mismatch between the politics of the press and parties has affected virtually all the papers. This is illustrated by Table 1, which summarises the postures of the press in 2005.

1. Editorial Endorsements and Press Partisanship

Paper	Owner	Sales (000s)	Party Support	Comments
Daily Express	Desmond	926	Con	Anti-Blair and anti-Labour
Daily Mail	United	2380	Con	Violently anti-Blair and anti-Labour
Daily Star	Desmond	851	None	Limited coverage of politics
Daily Telegraph	Barclay Bros	912	Con	Traditional partisan Tory
Financial Times	Pearson	427	Lab	Hesitant endorsement of Lab
Guardian	Scott Trust	367	Lab	Hesitant endorsement of Lab
Independent	O'Reilly	262	Lib/Lab	Grudging endorsement of Lab/anti Blair
Mirror	Trinity/Mirror	2185	Lab	Traditional partisan Labour
Sun	News Int.	3258	Lab	Endorsed Labour, preference for Tory policies?
The Times	News Int.	685	Lab	Endorsed Labour. Not time for a change
Total		12253		
Total pro-Conservative		4218	34.4%	
Total pro-Labour		7184	58.6%	

Sources: Circulation data from ABC.

Alone of the papers, the *Daily Telegraph* provided the Conservatives with 'partisan' support between 2001 and 2005. Lord Black's sale of the newspaper to the Barclay Brothers in the summer of 2004 did nothing to alter its political sympathies. The reasons for the *Telegraph*'s endorsement of the Conservatives were distilled into a simple equation: 'Small government + freedom + low tax = vote Tory'.[15] Even it, however, admitted to being not 'altogether happy' with the campaign in 2005 and considered immigration a distraction from the battles about tax and spending. The 'middle market' *Mail* had not endorsed William Hague in 2001, but it remained violently opposed to Labour. Between 2001 and 2005 it campaigned on the 'Conservative issues' of immigration, crime, and Europe. In the campaign it heaped abuse on Blair, labelling him 'a man who can no longer distinguish between truth and falsehood'. Its advice to its readers was blunt: 'However you vote, give Mr Blair a bloody nose'.[16] Of the Tories, it said 'even their greatest admirers would be hard-pressed to say that theirs has been an inspiring campaign'. It noted that 'they have rediscovered discipline and the will to win' under Michael Howard. The clinching argument was, however, negative: 'Yet if we're honest, our support for a Conservative victory—which we concede is unlikely—is superseded by an even greater imperative: to diminish the power of an overwhelmingly arrogant Mr Blair and restore a healthy democracy to this country'. Readers were provided with a helpful tactical voting guide on 'How to give Blair a bloody nose'.

The *Daily Express* and *Daily Star* had been bought by Richard Desmond shortly before the 2001 election. The deal was cleared by the Secretary of State for Trade and Industry on advice and was, coincidentally, followed by a donation of £100,000 to party coffers. Both publications dutifully endorsed Labour in 2001. As late as 2003, the *Express* declared, 'There is not a glimmer of hope that this newspaper could support to the Tories'.[17] The *Express* switched, however, in April 2004 when Blair announced his about-turn over the referendum on the EU constitution. The *Express* condemned Labour for its 'spin and deception', its failure to deliver on the NHS, its imposition of tax rises on the middle class and its surrender to the 'European super-state'. The real reason appears to have been that Desmond's short-term need for help with the regulators was over. The *Express* claimed 'Our stand does NOT mean that the Conservatives will get our unequivocal support. We shall be critical of them when they deserve it'. In 2005, however, it gave Michael Howard space to make his pitch directly to its readers and vigorously supported the Tories in the campaign. The *Daily Star* provided little political coverage in the four years preceding the election and next to nothing as 5 May approached. It eventually declined to endorse any party

Since 2001, the other Labour-inclined papers, the *Guardian* and *Independent*, had both become increasingly critical of Labour in government. The *Guardian* expressed concerns about the involvement of the private sector in public services, Labour's failure to adopt the Euro, its failure to respect the constitutional niceties, the erosion of civil liberties after 9/11, and aspects of the Iraq war. Its columnists varied from those who had lost all faith in Labour (the late Hugo Young), to its most eloquent advocates (Polly Toynbee). The *Independent* sought to establish a niche for itself as a campaigning 'viewspaper' under the editorship of Simon Kelner. Like their readers, both papers were repulsed by the Conservatives and indifferent between Labour and the Liberal Democrats. Moreover, both were acutely aware that their readers were evenly split between the parties of the left.

When it came to the question of endorsement, the *Guardian* frankly admitted to its difficulty saying 'It is an imperfect choice conducted under [an] imperfect electoral system'.[18] Having praised the Liberal Democrats, it finally came down for Labour: 'Only in a tiny handful of seats ... is it safe for Labour voters to switch to the Liberal Democrats'. The *Independent* freely admitted to being 'tormented' by its choice.[19] Having opposed the War, it felt it vital that Blair be held accountable for the 'most disastrous foreign policy decision since Suez'. It protested about an electoral system that forced them to choose, while recognising that 'It would be perverse if an anti-war protest vote inadvertently helped the Conservatives'. It concluded 'we seek an outcome in which there is a significantly larger force of Liberal Democrat MPs. And we hope that Mr Brown replaces Mr Blair as Prime Minister sooner rather than later'. To reinforce its ambivalence, Andreas Whitham-Smith provided a steer to the Liberal Democrats, while Steve Richards put the Labour case.[20]

The *Times*, the other Murdoch owned national daily, continued to be 'rather Catholic' in its political tastes and self-consciously judicious.

The threads that ran through its pages between 2001 and 2005 were a commitment to the market economy, pro-Americanism and Euro-scepticism. In 2004 it supported the Conservatives in the European elections and Simon Hughes, the Liberal Democrat candidate, for London Mayor. Like the *Sun*, it supported the decisions to invade Iraq and to introduce top up fees. It concluded that another Labour landslide 'would leave a distorted picture of public sentiment and stoke the arrogance of power'. It regretted the anti-American sentiment expressed by the Conservatives in the wake of the Iraq War. It advocated tactical voting to remove 'unreconstructed' Labour MPs such as Frank Dobson, but concluded, 'The best result for Britain would be a smaller but viable Labour majority and a larger and renewed opposition'. The force of its endorsement was diminished by one of its leading commentators, Simon Jenkins, who advised in the same edition, 'There's only one way to rap Mr Blair on the knuckles—vote Conservative'. The *Financial Times* endorsed Labour for the fourth election in a row, despite reservations about the growth of public spending and the erosion of civil liberties.

Table 1 shows that 58% of all readers took a newspaper that endorsed Labour in 2005. The significance of this statistic is unclear since not all papers are equally partisan and not all readers are equally suggestible. This figure includes the less than wholehearted support of the *Sun*, *Independent* and *Times*. Without these publications, Labour's share goes down to 21%. The nuanced and qualified nature of nearly all the endorsements must surely reduce their effect.[21] Dealignment in the press has produced mixed (but largely negative) messages about all the parties. These effects may be self-cancelling, may reduce turnout, or may favour the Liberal Democrats, as the anti-establishment party. Yet consumers choose newspapers that suit their lifestyles and political inclinations, and they are exposed to a range of sources. They are also moved by their direct experiences or those of their friends and family. The impact of the negative (and often highly personalised) messages in the press is a matter for further research (as is the effect of newspapers on party policies).

Table 2 displays the relationship between readership and vote intention in 2005. The strongest correspondence is for the *Mirror* and *Telegraph*, where two-thirds of readers supported the 'correct' party, the Conservatives. The next strongest relationships, however, are for the *Mail* (which indirectly beat the drum loudly for the Conservatives) and the *Star* (which provided no endorsement at all). Next is the *Guardian*, where 48% of readers voted Labour and only 7% voted for the Conservatives. In the case of the *Mail*, an astonishing one in four still intended to vote Labour despite being exposed to the most virulent propaganda. In two cases, the *Financial Times* and *Times*, the newspaper endorsed a party supported by a minority of its readers. If the consumer tail really does wag the newspaper dog, then these should both revert to supporting the Conservatives.

2. Vote Intention by Newspaper Readership (Percentages of Readers)

Newspaper Readership	Conservative	Labour	Lib Dem	Lab–Con
Daily Express	44	29	20	−15
Daily Mail	57	24	14	−33
Daily Star	17	53	13	+36
Daily Telegraph	64	14	18	−49
Financial Times	36	34	23	−2
Guardian	7	48	34	+41
Independent	11	38	43	+27
Mirror	13	66	15	+53
Sun	35	44	10	+11
The Times	44	27	24	−17

Source: MORI, first quarter of 2005.

The predictability of the Labour victory, the narrowness of the ideological differences between the parties, and the absence of any real dramatic incident conspired to limit election coverage. Research conducted by Peter Golding and colleagues suggests that campaign coverage was 'personalised and negative'.[22] Although policy issues became more prominent as the campaign wore on, most coverage was devoted to the election process (polls, postal voting, and the like). Fully three-quarters of tabloid front pages featured non-election issues.[23] The same research showed that the *Sun* and *Mirror* devoted ten times the column inches to David and Victoria Beckham's marriage than to debates about the Attorney General's advice relating to the Iraq War.[24] It could be that both did a service to Labour by shifting their focus elsewhere. It could, however, simply reflect the conviction that their readers would not be interested in anything as esoteric as the principles of constitutional government. In any event, the ennui experienced by the press may have contributed to the low turnout discussed in Chapter 8.

Television: trying its best

The broadcasters continued to take their public service commitments to inform and educate seriously in 2005, despite indications that viewers found election coverage a turn off. The BBC provided extensive coverage of the election, promising to cover it from 'all the angles'. It did not extend the *Six O'Clock News* as it had done in the past and, perhaps for that reason, viewing figures did not fall much. The *Ten O'Clock News* was extended by just a few minutes. Nevertheless, each bulletin devoted about fifteen minutes to the campaign and invariably led with election news. The *Six O'Clock News* Election Bus toured the country interviewing ordinary people. The regular shows such as *Breakfast News*, *Newsnight*, *The Daily Politics* and *Breakfast with Frost* continued to combine interview and analysis. The Corporation tried to enliven things by increasing the entertainment component. *Newsnight*, for example, sent Michael Crick around the country in a helicopter to embarrass politicians wherever he could. There was a regular 'Student

House' feature on first-time voters in Nottingham. The *Politics Show* even sent one of its reporters on a narrow boat tour from the North West to the West Midlands, stopping off at various points to interview people.

In addition to the staples, there were a whole series of election specials. Highlights included Jeremy Paxman's interviews with the leaders, which were broadcast at peak viewing time and attracted a great deal of comment. Despite fears that the BBC would be intimidated after Hutton, Paxman managed to be equally aggressive and rude to all the leaders. He asked Blair eighteen times how many illegal immigrants there were in the country, he questioned Kennedy whether his doctor was happy with how much he drank and smoked, and he forced Howard to concede that the 'tax take' would increase under the Conservatives. The interviews attracted audiences of 2.5 million and 229 complaints, mostly about Paxman's aggressive style. The BBC staged a special *Question Time* hosted by David Dimbleby, where each of the leaders faced the same audience. This attracted 4.1 million viewers, 73% of whom felt that it had helped them understand the parties' policies better and 87% of whom thought it was impartial.[25] The experiment was thought so successful that Helen Boaden, the BBC Director of News, declared the BBC might rethink their demands for 'American style' debates. *Election Call* on Radio 4 similarly gave listeners direct access to leading politicians.

ITV provided a range of programmes. Its news programmes, like the BBC, invariably led with election news and followed a similar style. It promised 'fun' election coverage and employed psychologist Geoffrey Beattie (who had previously been employed by the hugely successful *Big Brother* programme) to provide his interpretations of what politicians were 'thinking but not saying'. Special programmes included Jonathan Dimbleby's interviews with the party leaders, broadcast at the less than peak viewing time of 11.10pm. Another ITN feature 'Unspun' tried to pick out fact from fiction on the day's issues. The *Channel 4 News* 'Fact Check' website used journalists to scrutinise statements made by parties and politicians. Both performed a public service. The specialist news channels including *BBC News24*, *BBC Parliament*, *Sky News* and *The ITV News Channel* all carried live coverage of press conferences, keynote speeches and regular roundtable discussions on the campaign. For political anoraks with access to these stations, the 2005 election was paradise on earth.

Two trends noted in previous elections appeared to be continued in 2005. One was the continued growth of 'analytical mediation'. Most bulletins opened with the quotes from the leaders. These sound bites were invariably followed by an exchange between newsreader and political editor, or by further analysis by an expert who would dissect what had been said. In some cases this tactic undoubtedly increased understanding. The BBC's Economics Editor Evan Davis provided masterful summaries of each of the major parties' manifestos. Andrew Marr (BBC), Nick Robinson (ITV) and Adam Boulton (Sky) all provided excellent summaries of the day's events. Yet, as informative as these contributions were, it appeared that journalists were acting as both 'gate keepers' and 'nannies', selecting words and telling voters what they 'really' meant. Voters were often simply not trusted to work things out. The second striking feature was the increased use of the public to ask questions of politicians (possibly an extension of the trend to 'reality' television). ITN gave their *Ballot Box Jury* the opportunity to directly question leading politicians on issues. Tony Blair's questioning by Diana Church on *Question Time* about the perverse effects of targets on access to GPs provided one of the most memorable moments of the campaign. Like all politicians confronted with a 'real voter', he could not avoid her question, be rude, or patronising. Michael Howard was similarly embarrassed by a black policeman who accused him of making his job impossible every time he spoke about immigration. Both leaders simply squirmed with embarrassment. Informative or educative it may not have been; entertaining it certainly was.

Although the terrestrial channels continued to take the election seriously, their impact on the election was diminished. The massive growth of channels has provided voters with an enormous range of choices. The audience for the main news broadcasts has, therefore, fallen massively. In 1992 the main BBC1 news bulletins attracted total audiences of 14.6 million. By 2005 this had fallen to 9.6 million, a drop of 34%. The audiences for the main ITV bulletins over the same period fell even more dramatically, from 12.3 million to 7.1 million, a 42% decline.[26] It was, therefore, easier than ever to both watch a lot of television and yet avoid all but a passing acquaintance with the election issues. On election night itself, the average audience for the BBC results programme was 4.9 million, exactly the same as 2001, but down from 6.5 million in 1997.

The parties all made full use of their allocation of party election broadcasts: five apiece for Labour and the Conservatives and four for the Liberal Democrats. These gave each party the opportunity to state their case to the public without the need for mediation. Labour's first broadcast, directed by the Oscar-winning Anthony Minghella, consisted of a dinner table conversation between Blair and Brown designed to underline their long shared values. Other Labour broadcasts dealt with Michael Howard's record, the NHS, and the consequences of Labour voters staying at home. The Conservative broadcasts followed conventional formats: voters explaining why they would vote Tory, endorsements of Michael Howard by colleagues, and straight to camera work by the leader. Only the Liberal Democrats final broadcast about 'the little boy who called wolf', a parable about Tony Blair and Iraq, stood out (possibly for its dubious production values). The audience figures for the broadcasts remained healthy. Fully 12 million saw the first

Labour broadcast.[27] The Conservatives experimented with a cinema advert, 'Take that look off your face', which accused Blair of lying.

Television tried to stimulate interest and encourage debate in 2005. It was innovative, entertaining and comprehensive. It was also, as far as one can tell from the broadcasters own survey data, thought by the public to be impartial and even-handed between the parties. If turnout failed to increase substantially, the blame could hardly be laid at the door of the broadcasters. They tried their best.

The internet: failing to deliver?

The internet has promised to do so much for the conduct of electoral politics but it failed to deliver in 2005. To be sure, the major news websites attracted attention. The BBC website, for instance, generated 45 million impressions by 6 May 2005, and the *Guardian* website was particularly well used. It must be doubtful whether it attracted political virgins. It was probably electoral anoraks in search of their 'fix'. There was much interest in the emergence of election bloggers: individuals supplying their own idiosyncratic takes on politics, emphasising issues that were ignored or saying things that could not be expressed elsewhere. Some were witty, irreverent and innovative. Some were bitter, ranting or sad. Their overall effect on the quality of public debate was marginal.

One interesting development was a website (whoshouldyouvote-for.com), which asked people to respond to a series of political questions relating to Europe, freedom, defence, tax and spending, and then gave them a probability of voting for each party. An unusually large proportion of the 875,000 people who took the quiz were advised to vote Liberal Democrat. The same site added an 'electoral reform' quiz shortly after the election, but its designers denied any party associations.

The major parties largely used the web to distribute propaganda, their manifestos, press releases and leaflets. The Conservative website received many more hits than Labour, possibly because Labour received so much more attention in the rest of the media.[28] There was little sign that the web was used in order to plan party strategy or develop policy. The dominance and institutional conservatism of the major parties probably means that the possibilities for direct democracy opened up by the web are unlikely to be exploited to the full in the near future.

Conclusion

The continued decline in membership has limited the parties' abilities to reach voters directly and made them increasingly reliant on the media to carry their messages. The press and broadcasters are, therefore, still of vital importance to party campaigns despite the reduction in the market for both the national press and the major terrestrial channels. Newspapers are now distinctly non-partisan in their approach to politics and increasingly exploit their influence by attaching conditions to their support.

Given the widespread belief in the 'power of the media', the non-partisan press may, therefore, be more powerful than the partisan press ever was. Television newsrooms continue to be strongly influenced by the lofty ideals of public service broadcasting. Their rational and balanced approach to the reporting of politics, however, is no substitute for the mobilising potential of the partisan press. Electoral politics may have shifted to a less partisan, more rational and more conditional basis for choice, but it has also become less partisan, less intense, and less stimulating too.

1 J. Deans, 'BBC and ITV "more biased than Sky"', *Guardian*, 19.6.01.
2 P. Norris, J. Curtice, D. Sanders, M. Scammell and H.A. Semetko, *On Message: Communicating the Campaign*, Sage, 1999, p. #.
3 A. Sampson, *Who Runs This Place?*, John Murray, 2004, p. 207.
4 A. Rusbridger, *The Hugo Young Memorial Lecture*, University of Sheffield, 9.3.05.
5 I. Crewe, 'Party Identification Theory and Political Change in Britain' in I. Budge, I. Crewe and D. Farlie (eds), *Party Identification and Beyond*, John Wiley, 1976, p. 53.
6 P. Waugh, 'Murdoch praises Howard and Hints Blair may lose support of the *Sun*', *Independent*, 15.11.03.
7 *Sun*, 'It's time to make your mind up', 4.4.05.
8 *Sun*, 'Give them one last chance: Vote Blair & Brown', 21.4.05.
9 T. Kavanagh, 'Kicked in the ballots', *Sun*, 6.5.05.
10 *Sun*, 'Blair is handed wake up call', 6.5.05.
11 R. Greenslade, 'The Paper Ballot', *Guardian*, 11.4.05.
12 P. Morgan, 'Stop the f***ing lies', *Daily Mail*, 28.2.05.
13 *Mirror*, 'Prime Monster?', 14.3.03.
14 *Mirror*, 'Labour: The only choice', 6.4.05.
15 'Small government + freedom + low tax = vote Tory', *Telegraph,* 5.5.05.
16 'However you vote, give Mr Blair a bloody nose', *Daily Mail,* 4.5.05.
17 *Express*, 'Disastrous Tories pose a threat to democracy', 11.5.03.
18 *Guardian*, 'Once more with feeling', 3.5.05.
19 *Independent*, 'It is vital that the forces of liberalism prevail in this complex election', 4.5.05.
20 A. Whitham-Smith, 'Tony Blair has presided over a deceitful government: He must be voted out of office', *Independent*, 4.5.05. S. Richards, 'As he fends off cheap jibes and accusations, Blair seems a far more substantial figure', *Independent*, 5.5.05.
21 D. Deacon and D. Wring, 'Partisan dealignment and the British press' in J. Bartle, S. Atkinson and R. Mortimore (eds), *Political Communications: The General Election Campaign of 2001*, Frank Cass, 2001, pp. 197–211.
22 O. Gibson, 'Election 2005: Negative campaign a turn-off for voters: Media Research highlights lack of tabloid coverage of election', *Guardian*, 2.5.05.
23 O. Gibson. 'Negative campaign a turn off for voters', *Guardian*, 6.5.05.
24 Gibson, 'Negative campaign'.
25 BBC press release 'BBC election night and campaign audience data', 6.5.05.
26 http://uk.tv.yahoo.com/050427/344/fhfqk.html.
27 J. Day, 'First election broadcast cheers Labour', *Guardian*, 13.4.05.
28 'Tory site outstrips Labour', www.journalism.co.uk.

DOMINIC WRING

The Labour Campaign

Labour's second term in office was in sharp contrast to its first. Tony Blair and his government suffered a considerable, though not fatal, loss of authority following intense policy debates over health, education, and, most spectacularly, Iraq. The decision to support the US-led invasion stymied the development of the kind of permanent campaign Labour had effectively run in the first term. Despite Blair's protestations for the need to 'move on', the issue of Iraq continued to command attention, due to the controversies over the Prime Minister's relationship with President Bush, the illusory weapons of mass destruction that had been used to justify Britain's military involvement, the death of scientific adviser David Kelly, and the subsequent inquiries into his demise and the government's overall conduct. Cumulatively these matters undermined the public trust in Blair and foreshadowed his unprecedented announcement that his third term would be his last. The Prime Minister responded to his subsequent victory by claiming that he had 'listened and learned'. Yet it is difficult to envisage that this will involve meaningful consultations with a Labour party that has long been subordinate to government decree and dominated by three interdependent sets of actors.[1] First and foremost there are a group of powerful, mainly unelected advisers surrounding Blair who have effectively displaced key functions previously undertaken by the Cabinet, its Committees, ministers, the parliamentary party, the Annual Conference, the National Executive Committee, and the Policy Forum. Secondly, favoured media and think tanks have provided an important conduit enabling the Blair leadership to explore plans by 'spinning' them to journalists in a way that it would have been reluctant to do in a more formal public setting. Finally the views of the public have been constantly monitored through polling and focus group studies, especially of those voters whose support has been deemed critical to the government's survival. Together these actors have been central to the formation of Labour policy and its promotion, as the party attempted to win a third historic term in office.

'The people who count'

What Shaw terms the 'strategic community' came to dominate the internal workings of the Labour Party during the Policy Review of the

doi: 10.1093/pa/gsi064

late 1980s.[2] For a party that still promotes itself as 'new' a decade after it first started using the prefix, it is ironic that most if not all of the key people making decisions now (with the obvious exception of Neil Kinnock) are the same politicians, strategists, and officials who drove forward and sustained the Review. It was this process which arguably created the conditions that enabled Tony Blair to inherit the leadership and pursue a presidential style that would define his approach in opposition and then in government. Central to this arrangement has been an extensive network of unelected advisers whose primary loyalty is to the leader rather than the party. In 1998 the former party insider turned lobbyist, Derek Draper, identified the importance of this group when he argued that as few as five elected members of the Cabinet were among the '17 people who count' in government. Some doubted this judgement at the time, but it is instructive that these same ministers, together with Margaret Beckett, are the only ones who have enjoyed continuous service at the highest level of government ever since.[3]

The centralisation of power within Downing Street is a major reason why journalistic speculation over tension within the party has continually focused on the reportedly strained relationship between Blair and Gordon Brown, the number two on Draper's list. Though there have been minor policy differences, these have been exacerbated by the sometimes fierce rivalry that exists between the Blair and Brown camps and their media acolytes. Consequently the senior echelons of the government have as a result been described as resembling a feudal court driven by patronage and favour.[4] Preparations for the election were marred by speculation about the fate of Brown, following Blair's decision to appoint Alan Milburn as campaign coordinator in autumn 2004. The choice of former-Health Secretary Milburn proved controversial given his past differences with the Chancellor over foundation hospitals and because he now took on the role the latter had played in the previous two elections. Ironically Brown's displacement ultimately proved advantageous since his frontline intervention in the campaign, favouring Blair's stance on the Iraq war, was widely perceived to have shored up the Prime Minister's position.

Arguably the most revealing aspect of Draper's list was the numerical dominance of the ten appointees, some of whom were destined to become more influential and famous than many of the ministers they were nominally supposed to serve. The power of the advisers was personified in Alastair Campbell. His designation as Director of Strategy and Communication in 2001, promoted from the more high profile post of Prime Ministerial Press Secretary, did little to diminish his influence over elected ministers and the civil service, and he continued to play a crucial role in the informal decision-making structures that characterised Blair's 'sofa style' government. Special advisers are not solely, if only spin doctors, but, as the Phillis inquiry into government information services contended, effective communication should and did become as important as the core functions of policy formation and delivery to this Prime Minister.[5]

Concern about how initiatives would be received by the media and by target voters were important considerations for Blair and for aides like Andrew Adonis, John Birt, and Sally Morgan. Whilst these were rewarded with peerages, as were other similarly influential figures such as the intellectual Anthony Giddens and strategist Philip Gould, there was also a notable tendency among younger colleagues working as special advisers in No.10 and in other Departments of State to want to enter the House of Commons. Several succeeded in becoming MPs for safe seats, and, although they no longer exercised the same degree of influence, the career change afforded them a greater degree of job security and an opportunity to forge their own public profiles. Furthermore it is a noteworthy feature of this government how many of the former senior aides elected in 2001 have been disproportionately successful in becoming ministers when compared with the former trade union officials and councillors who dominate the backbench ranks of the parliamentary Labour Party. This trend looks set to continue with the arrival in parliament of another batch of ex-special advisers, including three of Gordon Brown's closest associates.[6]

The agenda setters

Labour's spin doctors have been routinely portrayed by journalists as manipulative, bullying, and generally unpleasant, but they could not have had the impact that they have had without the cooperation of some in the news media. It was the Policy Review that helped to forge the close links between spokespeople for the party leadership like Peter Mandelson and a select group of correspondents working for the *Guardian*, *Mirror* and other newspapers. These newspapers were most favoured and trusted by a wide section of a Labour party membership that began to vote on policy and internal matters as new forms of consultation were introduced. This process had the effect of marginalising Labour's more traditional representative decision-making structures. Following Blair's victory in the Clause 4 debate in 1994, leadership attention shifted from cultivating sympathetic opinion formers to forging a dialogue with a wider range of media proprietors, editors, and journalists in the hope of winning their audiences' votes. Gradually the 'Tory press' became the 'Tony press', as newspapers such as the *Sun*, *Star*, *News of the World* and *Express* emphasised their qualified support to Blair rather than to his party. Once in government, the leadership returned the favour by offering Trevor Kavanagh, the political editor of the best selling *Sun*, a series of scoops and exclusives. Though the newspaper shifted its partisan allegiance it did not markedly change an ideological stance and agenda that Labour has appeared willing and able to embrace ever since. It is noteworthy that the *Sun* provided some of the most strident criticism of the Fire Brigades Union during its dispute with the government over working conditions in 2003. Not for the first or last time the Labour leadership found itself ranged against one of the party's own affiliates, whilst being supported by one of the most vehemently anti-union news organisations in the country.

An influential, accusative media discourse of 'barons', 'vested' and 'producer interests', and their 'demands' had contributed to the weakening of the trade unions' political legitimacy since the 1970s. The forging of closer links between journalists and self-styled party 'modernisers' eventually led to a newspaper sponsored campaign to expel Labour's largest affiliates after the 1992 general election defeat.[7] The attempt failed, but it forced the unions on to the defensive. Their collective input into party affairs since has been further tempered by policy differences, ideological rivalries, declining memberships, and a determination that they would do nothing that might have harmful electoral repercussions. The turbulent second Labour term has, however, emboldened several general secretaries, including those leading the 'big four' affiliates, to mount sustained challenges to various government policies. Furthermore Blair lost the support of the traditionally rightwing Amicus when Sir Ken Jackson was defeated in internal elections by rival Derek Simpson in 2002. Even more dramatically the RMT and FBU, unions both led by prominent members of the so-called 'Awkward Squad' of left-wing leaders, were respectively expelled and disaffiliated from the party following separate disputes with the leadership. That said, the lead up to the 2005 election was marked by a rapprochement between the government and its remaining union allies which culminated with the Warwick agreement covering a wide range of employment-related issues.

The perceived success of the negotiations and the major union affiliates' preparedness to continue funding the party provided Labour with valuable support—most of the £9.14million they raised went into a campaign expected to cost an estimated £15million. The Warwick agreement has not, however, stemmed the amount of donations from corporate figures, led by Lord Sainsbury and Paul Drayson. It is noticeable that the government has gone to great lengths to maintain that it is the party of business by pursuing employers bodies, including the CBI and Institute of Directors. The growing company sponsorship of party events, the scale of money being given, and the allegations of funds for favouring wealthy businessmen like Laskhmi Mittal has, however, led to accusations that the government is now 'institutionally corrupt'.[8] The corporate sector has also indirectly attempted to promote a pro-business agenda within the party through funding debates and reports organised by think tanks with Labour associations, such as the Social Market Foundation, Demos, the New Local Government Network, the Foreign Policy Centre, the Institute for Public Policy Research, and the Fabian Society.

Party and public opinions

Labour has also engaged in determined and continuous monitoring of the 'opinion electorate' through feedback from polling and focus group studies.[9] The confidence to pronounce on the state of popular feeling has been a factor in the resulting top-down approach that has characterised Blair's style of party management and curtailed the influence of activists and union affiliates who are, by definition, viewed as being politically unrepresentative. Consequently opinion research has played a major strategic role, especially where it has been of the qualitative focus group kind involving those floating voters most likely to switch from Labour to the Conservatives and the loss of whose support would in effect count double in electoral terms. It was Blair's attentiveness to this target group that encouraged him to claim that his party was now 'the political wing' of the British people and led to consultations with President Clinton's former pollster Mark Penn.[10] The work of Penn, who specialises in developing psychological profiles of key target voters, complimented that of the existing research team led by fellow US Democratic consultant Stan Greenberg and Labour's chief strategist Philip Gould.

To underline its willingness to listen, Labour launched the Big Conversation in preparation for the 2005 general election and invited members of the public to submit their political views to what was billed as a major process of consultation. Yet what transpired was more a public relations exercise aimed at demonstrating this was a listening government after the controversies over tuition fees, foundation hospitals, and, most importantly, Iraq. The message to activists and core supporters was markedly different to that offered to mainstream opinion and amounted to little more than a warning that they should stick with Labour despite their doubts because the only alternative was a right-wing Conservative government. Given this somewhat complacent attitude it was hardly surprising that the dawn of a plebiscitary style party democracy proved illusory, precisely because it was an ad hoc arrangement reliant on leadership sponsorship. When participants to the Annual Conference, National Executive, or Policy Forum succeeded in challenging the platform, they were routinely dismissed by ministers or ignored by journalists who took a decreasing interest in these once important bodies. Blair's appointment of Charles Clarke to the new unelected post of Party Chairman in 2001 underlined the degree to which the party could be reorganised according to leadership whim. The degree of change in the party since it had last sought a third consecutive victory was further demonstrated by the brevity of the traditional Clause V meeting to ratify the 2005 manifesto; in 1979 the same meeting had been dominated by lively discussion.

The selection of parliamentary candidates remained one arena where members retained some influence, but even here choice was heavily

policed by the central party's insistence on prospective nominees undergoing vetting procedures. Certain activists also found limited expression
through media conscious groupings like the pro-leadership Progress on
the party's right or the centre-left Grassroots Alliance, but these and
other ventures did not stem a steep decline in membership that began in
1997. With activity down some CLPs became increasingly reliant on
those with incentives to participate such as elected councillors or the
growing number of professionals who have made a living out of politics, particularly since Labour came to power.[11]

'Forward, not back': the politics of positioning

The 2005 general election campaign provided a metaphor for the Blair
government in that it retained office having debated an agenda largely
determined by its opponents. The issue that had long dominated British
politics and elections past, namely the economy, was marginalised as a
media discussion point.[12] Understandably perhaps the Conservatives
took the view that there was little to be gained from them attacking
Labour on this terrain. It is a testament to the Tories' agenda-setting
success that the economy was not a prominent topic of debate in the
campaign, despite the government's best efforts to make it so through
the use of advertising, public relations, and Gordon Brown. The party
extolled Brown's last pre-election budget, his record on inflation and
unemployment, and longstanding government policies designed to promote 'redistribution by stealth' by giving 'a hand up not a hand out'
through work and related measures like the minimum wage, Working
Families Tax Credit, and New Deal programme. Perhaps more importantly the Labour manifesto confirmed the party would not raise direct
taxation, although increases elsewhere were not ruled out.

The perceived underlying strength of the economy was a positive factor in Labour's re-election despite public concern over the growing size
of personal debt, instability in the housing market, and a decline in
manufacturing industry that was spectacularly demonstrated with the
demise of Rover cars in the first week of the official campaign. None of
these reported problems was enough to dislodge Labour from its lead in
the polls, an enviable position the party had maintained with a few
exceptions since the European Rate Mechanism fiasco of September
1992. Even the government's controversial stance over Iraq failed to
drastically undermine Labour's support in the polls in the way that the
ERM debacle did for the Conservatives. Yet if the Millennium Dome
offered the most obvious symbol of government failings during the first
term, the second term equivalent will go down as Blair's support of the
Iraqi invasion based on what turned out to be illusory weapons of mass
destruction. The two policy crises were wholly dissimilar in nature but
underlined the very different challenges that faced Labour during its
two spells in office. Yet whilst the Dome was the source of much ridicule
and was often used to represent the Prime Minister's alleged hubris, the

first term government remained one of the most popular in history, and the leader a highly regarded figure.

Iraq helped erode public confidence in the government, led to a marginal fall in support for Labour, and, more spectacularly, contributed to the decline of trust in Blair himself. That said the fallout from the crisis did not have the devastating electoral impact it might have had, primarily because of the way that Iain Duncan-Smith, then Conservative leader, offered unwavering support for military action. This made it difficult for his successor Michael Howard to capitalise on the issue. Even the leaking of the controversial advice on the legality of backing the war in the memo to Blair from the Attorney General, Lord Goldsmith, failed to provide fresh impetus to Howard's blunt claim that the Prime Minister was a liar. Ultimately it was the anti-war Liberal Democrat and Respect parties who were better placed to benefit from the issue.

It was understandable that Labour approached the campaign underlining its intention to move on from Iraq and to concentrate all its efforts on promoting a primarily domestic agenda. Prior to 5 April, there was a concerted attempt to do this with the announcement of six pledges, although these did not play the role they had in the previous campaigns.[13] The Labour manifesto was drawn up under the supervision of Matthew Taylor, the former director of the Institute of Public Policy Research turned No. 10 Downing Street adviser. The document, *Forward, Not Back*, promoted the familiar Blair mantra of 'modernisation' without actually using the now somewhat hackneyed phrase in its title. For Labour, the term conveyed a preparedness to countenance the greater involvement of the private sector in the running of public services, and the manifesto linked this to the promise of giving citizens more consumer style choice in health, education, childcare, and other public services. Increases in direct taxation were again ruled out. The familiar brand conscious prefix 'new' Labour also appeared for a third election, despite having been first introduced over a decade before. In many ways Blair's pursuit of another mandate to reform public services laid him open to a charge that he was following a 'one more heave' strategy, a claim that fellow 'modernisers' had originally levelled at some of their more cautious Labour colleagues following the 1992 defeat.[14]

Another important dimension to Labour's positioning in the campaign was the renewed emphasis on the need for greater collective and individual security. These issues dominated the ambitious if unrealistic programme of legislation included in the Queen's Speech of autumn 2004. More importantly the event, often billed as a keynote address to the nation, provided the government with an ideal opportunity to launch its pre-campaign against the Conservatives. The attempt to seize the initiative and be 'tough' on crime, a policy area on which the leadership still felt vulnerable, was led by Home Secretary David Blunkett, who duly appeared on talk show programmes such as Channel 4's *Richard and Judy*. Blunkett attempted to reassure anxious voters that tackling crime was still a major priority for his government and could be achieved through the introduction of personal identity cards, more robust sentencing, and Anti-Social Behaviour Orders (ASBOs) to tackle persistent and nuisance offenders.

Labour's determined promotion of its crime and security agenda threatened to be undermined when David Blunkett resigned following embarrassing revelations over his granting of preferential treatment to former partner Kimberley Quinn and her nanny. Yet media preoccupation with the perceived threat from terrorists post-September 11, organised criminals, travellers, and violent and petty offenders kept public safety firmly on the political agenda and helped create a climate conducive to Labour's promotion of ID cards, ASBOs, house arrest, the abandonment of jury trials, and other measures designed to reinforce the party's robust stance on law and order. This authoritarian approach was further reinforced by lurid stories in the popular press about the activities of illegal asylum seekers. The issue became a major theme of the election when it found expression in the Conservatives' proposition 'Are You Thinking What We're Thinking', an advertising message accompanied by slogans attacking different government policies.

The particular focus on immigration and asylum-seekers during the election was widely interpreted as evidence of a 'dog whistle' campaign designed by chief Tory strategist Lynton Crosby to resonate with specific groups of anxious voters. A more appropriate prefix might have been 'fog horn' given the ensuing controversial debate and the strenuous denials of racism by leader Michael Howard. Labour attempted to neutralise the Conservatives' perceived advantage on immigration by promising swift action if re-elected. Arguably a 'dog whistle' had been sounded on this issue, but it had came from Home Secretary Blunkett much earlier in the parliament, when in 2002 he borrowed a phrase associated with Margaret Thatcher in speaking about public fears of being 'swamped' by illegal aliens. If much time and effort was expended in promoting or at least neutralising this particular concern during the formal campaign, by contrast there was comparatively little debate over housing, the European Union, pensions, transport, or the environment. Marginally more was made of health, education, and the other 'bread and butter' issues Labour politicians repeatedly suggested were those the electorate wanted discussed, although here the media focus tended to dwell on particularly contentious opposition preoccupations, such as the hospital 'superbug' MRSA or the impact of university top-up fees.

The 'air war': getting the message across

To promote its message Labour re-employed TBWA, the advertising agency first used in 2001 and headed by Trevor Beattie, a longstanding supporter who had first worked for the party in the mid-1980s. Beattie and his colleagues supervised the production of a range of outdoor and print advertisements, although none provoked the reaction that followed the appearance of images on the party's website shortly before the formal campaign began. One portrayed Michael Howard as a manipulative figure whom critics likened to the Shakespearean villain Shylock, whilst another depicted Howard and his Shadow Chancellor Oliver Letwin as flying pigs. The images originally appeared in an on-line feature offering party members the opportunity to vote on the best design from a choice of four but they reached a far wider audience following complaints about the alleged anti-Semitic slur on both politicians' Jewish heritage. Campaign coordinator Alan Milburn denied the accusation and took much of the media criticism. Subsequent adverts were less provocative and warned potential supporters that '*If you value it, vote for it*' and that Liberal Democrat support risked electing the Conservatives. Labour's series of Party Election Broadcasts conveyed similar messages with the help of celebrity endorsers, a reminder of Michael Howard's record in office and a documentary-style film by Oscar winning director Anthony Minghella featuring a relaxed Blair and Brown discussing their political and personal relationship.

The advertising was supported by an intensive public relations effort overseen by Matthew Doyle, assisted by Alastair Campbell from Labour's Victoria Street campaign headquarters and Director of Communications David Hill, who accompanied Blair. The Prime Minister played a major role in what was again a highly presidential-style election. The loss of confidence in Blair was not matched by any significant surge in support for his principal opponent Michael Howard; Charles Kennedy fared better but was not perceived to be either's main rival.[15] During the campaign Blair appeared in an unprecedented range of broadcast formats in a bid to reach the widest possible audience. Much was made of his attempt to reconnect with disaffected voters, especially women, through the so-called 'masochism' strategy. This started weeks before the election was called with a special day of guest appearances on four Channel 5 programmes featuring the kind of public access format that dominated the rest of the campaign. During these encounters Blair was subjected to robust questioning from a selected panel of voters, and although subsequent media reports focused on his female interrogators, some of the men also made compelling cases against Labour policies on Iraq, tuition fees, and faith schooling. The set piece debates during the campaign involving live audiences on the BBC's *Question Time* and ITV's *Ask the Leader* were similarly intense, uncomfortable experiences for Blair.

Labour strategists evidently made a decision that political programming, by its very nature, only appealed to a specific audience. Consequently they launched 'Operation Matrix' and sought to promote Blair's popular touch by placing him in less formal settings, including a light-hearted satirical interview on ITV1's *Saturday Night Takeway* in which presenters Young Ant and Dec visited Downing Street to ask him about underwear and other light-hearted matters.[16] Even more extraordinary was a surprise intervention by Blair on Jono Coleman's Heart FM radio programme when he thanked a retiring host who believed the caller was impersonator Jon Culshaw. The Prime Minister also discussed more weighty matters on programmes like *Richard and Judy* and GMTV and in interviews with a range of popular magazines and with Jamie Oliver, the television chief fronting a crusade to transform school catering. These formats afforded coverage of issues of particular interest to the 'school gate mums' and other members of their 'hard working families', a phrase developed by American consultant Bob Shrum and used in the manifesto and elsewhere.[17] The youth vote was courted by allowing Channel 4's T4 strand presenter June Sarpong to film Blair for a day and to chair a debate between him and a vocal collection of viewers. These and other appearances attracted cynical media commentary but enabled the Prime Minister to address a formidable audience that it was difficult to imagine Michael Howard being able to reach.

Efforts were made to cultivate national newspapers that had never been part of the Conservative press and that had tended to be neglected by Labour in previous campaigns. This election promised to be different, and these papers' readers were precisely the kinds of core supporters Blair needed to vote. Though the *Guardian* featured trenchant opposition as well as support for the government on its comment pages, there was also a discernible tendency for the paper to frame its news coverage, particularly on its front page, in ways that reinforced the Labour message, such as the alleged electoral threats from a well funded Conservative campaign, interventions from hunt supporters in key marginal seats, and the consequences of voter desertions to the Liberal Democrats. By comparison the *Mirror* was more blunt in its support for Labour, despite its restated opposition to the Iraq invasion. The absence of the vocal critic and former-editor, Piers Morgan, made the paper's reconciliation with the party somewhat easier, as was demonstrated with its publication of handwritten letters to readers from Tony Blair. The government failed, however, to regain the support of the staunchly anti-war *Independent* and its new allegiances were underlined when the paper led with a story on the defection of retiring MP Brian Segdemore to the Liberal Democrats during the campaign.

Prior to the election, Minister Douglas Alexander, the campaign coordinator in 2001, made a point of arguing that the party needed a different approach that would emphasise the importance of developing a rapport with local media as a means of reaching voters. Alexander's belated return to strategic duties during this election underlined his growing influence and that of his mentor Gordon Brown.[18] Regional journalists were perceived as more interested in the substantive policy issues and more in touch with their audience's concerns than their national media colleagues. Furthermore, the lack of previous contact between the local media and central government was likely to foster a more meaningful exchange, devoid of the cynicism, indifference, or sycophancy that characterised much Westminster coverage. Once the election was called, Blair travelled to the most marginal seat by helicopter, a mode of transport that enabled him to move rapidly around the country. The arrangement was made possible because of the party's decision to restrict access to a handful of journalists from the main news organisations: BBC, ITN, Sky, and the Press Association. In the previous election there had been particular trouble with correspondents who had complained about the lack of access to the Prime Minister whilst accompanying him on tour. These criticisms continued, but journalists, especially from the print media, now found it even harder to follow the leader's personal campaign.

The 'ground' war: getting the vote out

Blair's regional visits were controlled invitation-only events to prevent the possibility of an unseemly intervention by an irate protester dominating the news headlines. One of the most embarrassing tour moments came when Jessica Haigh, an invited student and daughter of a party activist, confronted the Prime Minister over Iraq, his relationship with George W. Bush, and for being too much like a Conservative. More typical were the visits in support of the two most vulnerable MPs in Dorset South and Dumfries, where Blair was greeted by the candidates and a photogenic entourage containing young people and children. Appearances by wife Cherie and son Euan reinforced Blair's image as a devoted husband and father. Deputy Prime Minister John Prescott was also dispatched on a bus tour of marginal seats and caused a minor stir when he accused a local journalist of being unprofessional, although there was nothing to compare with his melee with a Countryside Alliance supporter in the previous general election. Pro-hunting and other protesters were once again out in force, yet despite being able to disrupt House of Commons' proceedings they were unable to gatecrash Labour's heavily secured tour meetings.

The Blair and Prescott tours were the most public aspects of an ambitious and extensive operation involving several other ministers. The effort formed part of government attempts to convince voters that their own experience of improved local schools, hospital care, and other major programmes like Sure Start were far from isolated stories. The message that Labour's policies were making the difference was further promoted in a campaign of letter writing to local newspapers that was allegedly coordinated from the party's various regional press offices. Whilst this was a newer development, it appeared to be another example of the erosion in more traditional inter-personal forms of electioneering, such as door-step canvassing, speaker's meetings, and leafleting, due in part to the party's still declining membership.[19] The loss of genuine active volunteers encouraged the development of 'astroturfing' whereby paid professionals or 'real people', carefully selected because of their resemblance to target voters, were used to represent grassroots 'endorsers' during visits by Labour dignitaries. Activity also extended to providing teams of hecklers, complete with 'home made' placards, to hassle rival politicians at live events.[20] Other, more orthodox 'field operations' were coordinated by a temporary team of 120 organisers who included Karen Hicks, a former campaign manager for former US Democratic candidate Howard Dean.[21]

The remaining Labour membership and supporters who had given their details to the party via its website were targeted with messages from comedian John O'Farrell and leading politicians to volunteer or donate money to the campaign. The initiative bore the imprint of yet more American advisers, Joe Trippi and Zack Exley, both new media specialists with first-hand experience of how the tool had been used to build a dialogue between Howard Dean and his enthusiastic base of support. Information technology resources were also devoted to targeting different electoral groups, courtesy of sophisticated consumer research systems like Mosaic which could be adapted to help identify floating voters in marginal seats. Canvassing and leafleting was also conducted where necessary or feasible and supported by direct mailings, DVDs, and telemarketing operations based regionally or at a National Communications Centre in Tyneside able to contact an estimated 100,000 voters a month.[22] Affiliated trade unions replicated some of these efforts by targeting members living in designated key seats with mailings. Amicus, for instance, sent voters a DVD featuring *Star Trek* actor Patrick Stewart and leader Derek Simpson urging doubters to support the government because of the Warwick Agreement and to vote against the Conservatives and Liberal Democrats for various policy reasons.

Conclusion

'Operation Third Term' may have ended in another Labour victory, but it did not silence the criticism of Tony Blair from within his party and outside of it. Blair had again been the leading figure in another highly presidential election which saw him appear on an unprecedented range of media formats in a frenetic attempt to engage the British public. Yet some in his party argued that they won in spite of his contribution and that Labour would be more popular without him. Within a week of the election former Minister Glenda Jackson, a leading opponent of the Iraqi invasion, called on the Prime Minister to consider his position and claimed those former loyalists abandoning Labour had confounded Blair's basic strategic assumption that 'they had nowhere else to go'.[23] This is because the campaign underlined how many floating voters are not necessarily the least politicised of citizens nor the preserve of the two major parties. Labour's growing recognition of this became apparent during a campaign in which it relied heavily on the advice of several US Democratic operatives, all of whom recognised the importance of 'getting your vote out' from recent experiences on the American presidential trail. Iraq played a role here, and, although it was less important for many voters, those who did rank it as a major concern appeared willing to act accordingly on polling day. It is a testimony to the highly centralised, controlled and quiescent entity that Labour has become that it required a major electoral revolt to underline the extent of Tony Blair's political mortality.

1 D. Wring, *The Politics of Marketing the Labour Party*, Palgrave Macmillan, 2004, pp. 119–22.

2 E. Shaw, *The Labour Party since 1979*, Routledge, 1994, pp. 57–9.

3 Of the 17 'who count', the continuously serving Cabinet ministers were Blair, Gordon Brown, John Prescott, Jack Straw, and the then Chief Secretary Alistair Darling. The only other named ministers were Lord Irvine and Minister without Portfolio Peter Mandelson. The aides mentioned were Philip Gould and Downing Street staffers Alistair Campbell, David Miliband, Anji Hunter, Jonathan Powell, Geoff Norris, Sally Morgan, and Roger Liddle plus Brown advisers Ed Balls and Charlie Whelan (Wring, *Politics of Marketing the Labour Party*, 2005, p. 216).

4 F. Beckett and D. Hencke, *The Blairs and their Court*, Aurum, 2004. See also A. Seldon, *Blair*, Free Press, 2004.

5 D.Wring, 'Politics and the Media: The Hutton Inquiry, the Public Relations State and Crisis at the BBC', *Parliamentary Affairs* 2005/2.

6 2001 entrants David Miliband, James Purnell, and Andrew Burnham have all become ministers, as has 2004 by-election entrant Liam Byrne. If this trend continues, new MPs Kitty Ussher and Pat McFadden are set to join them as are Gordon Brown's former aides Ed Balls, Ian Austin and Ed Miliband.

7 Wring, *Politics of Marketing the Labour Party*, pp. 124–6.

8 D. Osler, *Labour Party plc*, Mainstream, 2003.

9 A. Panebianco, *Political Parties: Organisation and Power*, Cambridge University Press, 1988.

10 P. Hennessy and P. Sherwell, 'Blair recruits Clinton poll mastermind in the drive to capture more Tory voters', *Sunday Telegraph*, 23.1.05.

11 See comments by Patrick Seyd and others in I. Gaber, 'Parties over, time to say goodbye?', *Tribune*, 2.5.03.

12 The issue was eighth most prominent, well behind the postal balloting, asylum, and Iraq controversies. Loughborough University Communication Research Centre, *Guardian*, 2.5.05. For a discussion of Labour's economic record see D. Coates, *Prolonged Labour*, Macmillan, 2005.

13 The six pledges were: 'Your family better off' (economy); 'Your family treated better and faster' (health); 'Your child achieving more' (education); 'Your country's borders protected' (immigration); 'Your community safer' (law and order); and 'Your children with the best start' (childcare).

14 N. Lawson, 'New Labour is finished and the battle to succeed is on', *Guardian*, 2.4.05. The author had himself been a leading 'moderniser' and an aide to Gordon Brown.

15 Blair was rated as 'most capable leader' by 36%, Howard by 22%, and Kennedy by 14%, *Election Digest*, MORI, May 2005.

16 A. McSmith, 'Little Ant and Dec give the PM a thorough deep-fat frying', *Independent on Sunday*, 3.4.05.

17 J. Freedland, 'Something for everyone', *Guardian*, 23.4.05.

18 J. Ashley, 'Talkative strategist of a listening election campaign', *Guardian*, 15.9.03.

19 A report from an internal party pressure group estimated membership had declined by approximately half from 407,000 in 1997 to 208,000 by mid-2004. G. Johnson, *Has Labour a Future without the Party on the Ground?*, Save the Labour Party, 2004.

20 J. Kleeman, 'My Life in Labour's Lie Factory', *Daily Mail*, 21.5.05. The author worked undercover for a Channel Four Dispatches investigation *Undercover in New Labour* broadcast on 23 May.

21 T. Baldwin, 'Battle has been joined and the language is military . . . but don't mention the war', *The Times*, 6.4.05.

22 Ibid.

23 G. Jackson, 'Somewhere else to go', *Guardian*, 12.5.05.

ANTHONY SELDON AND PETER SNOWDON

The Conservative Campaign

In our chapter in the previous volume on the 2001 general election, we opened with the words 'From 1997 to 2001, the Conservatives experienced their most futile period in opposition in the last one hundred years. It was an utterly bleak period that could have been largely avoided with a steadier hand and a clearer strategic direction.' We concluded by saying 'whether the Party improves its fortunes in 2005 will have little or nothing to do with what goes on in the Tory Party, and almost everything to do with whether New Labour can hold together or whether it will implode'.[1]

The chapter thus posed a dilemma in its opening and conclusion. Was the plight of the Conservatives down to the errors and weaknesses of the leadership, or was New Labour's stranglehold so complete that there was little that the leadership could have done, bar waiting for the opposition to falter and then to seize the opportunity?

The years 2001–05 resolved which view of the Conservative Party in opposition was the more accurate. But before providing the answer, we need to look at the events that occurred during those four years, and the performance and key decisions of the Tory leadership.

The Conservatives in Opposition, 2001–05[2]

What might the leadership have learnt from the years 1997–2001? It should have learnt very clearly how *not* to do things. William Hague, leader throughout, offered neither clarity nor consistency, and provided no clear stamp of what the party believed as the new millennium opened: Hague's 'lack of strategic clarity [in the 2001 campaign] was the inevitable concomitant of a similar lack of clarity in the previous four years,' we wrote.[3]

What might a wise Conservative leadership have done from 2001–05? If they had learnt the lessons from the failure of 1997–2001, as well as from the more successful opposition periods in Conservative history, we might have expected the leadership to have done the following. Appoint a broadly-based and capable front bench and leave them in post so that they could gain widespread recognition and a reputation for competence. Insist on absolute discipline (as did Blair) across all levels

© Oxford University Press 2005
doi: 10.1093/pa/gsi069

of the party. Spend the first year researching deeply into the policies that would be true to Conservative principles, applicable to the problems facing Britain in the early twenty-first century, and which would command broad support. Realise that the party could only win if it reached out beyond its 'core vote' of some third of the electorate, to the voters in the centre-right ground who had traditionally supported the Conservatives but who had abandoned the party in the 1997 and 2001 elections. Tease out Labour's vulnerabilities, personal and policy, and pursue them relentlessly, while avoiding being seen as opportunistic. Build friends across business, academe, commentators, and the professions, not only among the centre-right but also with those on the centre-left who had become disillusioned with New Labour's ersatz Conservatism. Rebuild support across constituencies, particularly in urban Britain, and enlarge the party membership. Above all, repeatedly demonstrate that they were a principled party, deserving respect, and capable of regaining a reputation for trust and competence among all sections of the electorate. What the party had to avoid at all costs was being seen to 'flip-flop' on policy and to change tack at the first sign of trouble, or to fail to establish itself by 2005 with a range of familiar and trusted faces on their front bench. It should not have been beyond the Conservative Party to have achieved all, or at least much, of the above, as it did repeatedly throughout the twentieth century.

Iain Duncan Smith: 2001–03

But little of the above was achieved. One should perhaps have expected less of Iain Duncan Smith, who was elected leader in September 2001, only to fall two years later. Like Hague, he had to contend with a demoralised party, seemingly incapable of undertaking real thinking into the reasons for its unpopularity, and still deeply riven by ideological uncertainty and personality clashes. Duncan Smith's victory in the final ballot of party members, winning by a margin of three-to-two over Ken Clarke, settled the debate over Europe on the sceptical side, but otherwise it was a hollow victory. Unlike Hague, he failed to win support from a majority of his colleagues in the Parliamentary Party; indeed, in no ballot did he win more than a third of its votes. Popularity with the rank and file in the country was no compensation for the fact that many former ministers and Whips remembered him more for his rebellious activities during the mid-1990s rather than as a man of stature capable of commanding loyalty across the party. As Shadow Social Security Secretary and Shadow Defence Secretary under Hague, Duncan Smith had achieved a certain profile, but his personality, and his views on anything other than Europe, remained a little known quantity outside the precincts of Westminster.[4]

Duncan Smith began promisingly. Aiming to restore the Conservatives as the 'Party of ideas', he declared that a review of policy would be conducted with 'urgency and energy'. He instigated a reorganisation of the

Conservative Research Department, commissioned sophisticated polling and market research, and drew on a wider range of outside advice than his predecessor. All this suggested a more thoughtful and inclusive approach to policy renewal than had occurred under Hague. Duncan Smith sought to focus on the salient issues of the 2001 election—health, education, transport and crime—and called on the party to close down its discussion of Europe completely.[5] Reforming the public services and helping 'the vulnerable' in society were to become his mission, striking a very different tone from the kind of rightwing policies that those on the centre and left of the party feared he might espouse. Duncan Smith's vision of 'Compassionate Conservatism' (echoing President George W. Bush) stemmed in part from his Christianity and sense of social justice, but it still did not convince the political world that he had yet found a coherent agenda the party could pursue. His case was also weakened because key figures in his Shadow Cabinet (from both left and right) were not convinced about his 'compassionate Conservatism'.

Duncan Smith decided to steer clear of organisational reform, the focus of Hague's first two years as leader, and instead concentrated on the need to give the party a better public image. A marketing director and marketing department were thus established within party headquarters.[6] Under the Chairmanship of David Davis and then Theresa May, Central Office tried to encourage more women and ethnic minority candidates to apply and be included on the centrally approved candidates list, but hardly any progress was made and, as discussed in chapter 12, the Conservatives visibly lagged behind Labour in this area. Local associations continued to assert their autonomy, often choosing candidates that conformed to the white, male, middle class stereotype, though openly gay and ethnic minority candidates were selected in a handful of seats. Membership continued to decline after the 2001 election, but the party's revitalised youth wing, Conservative Future, saw its membership increase to over ten thousand by mid-2003.[7] Party finances showed little sign of improving, with corporate and individual donations remaining at relatively low levels. Worryingly for Duncan Smith, some former donors, including the spread betting tycoon, Stuart Wheeler, chose to withhold support from the party unless it changed its leader. Despite some progress in local government elections, the Conservatives remained in third place behind the nationalists in the 2003 elections to the Scottish Parliament and Welsh Assembly.[8]

In a claim that came to be seen as naïve and hubristic, Duncan Smith had announced that people would be able to form a judgement on his leadership after only three or four months. Only two days before his election as leader, the al-Qaeda attacks on New York and Washington heralded the beginning of the 'war on terror'. The world after 11 September 2001 offered Blair opportunities to ensure his international statesmanship would come even more to the fore, leaving Duncan Smith's Conservative Party in the shadows. The latter's pledge of unqualified support for military action against Iraq brought him short-term approval from Washington and plaudits from the right-wing press, but no long-term political gain. It shackled the party to wholeheartedly supporting a war and its prosecution although many clear-thinking Conservatives, including Ken Clarke and Lord Hurd, had significant qualms.

Continuing prosperity during Labour's second term ensured that Conservative efforts to dent the government's economic record made little impact. However, cracks in the New Labour edifice began to appear after 2001. Its divisions and policy difficulties, including university tuition fees and foundation hospitals, as well as over Iraq, offered Duncan Smith opportunities for making political capital that had not been available to Hague. Yet, by late 2002, Duncan Smith's stock had fallen so low with the press that his voice struggled to be heard.[9] His 'quiet man' image (launched at the 2002 Conservative Party conference) failed to excite the electorate, as opinion polls continued to show Blair and the Liberal Democrats' Charles Kennedy as more popular leaders. The Liberal Democrats capitalised electorally on the government's discomfiture, winning two Labour seats at by-elections. By contrast, the Conservatives' poor performances, particularly at the Brent East contest in September 2003, were the final straw for many Conservative MPs who lost whatever confidence they may have once had in their fledgling leader. As with Hague, he suffered from the fatal perception that no one saw him as a convincing Prime Minister-in-waiting. Despite exhibiting some promising instincts, such as trying to make the party again an inclusive, centrist force in politics, his fundamental weaknesses of personality counted too heavily against him.

Michael Howard: 2003–05

Iain Duncan Smith did at least set the Conservatives in the right direction, even if he failed to take the party far himself along that course. One could fairly criticise him for naively believing that he had the ability to lead the Conservatives, but at least he had the sense to depart like a "quiet man", leaving his successor time before the general election to do what was needed to make the party again a credible force as the principal challenger to Labour. Michael Howard began his leadership in November 2003 with advantages enjoyed by neither of his immediate predecessors. Blair was no longer seen as the impregnable figure of 1997–2001, or even of the first two years after the 2001 general election. The failure to find a speedy conclusion to the Iraq war, the death of government scientist Dr David Kelly, and questions over the war's legality were dragging him down, as were internal Labour Party divisions and his own health. Blair was no longer in his prime, and for a time in late-2003 and early-2004 he looked as if he might be on his way out. Unlike Hague and Duncan Smith, moreover, Howard had prolonged experience in office under two Prime Ministers, he had the benefit of being elected unopposed, and he had the gravitas to unite the Party after years of factionalism. Blair was not the only member of the political classes who expected great things from Howard.

Howard declared his candidacy speech for the leadership by insisting that 'when the government gets things right I won't oppose for opposition's sake'. The speech, drafted by Francis Maude and delivered at the Saatchi Gallery, indicated that he wanted to reclaim the moral high ground, almost unknown territory to the Conservatives for several years. It also suggested that he understood that the principal Opposition party had to look and sound like a government-in-waiting. However, as one colleague commented, 'the problem was that Michael didn't really connect with the words he uttered. He kind of did, but not fully. Before long, day to day pressures intervened.'[10] For all his qualities, the virtue most needed in a leader succeeding in 2003, strategic clarity and consistency, was the one he most conspicuously lacked.

Howard changed the tone of his Saatchi Gallery speech in the first three months of 2004. It was partly that the more consensual line he had articulated did not chime with the sympathies of those two assertive voices of Conservatism, the *Daily Telegraph* and *Daily Mail*. But it was also not in Howard's personality to be a consensual figure: he was by nature combative, and by profession a forensic lawyer, and these facts combined to make him want to be on the front foot against Labour. In the first quarter of 2004, he tried to convey his own personality and mission to the electorate. He set out to achieve this in a variety of ways, including his "I believe" statement, which listed, initially in a double page spread in *The Times* in January 2004, his personal credo. He developed his theme in a series of speeches. At Burnley he attacked the far-right British National Party, which revealed his passionate, as well as profoundly anti-racist, side. In Berlin he delivered a speech outlining his pragmatic Eurosceptic line towards the European Union, and at home he delivered another powerful 'British Dream' speech in which again he expounded on his vision for the country. The early signs were encouraging. In January 2004, one poll showed the Conservatives with 40% support, the highest since Black Wednesday, and ahead of Labour. The leadership also commissioned a far-reaching review of public spending under City troubleshooter, David James, to identity public sector 'waste' and propose savings in government expenditure to allow the Party to announce its new fiscal policy before the general election. Howard and his team hoped to build on this momentum when the Hutton Report on the build-up to the Iraq war was published (in February 2004), and expected it to be far more damning of Blair than it was. Instead of opting for a measured response, Howard acted as if he was the prosecuting counsel and he was portrayed as opportunistic: it was his first serious miscalculation as leader and, with hindsight, can be seen to be the turning point of his leadership.

Howard had still to entrench in the public's mind either his brand of Conservative policies, or indeed, the faces of his frontbench team. Instead of offering positive and constructive policies, he opted for pugnacity and negativity. From March to June 2004, under the influence of his new joint Party Chairmen, Maurice Saatchi and Liam Fox, he moved into a new phase which was a prolonged attack on Labour accusing it of having 'let down' the electorate. The view was taken that the forthcoming June local government, European and London Assembly elections should be viewed as a referendum on the performance of the Government and that the Conservatives would be seen to be failing if they did not lay bare the Government's weaknesses, as they saw them. The results were scarcely an unqualified success. The European Parliament elections in June 2004 provided the most disappointing result for the Conservatives. Although the Party came first in the poll, it only secured 27% of the vote (9% lower than Hague's performance in 1999) and saw a loss of eight seats. Labour's collapse (to 23% of the vote) and the success of the United Kingdom Independence Party obscured the fact that the Conservatives suffered their worst ever performance in a national election.[11] Far from challenging Labour in Parliamentary by-elections, the Party slipped into third place in Birmingham Hodge Hill and Leicester South and fourth, behind the (UKIP), in Hartlepool, on the eve of the party's annual conference. It was only in that summer's local government elections that the party built on the local recovery begun under Hague. Despite continuing progress in local government, becoming the largest party at a local level once again, Howard failed to match Hague's local election success of 2000, when the party won an estimated 38% of the vote.[12]

Yet another shift in strategy was now unleashed in the wake of these poor results. The summer of 2004 saw positive campaigning on the Conservatives' new policies on public services. Private polling suggested that health and education were seen as two negative issues for the Conservatives, so Howard determined that he should put forward fresh policies to counteract the criticisms that his party's policies were out of touch or unrealistic. However, it was again over Iraq where the Conservatives failed to win the argument that summer. In an interview in the *Sunday Times*, Michael Howard had suggested that he would have voted with the Labour rebels in March 2003 (while still supporting the war) if he had known the full facts about weapons of mass destruction at the time. This troubled the Parliamentary Party so that, when it came to the debate in the Commons on the Butler Report in July 2004, it was not fully behind the leader, and his performance lacked credibility and stature. Blair's conduct of the Iraq policy remained his greatest vulnerability, but Howard failed to push home his case, or, worse, even to identify a consistent Conservative line.

From the autumn, the final phase of Howard's leadership before the general election began: the so-called 'timetable for action'.[13] Based on focus group research undertaken over the summer, Saatchi in particular argued that the electorate was disillusioned with the failure of Labour to deliver on its promises. The leadership decided it needed to give not only specific policy pledges but also a clear timetable for delivery if it was to gain any credibility. Howard's speech to the Conservative conference in October set out the party's stall for the general election. Howard's personal qualities as a potential Prime Minister were also highlighted in contrast to what his team saw as an increasingly vulnerable Tony Blair.[14] But Howard's age (62) was perceived to be a drawback, while his televisual presence was not that much more convincing than that of his two predecessors.

By Christmas 2004, Howard had still failed to find an 'over-arching narrative' to explain what his Conservative Party was all about, and why people should vote for it rather than for Labour or Liberal Democrats. Poll after poll since March 2004 had shown little movement in Conservative support, languishing in the low 30s. In January 2004, The *Economist* had praised Howard for creating 'a resurgent and reinvigorated' party which was again 'a disciplined fighting force'. By November, it decided to write him off: 'the once impressive Mr Howard has shrunk in the job'.[15] Howard, however, lay great store by the Party's spending proposals, which would match (and in some areas exceed) the government's own plans for the public services. The James Review, which published its findings in January 2005, recommended £35 billion of savings, of which £23 billion Howard and Letwin pledged towards reinvestment in 'frontline' public services, while £8 billion would help to reduce government borrowing. The remaining £4 billion would finance 'targeted tax cuts', which were later announced during the election campaign (aimed at helping savers, first time buyers, and pensioners). But the party's proposal sent out mixed messages about their priorities on taxation and spending, leaving many commentators to conclude that Howard and his team were trying to please everyone, while satisfying none.

2005 Campaign

THE LONG CAMPAIGN: 'CORE VOTE PLUS' STRATEGY: By the beginning of 2005, a clear 'grid' outlining the precise strategy week-by-week was in place for the final stage of the 'long election campaign'. By then it was evident from private polling and published opinion polls that the government's lead on the key issues of the economy and public services was too large to reverse before the expected start of the official campaign in early April, let alone by polling day. Howard's team was now under the firm influence of celebrated Australian campaign director, Lynton Crosby (architect of the victories of Premier John Howard). He worked on the assumption that a positive promotion of Conservative policies in these areas would not make the impact the party needed to challenge

Labour.[16] Instead, the Conservatives should fight a highly disciplined but negative campaign on specific 'micro-issues', such as hospital-acquired infections and indiscipline in schools, where Labour's record was perceived to be weakest. It was believed that a strategy which sought to depress Labour's vote and boost the Conservative core vote with some additional support—a return to the 'core vote' strategy 'plus' new voters—could bring about a dramatic collapse in Labour's working majority.

For a time, Crosby's tactics appeared to bring dividends. By high-lighting individual cases where patients and pupils had suffered as a result of government policies and targets, such as Margaret Dixon, the 69-year-old whose shoulder operation was repeatedly cancelled, the Conservatives scored points against Labour as the long campaign reached its climax. The Conservatives had seized the news agenda, with the rightwing press rallying to its cause. Meanwhile the Labour strategy of highlighting £35 billion of 'Conservative cuts' to public services, led by Alan Milburn, faltered. The opinion polls began to show a steady narrowing in Labour's lead. But the 'hit and run' tactics belied the weaknesses in the Conservative strategy. While some aspects of the Conservative offensive appeared to work, others only served to rein-force the impression among many voters that the party was still unfit for office. Howard's attack in March on the abuse of planning laws by gypsies was designed to regain the initiative and reclaim the headlines after Brown's pre-election budget. But the attack invited more criticism than praise, reviving memories of the 'bandwagon populism' pursued by Hague in the pre-election period four years earlier.

What had begun as a tight and disciplined long campaign began to unravel only weeks before the start of the official campaign. Howard Flight, Party Deputy Chairman and one of the architects of the Con-servatives' tax and spending proposals, declared at a private meeting that the potential for efficiency savings was greater than those announced in the James Review. It gave the impression that there was a secret agenda drastically to cut public spending.[17] Determined to avoid the party being cast as untrustworthy on the public finances, Howard swiftly demanded Flight's resignation and de-selection as a candidate. His departure was damaging to party morale and cohesion on the eve of the official campaign and it also helped to revive Labour's beleaguered attempts to portray the Conservatives as a threat to the public services.

CAMPAIGN PREPARATION: The party was, however, in some ways more fully prepared for the 2005 general election than for those in 1997 or 2001. Activists were better mobilised, benefiting from an injection of younger recruits from the party's revitalised youth wing, and they were bolstered by more than 7,500 Conservative councillors (although this was still fewer than the 12,000 councillors who were able to campaign for Mrs Thatcher's first election victory in 1979). Conservative Central

Office was renamed Conservative Campaign Headquarters, and in July 2004 had moved to modern premises in Victoria Street, close to the Palace of Westminster. Crosby's disciplined approach quickly filtered throughout Campaign Headquarters and in the field, while an influx of donations after Howard became leader enabled the Party to invest in sophisticated computer software and equipment.[18] The 'Voter Vault' system, successfully pioneered by Karl Rove and the Republicans in the United States, which was procured by Liam Fox in mid-2004, enhanced targeted campaigning in marginal seats. The party's new machinery concentrated resources on 900,000 swing voters, and it was helped by a number of regional call centres, the largest based near Birmingham.[19] Despite efforts to boost the resources for candidates in a number of marginal contests, the party, however, still lagged behind Labour and the Liberal Democrats in channelling resources and manpower into target seats.[20] The task of winning all 164 target seats—far too many to select—to form an overall majority required a national swing of 11.5%; a task that was made all the more difficult by an electoral system that heavily favoured the Labour Party.[21]

THE OFFICIAL CAMPAIGN: MANIFESTO LAUNCH: The party nevertheless started the official campaign on 5 April in buoyant mood. In the first few days after Blair announced the election, polls showed the Conservatives trailing Labour by only 1 or 2%, on 35–36% of the vote, a far stronger position compared with the equivalent position in 1997 and 2001. Indeed, the British Election Study analysis revealed that the Conservatives were even ahead of Labour among those most likely to vote at the start of the campaign, particularly in marginal seats.[22] It was a picture which was to bring a false sense of security and confidence in the strategy adopted months beforehand. The Conservative manifesto, published on 11 April, several days before Labour's and the Liberal Democrats', was, at only 28 pages long, one of the thinnest ever produced. Its title, *Are You Thinking What We're Thinking? It's Time for Action*, was also the Party's main slogan for the first half of the campaign. But as *Sunday Telegraph* journalist Matthew d'Ancona pointed out, the message could be interpreted as one, not of empathy, but of 'grubby conspiracy: whispered words, and noses tapped' about concerns such as 'uncontrolled immigration.'[23] Another figure, Michael Portillo, called the Party's programme nothing more than a 'Victor Meldrew manifesto'.[24]

FOCUS ON 'CONTROLLED IMMIGRATION': Howard indeed pressed the message of 'controlled immigration' to the fore in the first two weeks of the campaign.[25] The other campaign themes, 'cleaner hospitals, school discipline, more police and accountability' came over less clearly as a consequence. Crosby, whose record in highlighting immigration in Australian elections was well known, later insisted after the election that Howard 'only gave one speech and one press conference on [immigration] in 34 days'.[26] This is utterly disingenuous. The Conservatives' emphasis and tone of the policy of yearly quotas and caps on both asylum seekers and immigrants exceeded the rhetoric used in Hague's unsuccessful campaign four years earlier. Howard's team asserted that immigration was a legitimate part of the leader's self-declared 'battle for Britain', and he blamed the media for hyping the issue.[27] But by the end of the second week, there were criticisms from senior Conservatives, including Lord Parkinson and Ken Clarke, that the 'public had enough of immigration' and that the Conservatives were in danger of becoming a 'one-issue Party'.[28] As most opinion polls indicated, immigration was high up in the list of salient issues before the official campaign began, but by 5 May it had receded in importance.[29] It is also clear from polls taken during the campaign that the public's rating of the Conservatives' campaign performance fell dramatically from +2% at the beginning to -18% at the end.[30] Leading pollster, Peter Kellner, pointed out that the party's lead on immigration actually fell during this period, indicating that the issue was a turn-off to potential supporters, and that there was little electoral gain to be made because 'the constituency that wants to be tough on immigration is much tougher than the Conservatives'.[31]

PREDOMINANCE OF HOWARD AND IRAQ: As the official campaign entered its final stages, it became clear that Howard had dominated the party's presentation. With private polling research continuing to suggest that Howard was perceived to be more in touch than Blair with the detail of people's problems, his advisers were keen to place him at the forefront of the campaign.[32] It was further felt that Howard needed to counter Blair's 'presidential' style of campaigning, but Conservative strategists either failed to notice or else ignored the fact that Blair never seemed far apart from Brown for most of the campaign. Oliver Letwin, the Shadow Chancellor, on the other hand was conspicuously absent in the last two weeks of the campaign, not just because he was fighting to save his own seat in Dorset. Indeed most of the Conservative frontbench were barely visible as Howard bestrode the campaign trail in front of a watchful media. Despite Blair's popularity ratings taking a tumble, the public's perception of Howard's prominence and performance went into freefall as the campaign drew to a close.[33] As discussed in chapter 11, only 21% by 5 May believed that he would make the best Prime Minister, fourteen points behind Blair.[34]

Realising, belatedly, that the Conservative campaign was weakening the party's support rather than strengthening it, the leadership sought to lower the temperature of the immigration theme and to broaden the party's message. *Are You Thinking What We're Thinking?* was replaced by *Taking a Stand on the Issues That Matter*, a slogan which also gave little indication about what the party stood for. The focus of the campaign, which had so far been predetermined by the Crosby grid, now veered off onto the territory of Iraq and the events which led to Blair's final decision to go to war in early 2003. Crosby admits that Iraq was a problem for the Conservatives in the final week of campaigning. 'People remembered why they had lost trust in Tony Blair', he argued, 'but they couldn't see any real difference between the Conservatives and Labour so we lost out on that.'[35] Howard's earlier claim that he would have gone to war irrespective of the Attorney General's advice sat uneasily with his accusations that Blair 'lied' in the case he made for war. Just as Howard was at sea after the Butler report into intelligence on Iraq's WMD, he now weakened his hand in the argument about the legality of the war in Iraq. The issue, which looked as if it would wound Blair deeply, and did to some extent, also did few favours for the Conservatives, who were already defined by their original support for the war.

Appealing to the electorate in the last days of the 2005 general election to wake up to a 'better, brighter Britain' by voting Conservative on polling day, Howard's almost only positive message of the campaign fell on deaf ears. Voters would not buy what Howard was selling. The long campaign had begun so promisingly. For the better part of the 'long campaign' and the first week of the official campaign, the party thought it had the edge over Labour. Only on the issues of asylum and law and order did the party enjoy leads over Labour and yet, even here, its advantage decreased by the end of the campaign.[36] On all other issues, including the economy, health and education, voters viewed Labour (somewhat grudgingly) as the more competent team on offer. Fighting on their chosen strategy, the Conservatives under Howard were highly unlikely to reach out beyond their core vote by more than 5%. The fact that the Party barely increased its vote on its 2001 performance is testament to a campaign that, for all its claimed discipline and vigour, failed utterly to offer the voters a convincing alternative to an unpopular government.

2005 general election: the verdict

But was the Party destined in 2005 to have performed no better? To answer this question requires a longer perspective. New Labour's command of the electoral landscape after 1997 had looked initially unassailable, with healthy leads over the Conservatives in every age and occupational group, except for the over 65s and AB professional classes.[37] The Party had to win back the 4.5 million deserting voters between 1992 and 1997, let alone the 1.2 million who had left the Conservative fold by 2001. In 2001 Labour and the Liberal Democrats continued their advance in seats lost by the Conservatives in 1997, whereas the Conservatives only improved their standing in their safest seats.[38] While a recovery in Scotland and Wales remained elusive, the party failed even to come second in any of the Manchester or Liverpool constituencies.

None of this made the prospects of defeating Labour in 2005 look encouraging. Howard and Crosby nevertheless believed that a disciplined and carefully targeted campaign could deprive Labour of a working majority—and indeed there were indications before the start of the campaign that this objective was within his grasp. Polling only 32.3% with fewer MPs than Michael Foot's disastrous performance for Labour, Howard claimed that the Party could 'hold its head up high' following a night of modest gains. But an analysis of the breakdown of the results suggests otherwise.

The Conservative performance varied considerably across the country on 5 May. Only in Greater London, the South East and Eastern England did the Party stage anything like a recovery. Yet even here the Conservative share of the vote only rose between 1 and 2% and the gains in seats were sporadic.[39] Aside from Wales and Scotland, where there was some progress, the Conservative share of the vote fell in five northernmost regions of England compared with 2001.[40] In the crucial battlegrounds of the East and West Midlands, the Party only gained six seats—well short of the number needed to displace Labour's majority. To form a government at the next election, the Conservatives have to win seats in the urban north, but the task will be made even harder now that the party invariably languishes in third place behind the Liberal Democrats in these areas.

More troubling for the Conservatives is the failure to reverse the socio-demographic trends in voting behaviour that first became evident in the mid-1990s. In some cases, the party has fallen back even on its 2001 performance. While New Labour's support consistently fell across all age, class and housing tenure groups, Conservative support improved only slightly, or even fell, compared with 2001.[41] Yet again, it was the Liberal Democrats who gained most at Labour's expense, rather than the main Opposition Party. Polling analysis of voter profiles and preferences in the 2005 general election suggests that women, once the most dependable source of support for the Conservatives, continue to desert the Party, while in the 25–34 age group the Party has been relegated to third place. Even among the AB professional and managerial classes, the Party's support has fallen by 2% since 2001, while the only improvement was among C2 and DE voters where Labour enjoys large leads.[42] In the crucial C1 category, the party simply trod water as the Liberal Democrats gained at Labour's expense. Despite Labour's downward trend in most social and occupational classes, it continues to lead the Conservatives among mortgage owners—a group that once placed its faith the party of Thatcher and Major, but now remains loyal to Blair and Brown.[43]

Clever targeting of resources and campaigning tools enabled the Party to make modest inroads into Blair's majority, but the story of the 2005 general election is much more about New Labour's success in holding onto just enough support to provide victory.[44] The Conservatives' failure in 2005 among women, AB voters and the young, in particular, point to the failure of the Howard/Crosby strategy, either to damage Labour, who have a solid working majority for its third term, or to provide a springboard for the Conservatives for the next general election. To see the 2005 campaign, and Howard's leadership as other than a complete failure, is not only disingenuous: it is also dangerous if the Conservatives are at last to learn lessons and move forward.

What now?

Thirteen years on since the Conservatives last won a general election in 1992, many in the Party had become accustomed to the feeling of defeat. The 2005 verdict was not a surprise; few commentators believed the party could overturn Blair's 2001 majority. But the aftermath of the 2005 general election was different to that of the previous two landslides. The scale of Labour's third successive victory was noticeably smaller, with many in the Conservative Party and the press behaving as if the government had had a narrow escape.[45] Although the near-collapse in Labour's vote was not mirrored by a strong recovery in the Conservative performance, the party nevertheless made their first substantial gains in seats since the 1983 general election. It was bolstered by an intake of 54 new MPs, many of whom were lauded for their talent and youth. Howard, in characteristically hubristic form, likened the 2005 newcomers to the 1950 intake, which boosted morale and injected energy in the party's ranks before Churchill's victory at the following general election.[46] Some more experienced figures, like the former Foreign Secretary, Malcolm Rifkind, also returned to Westminster and the frontbench to provide the experience the Conservatives badly needed. The Parliamentary Party also made steps to reflect more widely the population at large. Alongside two ethnic minority MPs, the tally of women Conservative Parliamentarians now reached 17, though this still only amounted to 9% of the Parliamentary Party—far less than Labour's female representation in the House of Commons (which was 35% after the 2005 election).

But amid some optimism about the future, Howard's announcement the day after the election that he would stand down once a new leader had been chosen under new rules, created inevitable uncertainty. His timetable for departure, which provided for consultation on changes to the Party's constitution during the summer of 2005, followed by the annual conference and an autumn leadership contest, elongated the period of uncertainty. While some, like Lord Heseltine, appealed for Howard to remain leader for at least a year, others argued that he should make way sooner rather than later to allow a new leader to assert his authority immediately against Blair, who was enjoying an 'Indian Summer' following his election success. Howard acted swiftly to reshuffle the shadow cabinet and proposed far-reaching organisational changes. Howard promoted the two 'rising stars' of the 2001–05 Parliament, George Osborne and David Cameron, to the positions of Shadow Chancellor and Shadow Education

Secretary, while battle-hardened figures like Tim Yeo and Nicholas Soames returned to the backbenches. Howard's new team was broader-based than any of his previous shadow cabinets, which merely highlighted further his earlier misjudgements in his appointments.

Returning to the frontbench after a four year absence, Francis Maude was given the task of steering the reform process as Party Chairman. Within weeks of the election, Maude and Raymond Monbiot, Chairman of the National Conservative Convention (the Party's voluntary wing) and Deputy Chairman of the Party, produced a consultation paper, *A 21st Century Party*, setting out a package of proposals to renew organisation at all levels and change the leadership election rules.[47] Maude declared that the party had been 'at its best and most successful' when it has been ready 'to embrace radical change, to renew itself so that it is fit to serve contemporary Britain'.[48] The proposals were certainly bold. They included merging moribund constituency associations in urban areas, widening the membership base, expanding the National Convention to include 800 representatives from across all wings of the party and scrapping the Hague system for choosing the leader, which gave grassroots members the final say. The recommendations encouraged a lively debate within the party during the summer of 2005 and, in the case of the latter, a strong reaction among the Parliamentary Party. Under Maude's preferred system, candidates would require the support of 10% of MPs to stand (unless one candidate received the support of over half the Parliamentary Party, in which case they would be declared leader). The National Convention would then vote on the candidates, with the winner being guaranteed a place in the final rounds of ballots among MPs. This method was roundly rejected by Conservative MPs at a meeting of the 1922 Committee in mid-June.[49] Instead of being bound by the Convention's preferences, backbenchers voted to strip grassroots members of their power to choose the leader directly by returning to the system where the Parliamentary Party has the final say.[50] Although the 1922 Committee vote was non-binding, it dealt a blow to Howard's diminishing authority and gave the impression of a divided Party, with voices such as Duncan Smith protesting at the disenfranchisement of the grassroots.

If divisions over party organisation were prevalent in the wake of the 2005 defeat, finding a consensus on the fraught matter of what policies the party should advocate after three defeats proved even more elusive. Apart from a few lone voices after the 1997 and 2001 defeats, there had been little fundamental debate over policy within the higher echelons of the party in eight years of Opposition.[51] Outclassed by New Labour's electoral machine and emasculated by Blair's cross-party appeal and Brown's management of the economy, which resulted in Labour winning the 'tax and spend' argument, the Conservatives were forced into the position of merely having to pledge to match Labour's spending plans. The Conservatives had been forced by Labour onto the back foot.

None of the three leaders after 1997 had been able to craft a convincing ideological position or devise a strong policy platform that could revive the party's fortunes.[52] In the stymied atmosphere of Howard's final months as leader, senior Conservatives went out of their way to praise the discipline of the 2005 campaign, but few broke rank to openly question the strategy pursued by Howard in the run up to the election.[53] Only Lord Saatchi, who left the shadow cabinet after the election, lambasted Howard's strategy for relying too heavily on focus groups, opinion polls and a lack of idealism.[54] Saatchi admitted responsibility for failing to challenge Lynton Crosby's tactics, yet he cannot escape culpability for his lack of influence as Party Co-Chairman since November 2003. The early frontrunner to succeed Howard, David Davis, argued that the Conservatives should not ditch their principles or indeed the Thatcherite inheritance, while David Cameron, Malcolm Rifkind, Ken Clarke and Alan Duncan called for a more centrist approach. Former leaders were also on hand to offer advice: Lady Thatcher called on the Party to return to 'first principles', whereas John Major insisted that the Party should reclaim the 'centre ground'.[55]

By mid-2005, however, some clarity emerged in the debate between competing Tory visions for the future. David Willetts argued in an important speech to the Social Market Foundation that the promotion of individual freedom was not enough. Modernising Conservatism meant emphasising the need for a strong society as well as a strong economy and that for far too long the party had not applied itself to questions of social justice.[56] For eight years, Willetts argued, the Party had been far too preoccupied with the question of leadership and organisation. For those like Liam Fox on the centre-right, 'freedom' had to be placed at the heart of the party's agenda. Influenced by the vitality of the American right, Fox declared to a right wing think tank: 'Freedom is our essence. Freedom is our core. Let freedom reign.'[57] But for others on the 'modernising' wing of the centre-right this would not simply mean a renewal of an economically-liberal prospectus. The inclusion of a socially-liberal agenda in tune with urban as well as suburban and rural Britain was espoused by David Cameron and others associated with the 'Notting Hill set'. As momentum gathered in his campaign in July 2005, David Davis appealed to the centre-left of the party by calling for a 'new Tory idealism' that speaks for 'one nation'.[58] With little in the way of policy flesh to be added to these intellectual bones, it will be the task of whoever succeeds Howard to not only add the details but also the timbre of the policies.

Conclusion

The period in opposition from 2001–05 was even bleaker for the Conservatives than 1997–2001, because it did not see the traditional recovery that the party had enjoyed after previous landslide defeats. Within four years of the 1906 election, the party had reached parity in seats with the Liberals. Five years after 1945, the party had recovered to within six seats of Labour. And four years after Labour's 1966 landslide, the Conservatives were back in power. Worse, the party showed little sign during 2001–05 of learning from history, or from Blair. From New Labour it learnt all the trivial lessons (setting up a 'war room', 'instant rebuttal' and other campaigning arts) but not the major lesson, that power will only be gained and retained by capturing and retaining the centre ground of the electorate, rather than merely courting the Conservative core vote, however ideologically satisfying and pleasing to the rightwing press that might be.

The answer to the question posed at the chapter's outset, was it inevitable that the Conservatives should continue to do so poorly given Blair's dominance of the centre ground, or were errors by the leadership to blame, can now be given. We would conclude that, while Hague had little room for manoeuvre in 1997–2001, he nevertheless might have achieved more against Labour had he adhered to the centre ground strategy more resolutely. The finger of blame can be pointed far more clearly at Duncan Smith, and above all Howard. Had Duncan Smith stuck to his centrist beliefs, and had the personality to impose his will on the party, real progress would have been made. But the real culprit is Howard, who managed to be so tactically and strategically inept. Blair and New Labour were no longer the forces in 2003–05 they had been. Howard's singular achievement was to let them off the hook, and hand them victory.

At the conclusion of our chapter on the Conservatives in Opposition from 1997–2001, we proposed that the new leader should spend four years saying that 'Labour will not deliver on its promises' on public services (he did not and they did not), while arranging for twenty of the party's best minds to go off to a Hebridean island for three years to think deeply about Tory principles and policy and report back.

Our advice now is even starker. The next leader must follow the advice set out at the start of the section above 'Conservatives in Opposition: 2001–05'. If he does so (and it will be a he), then the Conservative Party will be best placed to win the election in 2009. It will have met the minimum requirement of a principal opposition party—of looking and sounding like a government in waiting. Much of course will depend on Labour, and whether Blair goes quietly, and passes on power to a successor who can maintain Labour's (increasingly fragile) unity, and its broad appeal. But waiting for Labour to crack is not enough: the party, this time, has to act wisely. Another four years of myopia could weaken the party fatally.

1 D. Collings and A. Seldon, 'Conservatives in Opposition' in P. Norris (ed.), *Britain Votes 2001*, Oxford University Press, 2001, pp. 60–73.

2 The following sections lean heavily on A. Seldon and P. Snowdon, 'The Barren Years 1997–2005' in S. Ball and A. Seldon (ed.), *Recovering Power: The Conservatives in Opposition Since 1867*, Palgrave, 2005; and A. Seldon and P. Snowdon, 'The Conservative Party Under Blair: 2001–2005' in A. Seldon and D. Kavanagh (ed.), *The Blair Effect: 2001–05*, Cambridge University Press, 2005.

3   D. Collings and A. Seldon, 'Conservatives in Opposition', pp 60–73.
4   Iain Duncan Smith declined to serve (in a junior ministerial post) in the Major administration because of his opposition to its European policy. He was also the first leader of the Conservative Party not to have served as a Cabinet Minister before becoming leader. See P. Snowdon and D. Collings, 'Déjà vu? Conservative Problems in Historical Perspective', *Political Quarterly*, 2004/75.
5   G. Clark and S. Kelly, 'Echoes of Butler? The Conservative Research Department and the Making of Conservative Policy', *Political Quarterly*, 2004/75.
6   See J. Lees-Marshment, 'Mis-Marketing the Conservatives: The Limitations of Style over Substance', *Political Quarterly*, 2004/75.
7   *Sunday Times*, 29.6.03 and 2.11.03.
8   In Scotland, the Conservative vote rose by 0.6% compared with the 1999 election, while it improved by 3.3% in Wales.
9   Even the normally loyal Conservative commentator, Bruce Anderson, called on Iain Duncan Smith to resign, arguing that he did not possess the 'judgement, the personality, the intellect, the leadership skills or the self-confidence to lead his party anywhere near victory': *Spectator*, 5.5.03.
10 Private interview, 21.11.04.
11 In the Greater London Authority (GLA) elections, also held in June 2004, the Conservative share of the vote fell by 2% compared with 2000, despite the Conservatives becoming largest party on the GLA.
12 After the 2004 local elections, the party had over 8,000 councillors and had made important gains in urban areas in the Midlands and the North West. See House of Commons Research Paper 04/61, July 2004.
13 His office had decided that it would be 'inconceivable that the general election would be on any other date than in May 2005'. Private interview, 19.11.04.
14 'We want the general election to be a presidential contest between the two leaders,' one aide said. Private information.
15 *Economist*, 10.1.04 and 6.11.04.
16 Private information.
17 M. d'Ancona, 'The battle of the two Howards had to be fought', *Sunday Telegraph*, 27.3.03.
18 J. Fisher, 'Money Matters: the Financing of the Conservative Party', *Political Quarterly*, 2004/75.
19 P. Oborne, 'The Mean Machine', *Spectator*, 20.11.04.
20 *The Times*, 26.5.05.
21 M. Ashcroft, 'Smell the Coffee: A Wake-Up Call by the Conservative Party'. Conservative Party Report, June 2005.
22 See The British Election Study Rolling Campaign Survey, 2005: voter intentions among likely voters, University of Essex at http://www.essex.ac.uk/bes/.
23 M. d'Ancona, 'The battle of the two Howards had to be fought', *Sunday Telegraph*, 27.3.05.
24 M. Portillo, 'The Conservatives undone by their Victor Meldrew Manifesto', *Sunday Times*, 24.4.05.
25 The Conservative website boasted at the start of the campaign than Michael Howard had 'thrust immigration into the forefront of the campaign.'
26 A. Thomson, 'We lost but the Conservatives are back in the game', interview with Lynton Crosby, *Spectator*, 19.5.05.
27 Private information.
28 *Daily Telegraph*, 24.4.04.
29 See the final chapter this volume.
30 See The British Election Study Rolling Campaign Survey, 2005: campaign performance index, University of Essex at http://www.essex.ac.uk/bes/.
31 *Economist*, 14.5.05.
32 Private information.
33 Blair's performance in the campaign fell from –0.8 at the start of the campaign to -1.8 at the end, whereas Howard's dropped from –2.7 to –19.4. See the British Election Study Rolling Campaign Survey 2005: leader campaign performance index, University of Essex at http://www.essex.ac.uk/bes/.
34 See The British Election Study Rolling Campaign Survey, 2005: Who Would Make the Best Prime Minister?, University of Essex at http://www.essex.ac.uk/bes/.
35 A. Thomson, 'We lost but the Conservatives are back in the game', interview with Lynton Crosby in *Spectator*, 19.5.05.
36 The Conservative lead over Labour on immigration dropped from 11% to 8% by the end of the campaign, while the lead on law and order dropped from 6% to 0%. See ICM Research (http://www.icmresearch.co.uk/reviews/pollreviews.asp).
37 D. Butler and D. Kavanagh, *The British General Election of 1997*, Macmillan, 1997), pp. 244–6.
38 Labour held 23 of its 30 most marginal seats and increased its majorities in many of the leafy, suburban seats, such as Enfield Southgate, Wimbledon and Bristol West. P. Norris (ed.), *Britain Votes 2001*, Oxford University Press, 2001, p. 13.

39 Successes in Enfield Southgate, Putney and in a cluster of seats in Hertfordshire were offset by near misses in places like Hove, Harlow and Crawley, where Labour held on by the narrowest of margins.

40 See House of Commons Research Paper 05/33, 17.5.05; The British Parliamentary Constituency Database, 1992–2005.

41 See MORI's Aggregate Analysis, cited in *The Parliamentary Monitor*, May 2004, Issue 127.

42 Ibid.

43 Ibid.

44 See the final chapter of this volume.

45 Matthew d'Ancona wrote 'In the hours of Friday morning [6 May], the texture of the general election suddenly seemed unexpectedly silky for the Tories, and poll-defyingly scratchy for Labour.' *Sunday Telegraph*, 8.5.05.

46 *Daily Telegraph*, 10.5.05.

47 The Conservative Party, *A 21st Century Party: A Consultation Paper Setting Out Proposals to Reform the Conservative Party's Organisation*, 24.5.05.

48 Ibid.

49 BBC News online, 15.6.05.

50 Party members would be formally consulted under the option approved by backbenchers at the 1922 meeting, but MPs would not be bound by their preferences. Ibid.

51 One of these lone voices was David Willetts, who argued immediately after the 1997 landslide, that the party had to modernise itself without aping New Labour. See D. Willetts and R. Forsyke, *After the Landslide*, Centre for Policy Studies, 1997.

52 See A. Seldon and P. Snowdon, 'The Conservative Party under Blair, 2001–05' in A. Seldon and D. Kavanagh (eds), *Blair Effect II*, Cambridge University Press, 2005.

53 John Bercow was one of the few former frontbenchers to openly attack Howard's strategy in the immediate aftermath, calling the focus on immigration 'repellent' and the 'Right to Choose' policies in health and education an 'escape route' from the public services. Bercow was swiftly reprimanded by the leadership. See J. Bercow 'We must change: We looked nasty and visionless', *Independent*, 10.5.05.

54 M. Saatchi, *If This Is Conservatism, I Am A Conservative*, Centre for Policy Studies, June 2005, and *Daily Telegraph*, 20.6.05.

55 BBC News Online, 15.5.05.

56 D. Willetts, *What Does Modernising the Conservative Party Mean?* Speech to the Social Market Foundation, 2.6.05.

57 Dr L. Fox, *Let Freedom Reign*, speech to Politeia, 10.5.05.

58 D. Davis, *Modern Conservatism*, speech to the Centre for Policy Studies, 4.7.05.

ANDREW RUSSELL

The Liberal Democrat Campaign

In the immediate aftermath of the 2005 general election, Liberal Democrat leader Charles Kennedy hailed the party's performance, claiming that 'we now live in an era of three party politics', while a BBC political correspondent was quick to claim, 'Charles Kennedy has every reason to be delighted with the Liberal Democrats' performance in the general election'.[1] The Liberal Democrats increased both their representation in parliament and their share of the vote. The only party to increase their share of the vote in every region of Britain, they took seats from both of their main political rivals. Kennedy was the most popular of all three party leaders, and the public's assessment of the party's election campaign—unlike that for their opponents—was favourable throughout. Yet as the dust settled on the campaign it was clear that the Liberal Democrats had fallen short of their ambitions in 2005. Their electoral advance was skewed both politically and geographically; the Liberal Democrats had won a considerable amount of votes from Labour but had fared much worse against the Conservatives. Moreover, the detail of the party's results actually posed as many questions as it answered on the future strategy of the party.

The Liberal Democrats have become accustomed to historic performances. In 1997 the party's haul of 46 MPs had been their best since 1929, but it has now been further improved twice. In 2005 they garnered nearly six million votes and increased their national vote by nearly 4%. At the same time the Labour vote fell by over 5% and Conservative support improved by a mere .5%. The number of Liberal Democrat MPs increased again, this time to 62 MPs (the reduction in Scottish constituencies meant that the Liberal Democrats notionally held 51 seats from 2001), and the party was left with MPs across all regions of Britain.

The improvement in Liberal Democrat standings in Westminster ought to have been enough to lift morale but there was more good news for the party. In a contest that the public felt was characterised by negative electioneering, the Liberal Democrats' campaign was largely

© Oxford University Press 2005
doi: 10.1093/pa/gsi067

1. Liberal Democrat Regional Performance

	Vote Change	Seats	Seats (Net Change)
South East	+2.4	6	−2
East	+5.3	3	+1
Greater London	+4.6	8	+2
South West	+1.5	16	+1
West Midlands	+4.0	2	+1
East Midlands	+3.4	1	0
Yorkshire/Humberside	+3.7	3	+1
North West	+4.6	6	+3
North	+6.0	1	0
Wales	+4.5	4	+2
Scotland[a]	+6.1	11	+2
GB Total[b]	+4.0	62	+11

Note:[a] Changes based on Notional 2001 seats in Scotland; [b] GB Total does not include Staffordshire South seat where there was no contest on 5 May, or Glasgow North East the Speakers Seat and Wyre Forest where there was no Liberal Democrat candidate.
Source: The British Parliamentary Constituency Database, 1992–2005.

exempt from public criticism. For the second successive general election, Kennedy was alone among party leaders in being able to increase his personal rating over the course of the campaign.[2] During April, polling data put the Liberal Democrats ahead on two key issues, council tax and the environment, while the party's private polling is said to have shown a lead for the Liberal Democrats in three other campaign themes: tuition fees, long term care for the elderly, and Iraq.[3]

The 2005 British Election Study Rolling Campaign Panel Survey asked voters to list their voting intention throughout the campaign, and the fluctuations in reported vote intention were smoothed by using six day running averages. What is remarkable about these figures is that the Liberal Democrats were alone among the main parties to see their fortunes rise significantly over the campaign. While support for the Labour government among all voters remained stable or increased only slightly (from 35 to 35.7%, within the margin of error), Conservative support fell from 33.5 to 30.1%. Liberal Democrat support, however, improved from 19.4% to 24.8% over the course of the election campaign. As the book's conclusion suggests, this pattern was found in other opinion polls as well.

2. Contextual Change in Liberal Democrat Vote by Type of Battleground Seat

Seats Classified by the Party in 1st and 2nd Place after the 2001 Election	Change in % Liberal Democrat Vote Share in 2005
Con–Lab	+2.9
Con–LD	+0.5
Lab–Con	+4.7
Lab–LD	+7.7
LD–Con	+0.6
LD–Lab	+4.6
ALL	+4.0

Source: The British Parliamentary Constituency Database, 1992–2005.

Similarly, the public assessment of the campaign performances of the party leaders in the BES survey revealed that Kennedy's rating dipped during the beginning of the campaign (probably due to his high-profile gaffe on the detail of economic policy on his return to work after paternity leave), but improved dramatically during the final phase of the campaign. He ended the campaign with a positive performance index of +20.6, compared to Tony Blair's −1.8, and Michael Howard's −19.4[4]. The Liberal Democrats as a party also emerged the clear winner from the BES rolling campaign panel survey. On the final days of polling, the Liberal Democrats averaged a satisfaction rating of 17.0 for their campaign, compared to a rating of 3.6 for Labour and −18.2 for the Conservatives.[5]

The long and short campaigns

Although the official campaign lasted only four weeks, the 2005 general election inflicted the longest of long campaigns on the public. For the third time running the general election was timed to coincide with local elections. All parties had been on a war footing for a May 5 election for a considerable length of time. In fact although the announcement of the start of the official campaign had been delayed by the death of the Pope and the reorganisation of the marriage of the Prince of Wales, the parties had already begun their unofficial campaigning months ahead of schedule.

The length of the unofficial campaign caused the Liberal Democrats some significant problems. Without the benefit of the legally-required party balance in broadcast media's coverage before the election was actually called, the Liberal Democrats were surprised to find themselves so easily sidelined in the so-called 'phoney' campaign. Indeed the fear of being organised out of the coverage of the pre-election campaign was probably behind the Liberal Democrat media blitz on March 22 when the party broke with their recent tradition and spent £100,000 on a press conference to launch the party's programme and to pay for full page advertisements in three newspapers. The adverts, which featured Kennedy offering '10 good reasons to vote Liberal Democrat', may not have deviated markedly from the planned style of campaign, but they did represent a different style of political marketing. The party was attempting to recapture the spotlight which had been focused on the Conservative and Labour parties.

This event also marked a significant change in Liberal Democrat tactics from previous elections. The parliamentary party was now reaching critical mass in terms of size, and this growth required a new set of dynamic strategies in order to present the party as a coherent force. The March 22 launch represented the party's most ambitious advertising campaign since the formation of the SDP in the 1980s and demonstrated a determination to match local activism with a more prominent national campaign.

The campaign itself was a well-planned affair. The '10 reasons to vote Liberal Democrat' theme became the cornerstone of its branding theme the following month, being reworked into a set of 'We oppose: we propose' position statements. These included free personal care, opposition to tuition and top-up fees, the replacement of the Council Tax with a local income tax, and opposition to the war in Iraq. The campaign slogan—*the real alternative*—seemed to convey both positive imagery around the party and a sense of exasperation with their opponents. Meanwhile the campaign was characterised by a highly leader-centred drive, which included national and local press adverts and the nationwide roll-out of a billboard campaign—all of which were branded with the image of Kennedy.

After the hiatus caused by the birth of the Kennedys' first child in April, the Liberal Democrats settled into a daily routine designed to maximise the party's impact in the media. During the official campaign, the party held daily press conferences each morning. Whilst not universally popular with the journalists, the early start did enable the Liberal Democrats to beat their opponents to the punch and to lead the news agenda on occasion, something they had been worried about during the long campaign.

Coordination of the campaign was handled by the Campaign and Communications Committee (CCC) and a small number of key staff headed by Lord Chris Rennard, the party's Chief Executive, and Lord Tim Razzall, the Chair of the Campaign. The CCC would receive reports on target seat campaigning, market research, broadcasting strategy, and the preparations for the leader's tour. Each area of the campaign was largely autonomous, but the meetings of the CCC were designed as the constant checking point.

The relatively high-profile for the Liberal Democrat campaign was a marked change from recent elections. Largely, this was the result of necessity—the more successful the party becomes the more it needs a national rather than a local profile. Capability was also important: the Liberal Democrats received more money from donors than in previous elections. The biggest contributor to Liberal Democrat finance appears to have been Balearic-based businessman Michael Brown through his London financial company, Fifth Avenue Partners, which apparently accounted for roughly half of the £5m the party earmarked for spending over the course of the campaign. If the source of income was novel, however, the biggest drains on resources were more orthodox. Most of the Liberal Democrat spending went on campaign literature, advertising and broadcasting costs, the payment of staff, and the costs of the leader's tour.[6]

Education

At the previous two general elections, the Liberal Democrats had held a distinctive policy on education that would have seen an increase in the marginal rate of income tax of 1p to be ring-fenced and earmarked for spending on education. The hypothecated taxation policy was ditched in the run up to 2005, however, largely because Labour's increase in National Insurance rates had been aimed at the same outcome. Hypothecation had proved to be very popular in both 1997 and 2001, although the Liberal Democrats found it difficult to convert this popularity into votes. Its absence in 2005 might have led to a re-emergence of the traditional problem for the Liberal Democrats—that people did not know what the party stood for. Nevertheless, the party still found itself able to say something distinctive about education in 2005, announcing its intention to scrap the national curriculum, to replace A levels and GCSEs with a new diploma, and to further reduce class sizes in infant and junior schools. It was in the field of Higher Education, however, that the Liberal Democrats struck the most resonant chord. Labour's implementation of top-up tuition fees for students at university ran counter to their 2001 manifesto, and the Liberal Democrats sensed an opportunity to tap-in to opposition to the policy. The Liberal Democrats thus advocated the abolition of tuition-fees and pointed to the coalition with Labour in the Scottish Executive as the template for education policy. In Scotland, the party had been able to claim credit for the non-imposition of tuition fees for Scottish students in 1999, where most students will have to pay a graduate tax instead.

It was also felt that opposition to tuition and top-up fees would be popular with students. In April, the party produced a list of 27 parliamentary constituencies where the student vote could be vital to the election outcome. In truth many of these seats were Liberal Democrat targets anyway, but Liberal Democrat success in defeating six Labour MPs in Birmingham Yardley, Bristol West, Cambridge, Cardiff Central, Leeds North West, and Manchester Withington may have been assisted by student votes. Nevertheless, this commentary may have exaggerated the student-led Liberal Democrat swing. After all, the party failed to mount a sufficient student-led challenge in another eight Labour-held constituencies. Moreover, of the 13 student seats identified by the Liberal Democrats and held by the Conservatives, they only gained the marginal constituencies of Taunton, and Westmorland and Lonsdale. The student vote was a vital component in many places where the party was successful but was probably insufficient by itself to guarantee victory. For example, Leeds North West and Manchester Withington are seats with large university populations, but the student vote is notoriously difficult to harness, as many fail to register at their term time addresses, and many also fail to vote. University areas are also replete with recent graduates and, in particular, public sector employees, such as those who work in schools, hospitals, the media, and local government. All of these groups were equally susceptible to the Liberal Democrat message in 2005. Withington was an unexpected victory, but its genesis was standard for a Liberal Democrat gain based on local issues:

there were controversies surrounding two local hospitals, threats of closure to post offices, and the failure to extend South Manchester's Metrolink tram system to the constituency. These Manchester issues, in combination with Liberal Democrat advances at local elections in 2003 and 2004, reveal that the taking of Withington was no more remarkable than the capture of Sheffield Hallam from the Conservatives in 1997.

'We oppose: Bush and Blair on Iraq'

One of the aftermaths of the terrorist attack on the World Trade Center in New York on 11 September 2001 was its effect on British politics. The Labour government and the Conservative opposition found themselves close to the policies of President George W. Bush. By contrast, the Liberal Democrats expressed extreme unease with the wars on Afghanistan and then—particularly—Iraq. Kennedy told a rally in Hyde Park in February 2003 that there had been 'no just or moral case for war against Iraq', and over the next two years the Liberal Democrats became identified as the anti-war party. Indeed, pictures of Tony Blair were far more likely to be found on Liberal Democrat election addresses (usually in close proximity to President Bush) than on Labour campaign literature.

At the start of the official campaign, the Iraq War formed part of the subtext rather than the headlines of the election. Leading Liberal Democrat donor Greg Dyke, who lost his BBC job in the aftermath of the Hutton report, claimed that the issue was subsumed into the campaign theme of 'trust'. The war was never far away from the heart of the Liberal Democrat campaign and the party's ten reasons to vote Liberal Democrat included the pledge 'We oppose: Bush and Blair on Iraq. We propose: Never again'.

The Liberal Democrats had always intended to run the issue of the Iraq war during the campaign, but, knowing that once introduced it might dominate the rest of the campaign, they were anxious to portray other issues first. Hence the first two weeks of the campaign were dominated by the party's stance on tuition fees and council tax before they turned their attention to Iraq.

In the event, the leaking of a portion of the letter containing the Attorney General's advice on the legality of the conflict coincided with the gear-change in campaigning on April 25. The response over the next few days was to focus relentlessly on the Iraq war, but the Liberal Democrats tended to stop short of the Conservative tactic of labelling the Prime Minister a liar; instead they complained that the country had been 'misled' over the necessity for war.

In order to maximise their impact, the Liberal Democrats persuaded veteran Labour MP Brian Sedgemore to attend the early-morning press conference in order to announce his defection to the Liberal Democrats. As Lord Rennard, the party's Chief Executive explained, the Sedgemore defection, and the news stories about the legality of the Iraq

War, 'illustrated that the key differences on Iraq were not between Labour and the Conservatives but between Labour and the Liberal Democrats'.[7]

Apparently the party's internal tracking polls demonstrated that the Sedgemore defection was an advantage to the Liberal Democrats, adding to their media profile and campaign visibility. Moreover, according to Rennard, Iraq and top-up fees had provided the public with the evidence that the left-right scale was no longer relevant, being 'the type of thing you might expect from a Thatcherite Conservative government'. Moreover, he added:

If (Labour) move further to the right, you can understand why people on the left feel there is a vacuum, and might decide to vote for us. But we won't allow ourselves to be drawn into that vacuum and away from where we've always been.

However, this strategy may be easier to proclaim than to follow. Sedgemore was, after all, a veteran of Labour's left-wing, and the Liberal Democrats were attempting to draw support from both ends of the political spectrum simultaneously. In short, the party might have noted that their very attractiveness to those wishing to criticise the government from the left might alienate a potential audience from the right. When added to the party's stance on local income tax and the burgeoning critique of new Labour on civil liberties, the party's contemporary claim to be 'neither left nor right' ought be questioned in the context of the 2005 campaign.[8]

Either left or right?

Since the formation of the party, Liberal Democrat success in general elections has been based on taking seats from the Conservatives.

Vote Intention During the 2005 Campaign

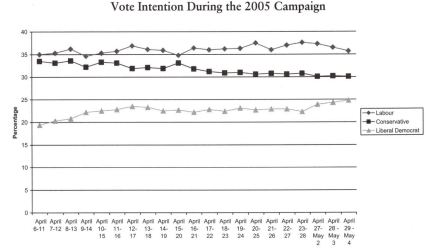

Source: 2005 British Election Study. Rolling Campaign Panel

Indeed, since 1992 the Liberal Democrats have won 42 Conservative-held seats over four general elections. In terms of the popular vote, the Conservatives were 24% ahead of the Liberal Democrats in 1992; after 2005, the Conservative lead over the Liberal Democrats in the popular vote is down to 10%.

After the 1992 election and the party's abandonment of equidistance, the Liberal Democrats joined a *de facto* anti-Conservative alliance, competing with Labour but fighting the Conservatives. As a result, Liberal Democrat advances were almost exclusively at the expense of the Conservatives and were predominantly in the south of England. If we are to believe the *Ashdown Diaries*, the extent to which the Blair-Ashdown axis found common cause was remarkable.[9] Following both the failure of Labour to deliver the promised electoral reform referendum and the change in Liberal Democrat leadership in 1999, distance between the Liberal Democrats and Labour increased. War in Afghanistan and Iraq drove a further wedge between the leadership of the two parties. At the autumn 2004 party conference, Kennedy reopened the possibility of equidistance, claiming that the Liberal Democrats would not enter a post-election pact with Tony Blair's Labour at Westminster.

There were also signs that the party was beginning to rethink its political and economic strategy. The party's reshuffle in 2003 saw the transfer of important domestic portfolios from the left to the right of the party: Matthew Taylor, closely associated with the hypothecation policy of 1997 and 2001, was replaced by Vincent Cable as Liberal Democrat treasury spokesman; Simon Hughes' home affairs portfolio went to Mark Oaten. The publication of *The Orange Book* (joint-edited by MP David Laws) in 2004 created controversy for the party, not least because it apparently opened the possibility that the Liberal Democrats could return to more traditional views of libertarianism and new visions such as the much heralded 'tough liberalism'.[10]

The party entered the 2005 contest trying to fight a war on two fronts. They attempted to build on recent success against the Conservatives and even attempted the audacious 'decapitation strategy' of removing senior Conservatives such as Oliver Letwin in Dorset West, David Davis in Haltemprice and Howden, and Theresa May in Maidenhead. As the 2005 contest drew ever nearer, however, the party seemed to pull back towards a set of policies that would seem more attractive to defectors from Labour than from the Conservatives. Opposition to the Council tax may be fairly widespread, but the appeal of a local income tax as its replacement for local authority finance may be more attractive to the left and to poorer groups. Certainly it was true that in the aftermath of 2005, at least, one outgoing MP blamed local income tax for defeat. This could be a developing area for Liberal Democrat strategists since Kennedy announced a review of taxation policy within a month of the election.

The party's Chief Executive remains adamant that the party cannot afford to allow itself to be defined solely in relation to its political rivals:

The truth is you look where the Liberal Democrats are, and you look at where we've got to go, and any strategy which is based on winning votes just from Labour or just from the Conservatives is doomed to failure.

The Liberal Democrats had captured Chesterfield from Labour in 2001. This was their first success against Labour since the mid-1980s, but it did not yet represent an equal battle with both Labour and Conservatives. With Labour and Tony Blair less popular in 2005, however, the Liberal Democrats were hopeful of making many advances at the expense of Labour in 2005. By-election victories in Brent East in 2003 and Leicester South in 2004 had demonstrated that the Liberal Democrats could attack Labour in their heartlands, particularly in seats with high proportions of black and minority ethnic (especially Muslim) voters. Furthermore, narrow by-election defeats in Birmingham Hodge Hill and Hartlepool had demonstrated the Liberal Democrats' ability to run Labour close in its working class powerbases of the Midlands and the North-east, where in the past the third party had always found it difficult to mobilise support. In short, despite the apparently unpromising starting point—they were within 5% swings of Labour in only seven parliamentary constituencies, three of them redistricted Scottish seats—the Liberal Democrats were optimistic that they could benefit in the election from increasing their criticism of Labour without harming their ability to fight the Conservatives.

The election of 2005 illustrated that the Liberal Democrats were particularly successful at gaining votes, and some seats, from Labour, but they made far less ground at the expense of the Conservatives. At the national level, the Liberal Democrat share of the vote increased by nearly 4%, but disaggregating electoral performance according to the constituency context is illuminating. The Liberal Democrat share of the vote rose most dramatically where they were competing in second place against Labour. In Con–LibDem seats, advances in the Liberal Democrat vote were sluggish in comparison. In Lab–Con seats, the Liberal Democrat vote increased by nearly 5%, indicating that the party probably was the recipient of Labour protest votes, despite the Prime Minister's rather exaggerated warning that such protests could lead to the formation of a Conservative government.

One aspect of the 2005 Liberal Democrat campaign concerned the ability of the party to react to being targeted—rather than ignored—by the other main parties. After all, the Liberal Democrats have grown accustomed to complaining about the media's failure to take the party seriously and to give them their fair share of the limelight. As late as March 26 the Prime Minister was talking of making 'common cause' with the Liberal Democrats against the Conservatives (*Guardian*,

26.5.05). However, as the campaign wore on, the focus of both Conservative and Labour parties was turned onto the Liberal Democrats, providing a stiff test for the party in 2005. Reasoning that it was better to be attacked than to be ignored, the Liberal Democrats chose, for the most part, to be flattered by the interest shown in them and to remain aloof, particularly from the bulk of negative campaigning during the election. Nevertheless, when the Conservatives attacked Liberal Democrat policies on the rehabilitation of prisoners and the mandatory life-sentence for murder, the party failed to mount the type of rapid rebuttal exercise that had characterised Labour's campaign in 1997. Similarly, when Labour claimed that even small-scale defections to the Liberal Democrats from Labour could lead to an unexpected victory for Michael Howard's Conservatives, the most effective counter-arguments came not from the party under attack but from the *Independent* and its resident academic psephologist, John Curtice.[11]

Liberal Democrat success and failure

Analysis of the new Liberal Democrat seats gained in 2005 is illuminating. It is clear that the Liberal Democrats had a very good election against the Labour government. On the other hand, the party ought to be relatively disappointed with how they fared against Michael Howard's Conservatives. Indeed it is possible to conclude that a different permutation of gains from the Labour and Conservative parties with the same net result would have been preferable for the Liberal Democrats.

Sarah Teather, the victor of the Brent East by-election in 2003, managed to retain the seat in 2005. This will have surprised only those who failed to note the 'stickability' of Liberal by-election victors over the years. Brent East may have been won on the back of a protest vote, but, like Simon Hughes in Bermondsey in 1982 and Sandra Gidley in Romsey in 2000, Ms. Teather has been able to overcome apparently unfavourable demographic conditions with the boost to her credibility given by her incumbency. The other Liberal Democrat by-election victory in the last parliament, Leicester South, reverted to Labour, perhaps because there was insufficient time between the by-election in 2004 and the general election for Parmjit Gill to make his mark as the constituency MP.

Liberal Democrat victories over Labour in Cardiff Central, Bristol West, Birmingham Yardley, and the newly redistricted Scottish constituencies of Inverness, Nairn, Badenoch and Strathspay, and Dunbartonshire East would have been welcome but expected since they required less than a 5% swing from Labour to the Liberal Democrats in order to fall. Nevertheless, all fell to the party with rather impressive increases in the Liberal Democrat vote and look relatively safe prospects for the next general election. The Liberal Democrats failed however, to take Aberdeen South in Scotland, and Oldham East and Saddleworth, which were within the 5% swing range.

More spectacular Liberal Democrat victories at Labour's expense came in Hornsey and Wood Green and in Manchester Withington, and the party came from third place in 2001 to take the Labour seats of Falmouth and Camborne and Leeds North West.

Rochdale returned to the Liberal fold after eight years of Labour incumbency, apparently assisted by the significant swing from Labour to the Liberal Democrats in the constituency's Muslim community. Nevertheless other seats which might have been winnable with similar shifts in the Muslim vote failed to be delivered—expected Liberal Democrat challenges in Blackburn, Pendle (where the Liberal Democrats came third), and Manchester Gorton were insufficient to dislodge Labour incumbents at this election. According to the 2001 census, there are nine seats where the Muslim population amounts to more than one fifth of the population. The Liberal Democrats failed to win any of these seats, and they came second in only two. Furthermore they were pushed into fourth place by Respect in no fewer than four of these seats. Even from the fifty seats with the largest Muslim populations, the Liberal Democrats managed to win only two (Rochdale and Brent East).

Despite the notable victory over Plaid Cymru in Ceredigion, the Liberal Democrats had less success against other parties than they did against Labour. In particular the Conservative vote seems to have hardened against the Liberal Democrat challenge in 2005. Despite the apparently unstoppable march of the Liberal Democrats in many Conservative seats since 1992, the Tories fought back in 2005, taking five seats from the Liberal Democrats while losing only three in the other direction. Given the nature of Liberal advance in the south-west in recent years, Liberal Democrat victory in Taunton seemed almost routine—and the Liberal Democrat victory in Solihull seems remarkable by any standard—but elsewhere the swing to the Liberal Democrats failed to materialise. Even in the south-west, the party had setbacks. The Liberal Democrat vote in Bridgwater, a target seat in 2001, collapsed, leaving the party third behind the Conservatives and Labour. The 'decapitation strategy' resolutely failed to deliver Conservative heads on a platter: David Davis, Oliver Letwin, Theresa May, and Michael Howard all saw their share of the vote increase at Liberal Democrat expense in 2005. The capture of Tim Collins' seat Westmorland and Lonsdale might represent the only victory for the decapitation strategy, but even then it seems to have owed more to burgeoning Liberal Democrat credibility based on local election success in recent years.

Defensive strategy

Compared to the last two elections, the Liberal Democrats were confident enough in 2005 to concentrate resources on winning new seats rather than pouring resources into defending previous victories. The extent of the party's confidence in their electoral machine was such

3. Liberal Democrat New Seats

	2001 Winner	New Liberal Democrat MP	% Change in the Vote, 2005
Birmingham Yardley	Labour	John Hemming	+8.1
Brent East	Labour[a b]	Sarah Teather	+36.9
Bristol West	Labour	Stephen Williams	+9.4
Cambridge	Labour	David Howarth	+18.9
Cardiff Central	Labour	Jenny Willott	+13.1
Ceredigion	Plaid Cymru	Mark Williams	+9.6
Dunbartonshire East	Labour[c]	Jo Swinson	+14.7
Falmouth & Camborne	Labour[b]	Julia Goldsworthy	+10.4
Hornsey & Wood Green	Labour	Lynne Featherstone	+17.5
Inverness, Nairn, Badenoch & Strathspay	Labour[c]	Danny Alexander	+10.8
Leeds North West	Labour[b]	Greg Mulholland	+10.3
Manchester Withington	Labour	John Leech	+20.4
Rochdale	Labour	Paul Rowen	+6.2
Solihull	Conservative	Lorely Burt	+13.9
Taunton	Conservative	Jeremy Browne	+2.0
Westmorland & Lonsdale	Conservative	Tim Farron	+5.1

Note: [a] Liberal Democrats won the 2003 Brent East by-election; [b] Liberal Democrats placed third in 2001; [c] Scottish 2001 results are notional after boundary changes.
Source: The British Parliamentary Constituency Database, 1992–2005.

that, unlike in 2001 where huge efforts were made to ensure that narrow victories in Richmond Park and Kingston and Surbiton were not overturned, relatively little attention was paid to defending the 2001 victories. In most cases this seems to have been successful; in Cheadle a Liberal Democrat majority of 33 turned into one of over 4,000, and the much-vaunted Conservative challenge in Norfolk North failed to materialise. Two 2001 wins, Guildford and Ludlow, were overturned, however, as were more established Liberal Democrat territories in Newbury and Weston Super Mare.

The Liberal Democrats concentrated their defensive strategy on seats where one of their sitting MPs had retired. This has often been a problem for the Liberal Democrats, since the profit from incumbency generally seems to be associated with the candidate as much as the party.

4. Liberal Democrat Performance in Seats Where Their Sitting MP Retired

	Outgoing Liberal Democrat MP	New Liberal Democrat MP	% Vote Change	Outcome
Berwickshire, Roxburgh & Selkirk	Archy Kirkwood[a]	Michael Moore[a]	−5.0	LD Hold
Cheltenham	Nigel Jones	Martin Horwood	−6.2	LD Hold
Cornwall North	Paul Tyler	Dan Rogerson	−9.4	LD Hold
Devon West & Torridge	John Burnett	David Walter	−5.0	Con Gain
Eastleigh	David Chidgey	Chris Huhne	−2.1	LD Hold
Richmond Park	Jenny Tonge	Susan Kramer	−1.0	LD Hold
Sheffield Hallam	Richard Allan	Nick Clegg	−4.2	LD Hold

Note: [a] Roxburgh & Berwickshire seat redrawn by boundary changes. Inheritor of notional seat was previously MP for Tweedale, Ettrick & Lauderdale.
Source: The British Parliamentary Constituency Database, 1992–2005.

The Liberal Democrat share of the vote fell in all seven seats where the sitting Liberal Democrat MP retired in 2005, but in six of these the drop in vote share was insufficient to dislodge the party. As such the Liberal Democrats can be fairly satisfied with this aspect of their defensive electoral strategy.

Conclusion

On the surface the 2005 election was good for the Liberal Democrats. They increased their share of the vote and their numbers in the House of Commons for the second successive election. The Liberal Democrat leader and campaign were held in high public esteem and, after several contests where the Liberal Democrats took seats almost exclusively from the Conservatives, the pattern was reversed. There are grounds for thinking that this tactic could be repeated in the next general election if Labour becomes less popular. Yet the success for the Liberal Democrats in drawing support against Labour masked a very disappointing return for them against the Conservatives.

In part this was due to the entrenched nature of British politics. It is almost counterintuitive but the unpopularity of both Labour and Conservative leadership elites may have harmed the ability of Liberal Democrats to harvest support. For the first time since 1997 the Conservatives were able to appeal to a sizeable anti-Labour sentiment, and this would have hindered the Liberal Democrat cause in Con–Lab seats. Similarly, the core Labour vote might have been diluted even more had the Labour leadership not put so much effort into persuading its heartland support that the Liberal Democrats could act as the Trojan horse for an unexpected Michael Howard victory. Furthermore, and for the first time since 1997, the Liberal Democrats look vulnerable to recovery from either (or both) of the main parties—both of whom are certain to be under new leadership and possibly under new direction—before the next general election.

Moreover, a strategic problem for the Liberal Democrats endures. Appeals in Conservative seats have traditionally been divided into a two-stage strategy. Firstly, Labour sympathisers are told that Labour cannot win in these areas. Then One-Nation Conservatives are told that the modern Conservative party no longer represents their views. When trying to replicate this tactic in Labour seats, a new conundrum has been revealed. In Labour seats, Conservatives can be told that they cannot win. But then the dilemma hits home. Labour is most prone to defection from its core left, not its centre. Hence the Liberal Democrats success at appealing not to the heart of New Labour's project in the south and the midlands but to its established heartland, a social democratic and socialist core who feels that new Labour's policy on civil liberties, education, and foreign policy is a betrayal of Labour tradition. The Liberal Democrats proved in 2005 that they could appeal to these voters, but they have yet to show that they can do this without alienating the One-Nation Tories necessary to deliver success against the Conservatives elsewhere. A long-term return to a strategy of equidistance may be the logical future for the party.

1   N. Assinder, 'What now for Kennedy?', *BBC News Website*, 6.5.05 (http://news.bbc.co.uk/1/hi/uk_politics/vote_2005/frontpage/4508949.stm).
2   D. Denver, 'The Liberal Democrat Campaign' in P. Norris (ed.), *Britain Votes 2001*, Oxford University Press, 2001.
3   YouGov's *Daily Telegraph* Election Trends polls had the Liberal Democrats leading on council tax and the environment throughout the campaign (http://www.yougov.com/archives/pdf/TEL050101014_3.pdf.), while the Sky News Election Day poll also run by YouGov found that Liberal Democrats were the most popular response for which party ran the best campaign (http://www.yougov.com/archives/pdf/RMW050101017_1.pdf).
4   This index simply subtracts the percentage of those respondents who said the leader was performing 'the worst' of all three main party leaders during the campaign from those saying they were performing 'best'.
5   Again this index is constructed by subtracting the percentage of those who feel the party was performing 'worst' of all three main parties during the campaign from the percentage of those who felt the party was performing 'best'.
6   According to the Party's campaign team.
7   This and other quotations from Lord Rennard were drawn from an interview with the author conducted in May 2005.
8   A. Russell and E. Fieldhouse, *Neither Left Nor Right? The Liberal Democrats and the Electorate*, Manchester University Press, 2005.
9   P. Ashdown, *The Ashdown Diaries: 1988–1997 Vol. 1*, Allen Lane, 2000, *1997–1999 Vol. 2*, Allen Lane, 2001.
10 D. Laws and P. Marshall (eds), *The Orange Book: Reclaiming Liberalism*, Profile, 2004.
11 See for example, 'Vote for Lib Dems will not let in Tories', *Independent*, 30.4.05, which quoted John Curtice: 'Labour would need to lose around one in four of its voters before its majority would be threatened, not just one in 10.'

PAUL WEBB

The Continuing Advance of the Minor Parties*

It is virtually a truism that the UK is an exemplar of the two-party system. It of course is not literally accurate to suggest that only two political parties are represented in the House of Commons, still less that that only two parties contest elections for Westminster or receive electoral support. The concept of a two-party system really implies that only two parties 'count', as Giovanni Sartori puts it, in understanding the essential dynamics of the system.[1] That is, the major parties in two-party systems receive most of the votes cast in elections and are consequently able to dominate the business of government to the extent of regularly governing alone rather than in coalition. This is the case in the UK. Yet it is widely recognised that since 1974 the two-party label has become a simplification which obscures almost as much as it reveals about party politics in the UK. The reason for this lies in the steady advance of the minor parties since that time. The general election of May 2005 confirmed the growing presence of the minor parties in British politics. The percentage of the vote jointly accounted for by Labour and the Conservatives has dropped significantly from an average of 90% between 1945 and 1970 to approximately 75% thereafter. In this context, 2005 marks a new low for the major parties, since their combined share of the vote across the UK fell to just 67.5%. The necessary concomitant of this trend, of course, is that minor parties are doing correspondingly better.

Minor party progress is further reflected in the greater fragmentation of the party system. A standard measure of fragmentation is the 'effective number of parties',[2] which takes account of both the number of parties in the system and their relative strength. It is an intuitive and useful yardstick since it tells us, for instance, that in any system comprised of just two equally strong parties, the effective number will be exactly 2.0, while a system consisting of three equally strong parties will generate an effective number of 3.0, and so on. This measure can be calculated either on the basis of party shares of the popular vote (the effective number of *electoral* parties [ENEP]) or on the basis of shares of seats won in parliament (the effective number of *parliamentary* parties

© Oxford University Press 2005
doi: 10.1093/pa/gsi063

[ENPP]). The ENEP has increased markedly since 1970, from an average of 2.36 between 1945 and 1970 to an average of 3.21 thereafter. The trend is less pronounced for the parliamentary parties due to the disproportional impact of the electoral system, addressed in Chapters 9 and 13. The growing fragmentation of the party system is still apparent, however, as the average ENPP increased from 2.05 to 2.21 between periods. In 2005, the increase in both measures became more pronounced, with ENEP jumping to 3.48 and ENPP climbing to 2.44—the highest either measure had been since 1945. In effect, there is now a two-and-a-half party system in the national legislative arena, but a clear multi-party system in the national electorate.

In winning more than a fifth of the popular vote and 60 seats in 2005, the Liberal Democrats can barely be considered a 'minor' party, and their impact on the election is examined at length elsewhere in this volume. In this chapter, I shall focus on the remaining actors in the system, seeking as far as possible to place their 2005 performances in the context of longer-term party system developments. In approaching this task, it is also helpful to bear in mind that the UK actually has more than one party system, with quite different patterns of party interaction to be found in England, Scotland, Wales, and Northern Ireland. Since party system dynamics in England are predominantly shaped by competition between the three main parties, I shall focus much of the discussion on the remaining constituent elements of the UK, where the 'other' parties are in fact not so minor, turning to England only in order to discuss the impact of the Greens, Respect, the BNP, UKIP, and Veritas.

Scotland

In 2005, the number of Scottish seats at Westminster was drastically reduced from 72 to 59. This was a response to the devolution of certain key powers to Edinburgh which, it was felt, rendered the previous over-representation of Scotland (per head of population) unnecessary. On the face of it, the two uniquely Scottish parties, the Scottish National Party (SNP) and Scottish Socialist Party (SSP), both lost ground in 2005, with the former ceding its position as Scotland's second party to the Liberal Democrats, who enjoyed an even greater surge of support at the expense of Labour than they did in England. While Labour continued to dominate Scottish representation at Westminster, the fragmentation of the Scottish electorate's support reached new heights, as illustrated by an effective number of electoral parties approaching 4 (see Table 1).

Westminster elections in Scotland are peculiar to the extent that the media and campaign tend to cover issues which are not always strictly relevant. For instance, health, education, and transport are all matters for which the policy, if not the funding, is decided at Holyrood. To that extent, it is not strictly logical that these issues should be the subject of a Westminster election campaign north of the border, and yet they often

1. Electoral Support and Representation in Scotland, 1974–2005

Date	Labour %	MPs	SNP %	MPs	Conservative %	MPs	Liberal Democrat %	MPs	Others %	MPs	Turnout %	ENEP	ENPP
Feb. 1974	36.6	40	21.9	7	32.9	21	7.9	3	0.3	0	79.0	3.17	2.40
Oct. 1974	36.3	41	30.4	11	24.7	16	8.3	3	0.3	0	74.8	3.47	2.44
1979	41.5	44	17.3	2	31.4	22	9.0	3	0.2	0	76.8	3.19	2.07
1983	35.1	41	11.8	2	28.4	21	24.5	8	0.2	0	72.7	3.60	2.37
1987	2.4	50	14.0	3	24.0	10	19.2	9	0.4	0	75.1	3.45	1.93
1992	39.0	49	21.5	3	25.6	11	13.1	9	0.8	0	75.5	3.51	1.99
1997	45.6	56	22.1	6	17.5	0	13.0	10	1.8	0	71.3	3.29	1.59
2001	43.9	56	20.1	5	15.6	1	16.4	10	4.0	0	58.2	3.52	1.59
2005	38.9	40	17.7	6	15.8	1	22.6	11	5.0	0	60.6	3.87	1.91

Notes: 'Liberal Democrat' refers to the Liberal Party for the period 1974–79 and the SDP-Liberal alliance in 1983 and 1987. ENEP refers to the effective number of electoral parties; ENPP refers to the effective number of parliamentary parties. Sources: Jessica Yorwin, *UK Election Statistics House of Commons Research Paper 04/61*, July 2004; Scottish Parliament website (http://www.scottish.parliament.uk).

are in reality—the NHS being a prime example.[3] Opinion research for BBC Scotland suggested that the voters' preferred campaign agenda in Scotland placed taxation and public expenditure first in order of priority, followed by pensions, immigration, identity cards, and the war in Iraq.[4] The issues which featured most prominently in the SNP and SSP campaigns included a number of common points, including Iraq, Tony Blair, taxation and public services, and the fate of Scottish army regiments which the government in London planned to merge.

The SSP professes to stand for 'the break-up of the British state and the creation of a free Scottish socialist republic'. It was established in 1998 and succeeded in returning the former Militant Tendency activist Tommy Sheridan to Holyrood as a Member of the Scottish Parliament in the first devolved elections of May 1999; four years later he was joined by five other Scottish Socialist MSPs. At the general election, the party stood on a manifesto in which the central pledges related to opposition to the Iraq war, free school meals for all children, the minimum wage, public sector job creation, abolition of the Private Finance Initiative in funding public services, and reform of local taxation. The party contested all Scotland's Westminster seats bar East Kilbride, Strathaven and Lesmahagow, winning 1.9% of the vote in Scotland overall (a loss of 1.2 percentage points on its 2001 result) and gaining no seats. Its strongest performances were by John Aberdein in Orkney and Shetland (5.6%), Keith Baldassara in Glasgow South West (5.4%), Les Robertson in Dunbartonshire West (4.1%), and Marie Gordon in Glasgow Central (4.0%).

The protagonist unique to Scotland which contributes most to its distinctive party system is of course the Scottish National Party. Maintaining its traditional left-of-centre stance, the SNP's manifesto for 2005, *Make Scotland Matter*, was championed as the Scottish option that would avoid the 'no choice' election between Howard and Blair—'a

Tory who introduced the Poll Tax or . . . the Tory who took us into an illegal war'. Its major themes included economic growth and job creation schemes, more opportunities for young people in Scotland, improved pensions, and a 'nuclear-free Scotland'.[5] The party accused the Labour government in London of planning to scrap the Barnett Formula[6] with inevitable consequences for spending on public services—a claim that was strenuously denied by Labour. As in the UK generally, however, it was the issue of Iraq that became increasingly prominent as the campaign entered its later stages. Indeed, it was not only the SNP, but the Liberal Democrats, Greens, SSP, and various independent candidates who campaigned against Labour on these grounds. The most notable among these was probably Rose Gentle, the mother of a teenage soldier who lost his life in Basra. She stood against the former Armed Forces minister, Adam Ingram, in East Kilbride, Strathaven and Lesmahagow, campaigning on behalf of bereaved families who were demanding a full public inquiry in to the war. She eventually took 3.2% of the vote and came sixth in the constituency. As with all of Labour's main opponents in Scotland, including the pro-war Conservatives, the SNP used the Iraq issue to campaign on the issue of trust in Tony Blair. Leader Alex Salmond even revived the prospect of an impeachment process against the prime minister for having allegedly lied to the Commons and taken Britain into an 'illegal war'.

At first blush, Table 1 seems to suggest that the results were somewhat disappointing for the SNP. The party won nearly 18% of the vote, 2.4 percentage points less than in 2001 and 4.4 percentage points less than in 1997. However, the SNP did manage to win six seats, one more than in 2001, and this despite the drop in the number of Scottish seats. Moreover, while the extensive boundary changes affecting Scottish constituencies in 2005 render direct comparison with 2001 impossible, 'notional' estimates of how the new constituencies might have voted in 2001 can be made,[7] and on this basis the SNP can be said to have gained two seats. The party's major successes included the Western Isles (*Na h-Eileanan an Iar* in Gaelic), where Angus MacNeil took the seat from Labour's Calum MacDonald, the constituency returning to the SNP for the first time since 1987, on the back of a campaign fought around local issues, including transport problems and a controversial government plan to construct Europe's largest wind farm on Lewis. With new boundaries, the constituency of Dundee East also fell to the SNP, their candidate Stewart Hosie edging out Labour's Iain Luke by just 383 votes. The Western Isles and Dundee East were the first Labour seats to fall to the SNP since 1974.

Wales

As with Scottish nationalism, the electoral growth of Welsh nationalism became evident in the decade following the middle of the 1960s; by-election success for Plaid Cymru (PC) at Carmarthen in 1966 was followed by an electoral breakthrough in February 1974, with PC securing over 10% of the vote in Wales and returning two MPs to Westminster. This level of electoral support has been broadly maintained for elections to Westminster, though the number of representatives elected to the Commons increased to four in 1992. That said, Plaid Cymru's support is concentrated in the Welsh-speaking counties of Gwynedd and Dyfed.[8] All of the Westminster seats which the party has held in its history (Camarthen, Ynys Mon, Caernarvon, Merionnydd Nant Conwy, and Ceredigion) have been located in this north Wales stronghold, while it has often struggled to make an impact in seats outside the North and West. Given Labour's traditional political dominance in Wales, reflected in the low effective number of parliamentary parties there (see Table 2), it can be thought of as having a dominant party system. As in Scotland, the primary opposition to Labour has often been on the centre-left, whether nationalist or Liberal Democrat, rather than the right.

Given that it finds itself occupying devolutionist and left-of-centre territory in common with Labour, it is not surprising that Plaid Cymru generally seeks to distinguish its own brand of 'community socialism' from Labour's 'state socialism', a distinction that draws on long traditions in Wales and is more than merely rhetorical. In 2005, the party placed the need to support and strengthen public services, especially the NHS, and to remove injustice and inequality at the centre of its campaign. Greater investment in housing and transport, environmental concern, and the demand for greater devolution of power to a reformed Welsh Assembly also featured prominently in its manifesto, *We Can Build a Better Wales*. The party devoted much analysis to the claims that inequality had grown under New Labour, that the governing party in London offered little that was distinct from Thatcherism, and that

2. Electoral Performance and Representation in Wales, 1974–2005

Date	Labour %	Labour MPs	Conservative %	Conservative MPs	Liberal Democrat %	Liberal Democrat MPs	Plaid Cymru %	Plaid Cymru MPs	Others %	Others MPs	Turnout %	ENEP	ENPP
Feb.74	46.8	24	25.9	8	16.0	2	10.8	2	0.5	0	80.0	2.97	2.00
Oct.74	49.5	32	23.9	8	15.5	2	10.8	3	0.3	0	76.6	2.90	2.14
1979	48.0	22	32.2	11	10.6	1	9.2	2	0.0	0	79.4	2.76	2.13
1983	37.5	20	31.0	14	23.2	2	7.8	2	0.5	0	76.1	3.34	2.39
1987	45.1	24	29.5	8	17.9	3	7.3	3	0.2	0	78.9	3.03	2.20
1992	49.5	27	28.6	6	12.4	1	8.9	4	0.6	0	79.7	2.80	1.85
1997	54.7	34	19.6	0	12.3	2	9.9	4	3.5	0	73.5	2.71	1.36
2001	48.6	34	21.0	0	13.8	2	14.3	4	2.3	0	61.6	3.13	1.28
2005	42.7	29	21.4	3	18.5	4	12.6	3	4.8	1	62.4	3.59	1.34

Note: 'Liberal Democrat' refers to the Liberal Party for the period 1974–79 and the SDP-Liberal alliance in 1983 and 1987. ENEP refers to the effective number of electoral parties; ENPP refers to the effective number of parliamentary parties. In Welsh constituencies represented at Westminster; the independent MP for Blaenau Gwent (Peter Law) is taken into consideration in making this calculation for 2005. Sources: Jessica Yorwin, *UK Election Statistics House of Commons Research Paper 04/61*, July 2004; BBC News website.

economic opportunities remained far worse in Wales than in the South
East of England. Greater devolution was seen as an essential part of the
solution to these problems, for the people of Wales needed power in
their own hands to effect the changes that would bring more democracy
and better economic opportunities.[9] Interestingly, in contrast to the
SNP, Plaid Cymru also called for the abolition of the Barnett Formula
for allocating public expenditure across the UK. In place of this 'popu-
lation-based' formula for allocating resources, it demanded a 'needs-
based' mechanism which would benefit Wales.[10]

In the event, the outcome of the election continued the recent pattern
of disappointment for Plaid Cymru. As across much of the rest of Britain,
Labour lost support at the expense of the Liberal Democrats and the
Conservatives, but, as in Scotland, nationalist support was also eroded,
by 1.7 percentage points overall. However, unlike the SNP, Plaid
Cymru paid the price in terms of representation at Westminster, losing
one of its four seats. Ceredigion was taken from Simon Thomas by the
Liberal Democrats on a swing of 6%. Further disappointment came in
the failure to win the key target seat of Ynys Mon (Anglesey), where a
swing of 0.6% to Labour enabled Albert Owen to hold the seat. This
proved to be a rancorous campaign in which tensions ran particularly
high between the Plaid Cymru candidate Eurig Wyn and the independent, ex-Conservative member of the Welsh Assembly, Peter Rogers,
who was blamed for splitting the anti-Labour vote in the constituency.
However, Hywel Williams held Caernarfon for the nationalists (enjoying a swing of 3.3% from Labour), while Adam Price replicated the feat
in Camarthen East and Dinefwr (on a 5.4% swing), despite a concerted
effort by Labour to unseat the MP who had played a leading part in the
campaign to impeach Tony Blair over the war in Iraq. Finally, the
parliamentary party leader Elfyn Llwyd retained Meirionnydd Nant
Conwy, on a swing of 2.6% from Labour.

The general election came on the back of a disappointing performance in the devolved elections of 2003, in which Plaid Cymru lost five
of its 17 seats. In the aftermath of that campaign, the party had in effect
been led by a triumvirate consisting of the Welsh Assembly leader Ieuan
Wyn Jones, parliamentary leader Elfyn Llwyd, and party president
Dafyyd Iwan. In the wake of the general election, this leadership structure came under fire from, among others, the vanquished former MP
for Ceredigion, Simon Thomas. Early indications are that, despite this
criticism, the present structure and personnel will remain in place.

One other result in Wales is worthy of note—the extraordinary victory of the independent candidate Peter Law in the Labour stronghold
of Blaenau Gwent. Law was a Labour member of the Welsh Assembly
who left the party in protest at the imposition use of an all-women
shortlist. The selection of Maggie Jones, a Unison official, had provoked the resignations of most of the local party executive. Law then
announced that he would fight the seat as an independent, despite

undergoing surgery to have a brain tumour removed in early April.[11] The result in Blaenau Gwent was extraordinary: Labour's safest seat in Wales, formerly held by the likes of Aneurin Bevan and Michael Foot, fell to Peter Law on a swing of 58.2%.

Northern Ireland

The dimensions and dynamics of party interaction in the province of Northern Ireland are quite unlike those found in any other part of the United Kingdom. The less salient of the two main dimensions of competition is the classic left-right axis of distributional politics, while the most important dimension is the nationalist one, pitting Irish national identity against loyalty to Britain. In Ulster, identification is at least as important as competition when it comes to understanding the nature of party/voter linkages; traditionally, most voters have identified with either British or Irish nationality, and there has consequently been very little scope for direct electoral competition *between* unionists (British) and nationalists (Irish), although competition for electoral support has undoubtedly become very intense *within* each bloc in recent decades.

Since the early 1970s Unionism has fragmented, with the birth of Ian Paisley's Democratic Unionist Party (DUP) in 1971 being particularly significant. The DUP has come to represent a more militant and populist unionist voice than the Ulster Unionist Party (UUP). The distinction between the two main Unionist parties can be drawn in terms of both constitutional and class ideology. The DUP has been able to appeal to the economic insecurities of the Protestant working class, while the UUP has traditionally been the party of the dominant Protestant middle class. Thus, the former claims to be the more left-wing of the two Unionist parties, and social class has a significant impact on which of these parties loyalists vote for; indeed, left-right ideology 'not only cross-cuts the effects of constitutional ideology, (but) it is a more powerful predictor of intra-communal political division than is the constitutional issue'.[12] This is not to deny, however, that the DUP's stance on the Union has also generally been more radical. While both parties broadly favoured the maintenance of the link with mainland Britain, the more conciliatory UUP became the key Protestant interlocutor in the Good Friday Agreement of 1998. The DUP, in contrast, has consistently refused to compromise its stance and has frequently criticised aspects of the settlement. Most notably, it has remained steadfastly hostile to the idea of sharing power with Sinn Fein while the IRA remains in existence.

The nationalist parties in Northern Ireland are motivated both by the goal of a reunited Ireland and by the desire to enhance the lot of the Catholic population in the province. Until recently, the major nationalist party has been the Social and Democratic Labour Party (SDLP), founded in 1970. The SDLP quickly came to represent the legitimate face of nationalism for most observers and certainly became the party of the majority of Catholics in the North, broadly winning from one-fifth to one-quarter of all votes cast in the province at general elections after 1974 (see Table 3). The other major nationalist force is Sinn Fein. The origins of this party lie in the organisation founded in 1905 to fight for an independent Ireland, though the present organisation in Northern Ireland really dates from the enormously volatile period of the early 1970s.

Since both the SDLP and Sinn Fein occupy left-of-centre positions on class ideology, the dimension of constitutional ideology is all-important in explaining intra-bloc differences in the nationalist community. The SDLP has always supported the reunification of Ireland by peaceful constitutional means and the devolution of government in Northern Ireland based on consensual and power-sharing structures. Sinn Fein has distinguished its position from the SDLP in a number of ways, including its notable reluctance to condemn the IRA's strategy of violent confrontation and, although it was brought into the peace process thanks to the IRA ceasefire, its own leadership's acceptance of the 'Mitchell principles' of democracy and non-violence. Sinn Fein's participation was eventually achieved through the considerable efforts of the former SDLP leader John Hume and the UUP's David Trimble to accommodate it. Thus, Sinn Fein has come a long way towards the legitimate political mainstream since the 1970s and has derived a handsome electoral reward over the last decade.

The 2005 general election was held in a somewhat depressing political context for Northern Ireland. Successful implementation of the Peace Agreement seemed more distant than ever, thanks to the suspension of devolution because of evidence of IRA intelligence gathering at Stormont in 2002. Talks aimed at restoring devolved government stalled in 2004, and the run-up to the election campaign was dominated

3. Electoral performance and representation in Northern Ireland, 1974–2005

Date	UUP %	MPs	DUP %	MPs	APNI %	MPs	SDLP %	MPs	SF %	MPs	Other %	MPs	Turnout	ENEP	ENPP
1974F	45.5	7	8.2	1	3.2	0	22.4	1	–	–	20.8	3	69.9	3.24	2.40
1974O	36.5	6	8.5	1	6.4	0	22.0	1	–	–	26.7	4	67.7	3.83	3.00
1979	36.6	5	10.2	3	11.9	0	18.2	1	–	–	23.2	4	67.7	4.18	3.60
1983	34.0	11	20.0	3	8.0	0	17.9	1	13.4	1	6.0	1	72.9	4.63	2.17
1987	37.8	9	11.7	3	10.0	0	21.1	3	11.4	1	8.0	1	67.0	4.53	2.86
1992	34.9	9	13.1	3	8.7	0	21.8	4	10.0	0	11.5	1	69.8	4.44	2.70
1997	32.7	10	13.6	2	8.0	0	24.1	3	16.1	2	5.6	1	67.1	4.53	2.75
2001	26.8	6	22.5	5	3.6	0	21.0	3	21.7	4	4.4	0	68.0	4.61	3.80
2005	17.7	1	33.7	9	3.9	0	17.5	3	24.3	5	2.9	0	62.5	4.22	2.79

Note: UUP—Ulster Unionist Party; DUP—Democratic Unionist Party; APNI—Alliance Party of Northern Ireland; SDLP—Social Democratic & Labour Party; SF—Sinn Fein; 'Other' includes Vanguard Party, pre-1974 Faulknerites, PUP, UDP, UKU, various Loyalist groups, the Northern Ireland Labour Party, and various independent candidates. ENEP refers to the effective number of electoral parties; ENPP refers to the effective number of parliamentary parties. Sources: Jessica Yorwin, *UK Election Statistics House of Commons Research Paper 04/61*, July 2004; BBC News website.

by a £26.5 million raid on the Northern Bank in December 2004 and the murder of Robert McCartney in January, both crimes widely attributed to the IRA. The pressure on Sinn Fein as a result was considerable, and on April 6th Gerry Adams publicly asked the IRA to commit itself to pursuing its objectives by purely peaceful and democratic means; three weeks later he reported that it had started an internal debate on whether it should do so. The party's manifesto emphasised issues relevant to the peace process, including the full implementation of the Good Friday Agreement, the transfer of powers on policing and justice, the 'de-militarisation' of Northern Ireland, and new measures of cross-border cooperation and integration, plus an anti-poverty strategy, public services investment, and rural development. The party's recent electoral progress continued: as Table 3 shows, it gained 2.6 percentage points and one seat (Newry and Armagh from the SDLP) in net terms. This left Sinn Fein in the position of being Ulster's second party overall and the leading nationalist party in the province.

The reverse side of Sinn Fein's story of progress is that of the SDLP's continuing decline. In 1997 the SDLP still accounted for nearly a quarter of all votes cast in the province and took three seats at Westminster. Although it managed to retain those three seats in 2005, the recent trend of electoral loss continued, with only 17.5% of voters supporting the party's candidates. Standing on a platform of support for the implementation of the Good Friday Agreement, the SDLP criticised both Sinn Fein and the DUP for 'ignoring the democratic will of Ireland' and creating the stalemate which had led to the reimposition of direct rule from London. In addition, the party proposed closer cross-border institutional integration and greater investment in public services. Party leader Mark Durkan fended off a strong challenge from Sinn Fein's Mitchell McLaughlin to win Foyle for the SDLP, while Alasdair McDonnell took South Belfast and Eddie McGrady held on to South Down.

Perhaps the major story of the 2005 election relating to Northern Ireland concerns the dramatic changes affecting Unionism. For many years *the* party of six county politics, the UUP was reduced to just one seat, while the DUP surged to a new high of nine seats at Westminster. These figures represent a complete reversal of the situation less than a decade previously; since 1997 the swing in voter share from UUP to DUP is a remarkable 17.6%. In its centenary year, the UUP shed four of its MPs. Most shockingly of all, party leader David Trimble—joint Nobel Prize winner with the SDLP's John Hume for his work in forging the Good Friday Agreement—lost his Upper Bann stronghold to the DUP candidate David Simpson on a swing of 8%. He immediately resigned the party leadership. This left Lady Sylvia Hermon, wife of the former Chief Constable of the Royal Ulster Constabulary, as the sole remaining UUP member at Westminster, representing the constituency of North Down. She declined to stand for the leadership, citing her commitment to her sick husband (Sir John Hermon suffers from Alzheimer's disease).[13] The UUP was thus left in awful disarray, suffering the consequences of years of walking a political tightrope between the various communities and governments with stakes in Northern Ireland. While the DUP and elements of the UUP itself were implacably anti-Agreement—Trimble had survived several attempts in the party's ruling council to remove him from the leadership—Sinn Fein, the SDLP, and the British government generally pushed in the opposite direction. Although Trimble had survived every attempt to unseat him as leader, protestant voters were less and less inclined to regard his version of unionism as credible in the light of problems over the de-commissioning of paramilitary weapons and claims of continuing IRA violence. This does not necessarily express itself in direct vote-switching from UUP to DUP, but rather in protestant middle class political disengagement as former UUP voters appear less likely to turn out than DUP supporters.

The great beneficiaries, of course, were the DUP, now incontrovertibly Northern Ireland's leading political force. Campaigning with the slogan 'unionism is finally on top—don't let Trimble wreck it', the DUP fed off the very success of Sinn Fein within the nationalist community to consolidate its own growing supremacy within unionism: 'Northern Ireland cannot afford for Sinn Fein to be the largest party and only the DUP can stop this'.[14] While the UUP had made concession after concession to Sinn Fein, argued Democratic Unionist leader Ian Paisley, the DUP could be relied upon to stand up to an organisation 'inextricably linked with terrorism and criminality'. Thus, the polarisation of Northern Ireland's politics around Sinn Fein and the Democratic Unionists seems to have developed according to a self-serving logic of mutual antipathy. The DUP's successes included some spectacular gains from the UUP, among them Jeffrey Donaldson's victory in Lagan Valley on an extraordinary swing of 38%, Sammy Wilson's in East Antrim on a swing of nearly 12%, and William McCrea's in South Antrim on a swing of nearly 6%. These triumphs were cemented by further resounding successes in the local elections which were also held on 5 May: the DUP took 30% of the votes cast in 26 councils elections, winning 182 councillors in all, while Sinn Fein won 24% of the vote (126 councillors), UUP 18% (115 councillors), and the SDLP 17% (101 councillors).

Radicals and populists, left and right

Other than the three main parties, some 85 organisations contested seats across England and Wales, 54 of which only put up a single candidate. In Scotland, 18 parties or independents stood other than the 'big three', and in Northern Ireland nine parties contested seats (all of them more than one each).[15] Table 4 reports the details.

Apart from Peter Law in Blaenau Gwent, one other independent candidate was successful in winning a place in parliament; this was Richard Taylor who, despite a 14% swing to the Conservatives, retained the

4. Minor Party Candidates in 2005

England and Wales

United Kingdom Independence Party (450)
British National Party (114)
Plaid Cymru (36)
RESPECT: The Unity Coalition (26)
Legalise Cannabis Alliance (20)
Vote For Yourself Rainbow Dream Ticket (16)
National Front (11)
Workers' Revolutionary Party (9)
Forward Wales (5)
Mebyon Kernow (4)
People's Choice Making Politicians Work (3)
UK Community Issues Party (3)
Clause 28 Children's Protection
Christian Democrats (2)
Peace Party (2)
S-O-S! Voters Against Overdevelopment
of Northampton (2)
Your Party (2)
Plus 54 other single-candidate 'parties'.

Green Party of England and Wales (183)
Veritas (62)
Socialist Labour Party (34)
Socialist Green Unity Coalition (26)
Official Monster Raving Loony Party (20)
Liberal Party (13)
Christian People's Alliance (9)
Communist Party of Britain (5)
Community Action Party (4)
Alliance for Change (3)
Progress Democratic: Party Members Decide Policy (3)
Progressive Democratic Party (3)
English Democrats (2)

Senior Citizens Party (2)
Third Way (2)

Scotland

Scottish National Party (59)
United Kingdom Independence Party (20)
Operation Christian Vote (10)
Free Scotland Party (3)
Plus 10 other single-candidate 'parties'.

Scottish Socialist Party (58)
Scottish Green Party (19)
Socialist Labour Party (10)
British National Party (2)

Northern Ireland

Ulster Unionist Party (18)
Sinn Féin (18)
Alliance Party of Northern Ireland (12)
Workers Party (6)
Socialist Environmental Alliance (1)

Democratic Unionist Party (18)
Social Democratic and Labour Party (18)
Vote For Yourself Rainbow Dream Ticket (6)
Conservative Party (3)

Notes: The numbers in parenthesis indicate how many candidates were run by each organisation. The Socialist Green Unity Coalition stood candidates as Alliance for Green Socialism, Democratic Socialist Alliance—People Before Profit, Socialist Alternative, or Socialist Unity.

Wyre Forest seat he had won in 2001 as the Independent Kidderminster Hospital and Health Concern candidate. Of the various organisations listed in Table 4, I shall focus the remainder of the discussion on the five parties that succeeded in attracting the most media attention in the campaign: Respect, the Greens, the British National Party (BNP), the United Kingdom Independence Party (UKIP), and Veritas. This group of political actors takes us from the radical and post-materialist left through to the populist far right.

Respect

The only one of these parties that actually succeeded in winning a seat was Respect. An acronym for 'Respect, Equality, Socialism, Peace, Environmentalism, Community and Trade Unionism', the new party was formed in January 2004. Though not a single-issue organisation, it was born in the context of protest against the war in Iraq, which generated a motley coalition of support, including various far left organisations such as the Communist Party of Great Britain (Provisional Central Committee), the Socialist Workers' Party, the Socialist Alliance, the Socialist Unity Network, and the International Socialist Group, plus the Muslim Association of Britain. While the official party leader is barrister and former *Militant* editor Nick Wrack, the party is actually run by its national council, a collective leadership. There is no doubt about its most high-profile individual, however: this is the controversial former Labour MP George Galloway. Having represented the Glasgow seats of Hillhead and Kelvin since 1987, Galloway was expelled by Labour in 2003 for his public stance on Iraq, in particular for comments which many interpreted as incitement for British troops to mutiny. Respect contested the European parliamentary elections and the London Assembly and Mayoral elections of 2004, doing well enough to claim that that it had attracted more votes than any far left organisation in the country's electoral history. It gained 1.7% of the European parliamentary vote and nearly 5% of the vote in London. For all its left-wing credentials, there appears to be a clear correlation between support for Respect and the concentration of Muslim voters, with particular areas of strength emerging in East London, Birmingham, and Leicester.

The party's manifesto for 2005, *Peace, Justice and Equality*, argued that 'there is an alternative to imperialist war, unfettered global capitalism and the rule of the market', and proposed a number of eye-catching policies, including: ending 'the occupation of Iraq', renationalising public services, especially transport, investing more in the NHS, creating comprehensive secondary schools, establishing earnings-linked state pensions, abolishing tuition fees, increasing the minimum wage, repealing 'anti-union laws', increasing taxation on corporations and the wealthy, and opposing the government's proposals for individual identity cards.

In the election, Respect put up 26 candidates, winning 0.3% of the overall vote cast across the UK and an average of 6.9% in the constituencies it contested. By far and away the most impressive of the organisation's results was George Galloway's victory in Bethnal Green and Bow, where he ousted Labour's Oona King on the back of a 26% swing. Iraq featured prominently in a campaign directed heavily at the large local Muslim population of nearly 45,000. King was an unusual parliamentarian in so far as she was female and a member of more than one ethnic minority (as a Black Jew). A Blair loyalist first elected in 1997, she paid the price for staunchly defending the prosecution of the war. The campaign in Bethnal Green was notably vituperative: while she accused Galloway of grovelling at the feet of Saddam, he retorted that King was responsible for 'the deaths of many people in Iraq with blacker faces than hers'. She was allegedly targeted by Islamic fundamentalists and anti-Semites who slashed the tyres on her car, pelted her with eggs and vegetables, and made threats to kill her. Galloway also claimed to have received death threats, and at various times in the campaign both candidates required police protection.

Elsewhere, Respect candidates did especially well in Birmingham Sparkbrook (where Salma Yaqoob enjoyed a 24% swing to win more than a quarter of the constituency vote, but could not unseat Labour's Roger Godsiff[16]); East Ham (where Abdul Khaliq Mian won 21% of the vote); Poplar and Canning Town (where Oliur Rahman won 17.2% of the vote); and West Ham (where former London mayoralty candidate Lindsey German won 19.5%). When detailed individual-level analysis is possible, it will be interesting to estimate how far Respect's success at the election was due to Muslim anti-Labour sentiment rather than a surge in radical left-wing politics in the electorate. The answer to this question can be expected to bear heavily upon the future strategy and prospects of Respect. Initial analysis of British Election Survey data that have recently become available provide a number of clues.[17] First, Muslim respondents are more likely than other voters to disapprove of the war; while 67.1% of all voters in the sample disapproved, some 83.1% of Muslims did. Second, Muslims were far less likely to regard the war as having been a success than the average respondent; on a scale running from zero to ten, with zero equalling 'complete failure' and ten equalling 'complete success', the average score for Muslims was only 2.27, compared to 3.46 for all respondents. This confirms—as anyone living in the UK between 2003 and 2005 would surely have surmised—that British Muslims were generally very unhappy about Iraq. At the same time, however, Muslims do not tend to regard themselves as generally politically radical. When asked to place themselves on a left-right ideological scale, with zero equalling far left and ten equalling far right, Muslim respondents score 5.14 on average, which is certainly not significantly different to the overall sample mean of 5.69; their ideological self-placement is approximately normally distributed, with the bulk regarding themselves as centrist. Though rudimentary, this initial analysis suggests it is unlikely that Respect represents a sudden groundswell of radical leftist sentiment in the country in 2005; it seems more likely that it simply benefited in certain constituencies from Muslim anger about Iraq.

The Greens

Formally distinct entities, the Green Party of England and Wales and the Green Party of Scotland, ran 202 candidates between them. Although no Green MPs have ever been returned to Westminster, the Greens have enjoyed a degree of electoral success at other levels of political jurisdiction in recent years. At the time of the general election, the party in England and Wales had 64 local councillors, plus two members of the European Parliament (Caroline Lucas for the South East and Jean Lambert for London), two members of the Greater London Assembly (Darren Johnson and Jenny Jones), and one member of the

House of Lords (Beaumont of Whitley). It has no formal leadership as such, but its principal speakers are Caroline Lucas and Keith Taylor; the latter is a councillor in Brighton and Hove and was a candidate in the general election for the seat of Brighton Pavilion. The Scottish Greens were able to boast seven Members of the Scottish Parliament, two of whom (Shona Baird and Robin Harper) are the party's 'co-convenors'.

The party's campaign rhetoric and their manifesto, *The Real Choice for Real Change*, emphasised opposition to the war in Iraq and to the use of the Private Finance Initiative to fund public services. The manifesto also proposed radical reform of the tax system: a higher marginal rate of income tax; the replacement of VAT with 'eco-taxes' such as aviation fuel tax and plastic bag tax; the substitution of council tax by land-value tax; extra funding for the NHS and public transport; the scrapping of road-building schemes; massive investment in renewable energy; and a 20% reduction in Carbon Dioxide emissions within five years. The governing party was criticised by the Greens for failing to deliver on EU legislation regarding emissions and for promoting the expansion of aviation. The Liberal Democrats were also targeted for supporting major road schemes, opposing congestion charging in cities, supporting GM crop initiatives, and only opposing military intervention in Iraq 'after opinion research told them to'.[18] The strategy of the party was designed principally to appeal to disaffected Labour supporters, and the Greens recognised that they were competing directly with the Liberal Democrats in this respect.

Overall the Greens won 283,084 votes or 1.07% of the vote, up from 0.7% in 2001. In part this can simply be explained by the fact that they ran over a third more candidates than in 2001. However, they achieved an average of 3.4% of the vote in the seats they contested, an increase of 0.6% on 2001, their previous best. Their best result in 2005 occurred in Brighton Pavilion, where Keith Taylor won 22% of the vote to take third place. The party's other notable results included the neighbouring constituencies of Brighton Kemptown (where Simon Williams achieved 7.1%) and Hove (where Anthea Ballam took 5.7%), as well as Lewisham Deptford (where MLA Darren Johnson won 11.1%) and Norwich South (where Adrian Ramsay won 7.1%). In the local elections, the Greens made a modest net gain of six seats.

BNP

On the radical and populist right two minor parties merit attention: the British National Party and the United Kingdom Independence Party (plus the latter's offshoot, Veritas). Each of these parties speaks primarily to the libertarian-cosmopolitan/authoritarian-nationalist dimension of ideological polarity, rather than the state/market tension between socialism and capitalism. Specifically, the issues around which they have sought to mobilise support are immigration, asylum-seekers and refugees, law and order, and Britain's relationship with Europe.

The BNP formed as a breakaway from the National Front (NF) in 1982. The latter had been created in 1967 but had never managed to win the support of 1% of the national vote, hampered as it was by three factors: first, its image as an extremist organisation whose foot-soldiers were skinheads and hooligans; second, Margaret Thatcher's notorious claim that she understood British fears of being 'swamped by people with a different culture', a coded message about a shift in Conservative policy towards immigration in the run-up to the 1979 election that was followed by the passage of the British Nationality Act 1981 which tightened the definition of citizenship; and, third, the electoral system worked against the NF as it does against all minor parties lacking strong geographical concentrations of support.

Since 1999, the BNP has been led by Nick Griffin and has pursued the so-called 'Euronationalist' strategy, which is a process by which far right parties seek to enter the political mainstream through downplaying their extremism and aiming for a more 'respectable' image. This entails, among other things: a rejection of extra-parliamentary action and a stress on electoralism; hostility towards further immigration, while generally accepting existing ethnic minority communities; antipathy or scepticism towards the EU; a traditionalist, or authoritarian, stance of social morality; rejection of unfettered neo-liberal economics; and heavy criticism of the political 'establishment'.

The BNP has had some modest success in pursuing such an approach. In 2001, it contested 34 parliamentary seats, achieving an average score of 3.7% of the vote in these constituencies and 0.2% of the UK vote as a whole. It has also had some notable successes at local level, especially in Burnley and Oldham, where there are substantial Asian populations. In total, there are currently 24 BNP councillors, a total that is put in perspective when one remembers that there are more than twenty thousand councillors overall. The BNP fielded a record number of local candidates (309) in the June 2004 local elections in England and Wales, winning an average of 16.1% of the vote in the wards they fought. In the European parliamentary elections, which were held simultaneously, the BNP won 4.9% of the vote and no seats.

The 2005 BNP manifesto (*Rebuilding British Democracy*) offered the electorate a range of radical policies, including: withdrawal from the EU; an immediate end to immigration; a scheme of assisted voluntary resettlement to immigrants and their descendants; an end to the 'Islamification of Britain'; the reintroduction of capital and corporal punishment for certain crimes; the repeal of the legal prohibitions on individual gun ownership imposed after the Dunblane school massacre in 1996; the introduction of Citizens' Initiatives and an English parliament; repeal of laws inhibiting free speech on matters of race and religion; increased health spending; a system of 'Britain first economics' which would emphasise national self-sufficiency as far as possible; the replacement of income tax by consumption tax; an independent foreign policy based on ending 'spineless subservience to the USA'; and the immediate with-drawal of troops from Iraq.

The BNP ran 119 candidates across England, Scotland and Wales, polling a total of 192,850 votes, an average of 4.2% across the seats in which they stood and 0.7% across Britain as a whole. The party's most notable results occurred in Barking, where Richard Barnbrook won 16.9% of the constituency vote and came third; Dewsbury, where David Exley took 13.1% and came fourth; Burnley, where Len Starr won took 10.1% and came fifth; and Keighley, where party chairman Nick Griffin took 9.2% of the vote and came fourth. In 70% of the seats where they stood, BNP candidates came in fourth or better, and their average vote increased by 0.5 percentage points on 2001. This could therefore be regarded as a relatively successful election for the BNP in which they were perhaps less overshadowed by UKIP than in 2004.

UKIP

The UK Independence Party was founded in 1993 as a successor to the Anti-Federalist League. The latter had formed in 1991 to campaign against the Treaty of Maastricht. Its principal spokesman was Dr Alan Sked, who led the way in the formation of UKIP as a body which would campaign for British withdrawal from the EU. In the 1997 general election UKIP was over-shadowed by James Goldsmith's short-lived Referendum Party, but the party benefited from an influx of support from the latter after Goldsmith's death. In 1999, UKIP won 7% of the vote and three seats in Britain's European parliament-ary elections, a feat surpassed five years later when this was increased to an impressive 16.1% of the vote and 12 members of the European Parliament (MEPs). It also picked up a handful of local council seats and two places in the Greater London Assembly. In 2001, it ran 420 candidates at the general election and won 1.5% of the vote nationwide. This was undoubtedly rapid progress for a minor party in Britain, and the party's hopes were high going into the general election, at which UKIP ran 495 candidates.

However, there was a cloud on UKIP's horizon: Robert Kilroy-Silk. Having been sacked by the BBC in January 2004 for authoring a con-troversial newspaper article that was widely regarded as anti-Arab, the former Labour MP and daytime TV presenter stood as a UKIP candid-ate in the European parliamentary elections later that year, winning a seat in the multi-member East Midlands constituency. Almost immedi-ately, Kilroy-Silk publicly stated his ambition to replace former Con-servative MP Roger Knapman as party leader, but he was firmly rebuffed by Knapman, who was able to point to the fact that Kilroy-Silk enjoyed little support in the party branches. In January 2005, Kilroy left UKIP and formed his own new organisation, Veritas ('the straight-talking party').

UKIP's manifesto for the general election (*Let's Get Our Country Back!*) made withdrawal from the EU its foremost proposal, on the grounds that the EU is costly, prone to corruption, undemocratic, and undermines British sovereignty. It claimed that bilateral trade agreements with Europe would continue to flourish even after British withdrawal, while trade with other parts of the world could be expected to grow. On the economy UKIP proposed 'wholesale deregulation, especially for small businesses', an increase in borrowing in order to fund tax cuts, and an increase in state pensions. On internal affairs, UKIP proposed more 'bobbies on the beat', reduced bureaucracy, a review of sentencing, and more prisons. On immigration, a new 'points system' would be introduced for evaluating work permit applications, border controls would be reinstated, and 'Britishness' tests would be introduced to encourage those settling in the country to assimilate into society. 'More rigour' was promised in deporting asylum-seekers who are refused the right to stay. On governance, UKIP emulated the BNP's demand for citizen initiatives, demanded decentralisation of state power, and promised to repeal the Human Rights Act, 'preferring to rely on British custom, our common law and the principles of the European Convention of Human Rights'. Though briefer, Veritas' manifesto was essentially identical in terms of its major proposals.

On 5 May, UKIP gained 618,000 votes, or 2.3% of the total votes cast in the election and 2.8%, on average, in the constituencies where they contested seats. Although this placed them fourth in terms of total votes cast and represented some slight progress on the 2001 result, there was a palpable sense of disappointment in the party as they did not even come close to achieving their stated targets. Roger Knapman had claimed that the party was confident of doing well in 21 seats and that it had genuine designs on winning at least one, with Thanet South as the prime target. However, the MEP Nigel Farage, who was UKIP's candidate there, won just 5% of the vote, well below the 20% which the party had expected. Modest progress came in the 45 saved deposits which UKIP managed, up from only six in 2001. Their best performance was in Boston and Skegness, where Richard Horsnell came third with 9.6% of the vote. Knapman himself managed 7.7% in coming third in Totnes. Things hardly went better for Robert Kilroy-Silk, who, in contesting the Derbyshire constituency of Erewash, garnered 2,957 votes (5.85%). Still, he had at least vanquished candidates representing UKIP and BNP, not to mention the Church of the Militant Elvis Presley. Overall, Veritas ran 62 candidates and won an average vote of just 1.5% in these constituencies. The best performances other than Kilroy's were by Colin Brown in Leicester East (4.0%), Tony Martin in City of Durham (3.6%), John Burdon in Hemsworth (3.4%), Stephen Wallis in Hull West & Hessle (3.2%), and Patrick Eston in Tamworth (3.0%).

Conclusion

The long-term erosion of traditional party loyalties, the emergence of new social fault-lines, and disillusionment with the major parties are all factors which can be expected to facilitate the growth of protest voting and minor party support. Moreover, three specific issues fostered minor party support in 2005: immigration, Iraq, and Europe. While immigration was grist to the mill of the populist right, Iraq particularly fed the agenda and appeal of the radical left. The European project helped both. Although neither is expressly anti-European, Respect and the Greens share a common rejection of an EU driven by the logic of economic neo-liberalism and free trade; indeed, this stance led both to reject the doomed European constitution in 2005. The minor parties of the radical right are more intrinsically and viscerally anti-European, principally on the grounds that the EU erodes British identity and sovereignty.

None of these issues or factors, including Iraq, seems likely to disappear from the agenda of British politics in the near future. When one further considers that the cleavages which gave birth to the nationalists in Scotland and Wales and to Northern Ireland's unique party system are unlikely to weaken any time soon, it becomes hard to imagine a reversal in the steady advance of the minor parties at Westminster. Furthermore, in the immediate aftermath of the general election, pressure grew on the main institutional bulwark against the minor parties, the Single Member Plurality electoral system, as critics loudly lamented the formation of a single-party government with the support of little more than a fifth of the registered electorate. This is not to underestimate the limits to growth of parties such as the BNP or UKIP which are imposed by their extremist images, especially in the former case, and the strategic adaptations of the Conservative Party. Individual organisations may wax and wane, and it is hard to imagine any one of them making a dramatic breakthrough in the foreseeable future, but, on the whole, the place of minor parties at Westminster continues to become incrementally more prominent.

* I am very grateful to David Denver, Roger Scully, Jonathan Tonge and Christopher Wlezien for their valuable comments on earlier drafts of this article. The usual disclaimer of responsibility applies.

1 G. Sartori, *Parties and Party Systems: A Framework for Analysis*, Volume 1, Cambridge University Press, 1976, pp. 122–3.

2 M. Laakso and R. Taagepera, 'Effective Number of Parties: A Measure with Application to Western Europe', 12 *Comparative Political Studies*, 1979, pp. 3–27.

3 The Scottish parliament is empowered to take responsibility for domestic policy in Scotland over areas such as education, health, housing, the legal system, the environment, and transport. A number of matters remain the preserve of Westminster, including foreign and defence affairs, constitutional issues, economic policy, energy, and social security. The parliament in Edinburgh also has the right to adjust public expenditure by varying the income tax imposed on Scots by plus-or-minus 3% with respect to the level set by the national government in London.

4 S. Herbert, R. Burnside and S. Wakefield, *UK Election 2005 in Scotland*, Scottish Parliament Information Centre Briefing 05/28, Edinburgh, 2005, p. 28.

5   See *If Scotland Matters to You, You Can Make it Matter in May*, Scottish Nationalist Party, 2005.

6   Named after the late Chief Secretary to the Treasury in the Callaghan government of the 1970s, Joel Barnett, this non-statutory formula is part of the mechanism for determining the budgets of the Scottish, Welsh, and Northern Ireland Offices. The formula has been widely seen as favourable to Scotland compared to the English regions.

7   For detailed information on the notional results for 2001, see D. Denver, C. Rallings and M. Thrasher, *The Media Guide to the New Scottish Westminster Parliamentary Constituencies*, Local Government Chronicle Elections Centre, 2004.

8   P. Norris, 'Anatomy of a Labour landslide' in P. Norris and N.T. Gavin (eds), *Britain Votes 1997*, Oxford University Press, 1997, pp. 1–24.

9   Specifically, PC called for the implementation of the Richard Commission's proposal to replace the Welsh Assembly with a 'real' legislature along the lines of the Scottish Parliament. Such a body would have primary law-making and tax-raising powers: the present Assembly only has the right to making secondary laws, designed to effect the implementation of primary legislation made at Westminster. This proposal is also supported by the Liberal Democrats, a majority of Labour members of the Welsh Assembly (but not the party's MPs in Wales), and several Conservative Assembly members.

10 See I. McLean and A. McMillan, 'The Distribution of Public Expenditure across the UK Regions', 24 *Fiscal Studies*, 2003, pp. 45–71.

11 Note that a side-effect of Law's resignation from the party was to deprive Labour of its majority in the Welsh Assembly.

12 G. Evans and M. Duffy, 'Beyond the Sectarian Divide: The Social Bases and Political Consequences of Nationalist & Unionist Party Competition in Northern Ireland', 1 *British Journal of Political Science*, 1997.

13 On 23 June, Sir Reg Empey, Northern Ireland Assembly member for East Belfast, was eventually elected leader.

14 *Leadership That's Working: Parliamentary and Local Government Manifesto 2005*, Democratic Unionist Party, 2005.

15 This includes three Conservative Party candidates who might be considered minor party representatives in the context of Northern Ireland.

16 Note that Salma Yaqoob launched a petition against the result in Birmingham Sparkbrook on 1 June, alleging irregularities in the poll. The constituency includes part of Bordesley Green, one of the wards where five Labour councillors rigged postal voting in local elections in 2004.

17 I am grateful to the directors of the British Election Survey for making the pre-election cross-sectional data available so soon after the election. Note that the data are weighted to provide a representative sample of England in the brief analysis offered here, since Respect only ran candidates in England.

18 M. Tempest, 'Greens turn fire on Lib Dems', *Guardian*, 5.3.05.

JOHN CURTICE

Turnout: Electors Stay Home—Again

One feature of the outcome of the 2001 election sent shockwaves through politicians of all parties. Just 59.1% of the electorate in Great Britain voted.[1] Not only did this represent a drop of 12.4% on the turnout in 1997, it was the lowest recorded level of voting participation since 1918. Given that many troops were still abroad in that post-First World War election, it is probably the case that more of the electorate abstained voluntarily in 2001 than in any previous UK election since the advent of the mass franchise. It appeared that the British political class had become seriously disconnected from the public it sought to serve, thereby raising some important questions about the effectiveness of British democracy.

Turnout was little better in 2005. Just 61.2% of the electorate in Great Britain voted, an increase of no more than 2.1% on the record low of four years previously. At least things had not become any worse, but turnout was still well below the norm in British general elections. Between 1970 and 1997 turnout had never dipped below 71.5%, and it had even been as high as 79.1% in February 1974. In other words, turnout in 2005 was still about ten points below what had hitherto been its low water mark.

Moreover, turnout was once again so low despite the fact that it was possible for any elector to vote by post in the comfort of their own home. No longer was access to a postal vote confined, as it had been previously, to those who were ill, away on business, or on holiday. The new more liberal regime had been in force at the time of the 2001 election, but as the new regulations had only been introduced some five months previously, there had been relatively little opportunity for people to become aware and to take advantage of the new facility. So while the number of postal voters doubled in 2001, the proportion of the electorate registered to vote by post was still no more than 4%. It might be anticipated that postal voting on demand would have had rather greater impact in 2005.

This chapter therefore examines two main issues. First, why was there only a modest increase in turnout compared with 2001? Does it

doi: 10.1093/pa/gsi066

mean that British democracy does indeed face some kind of 'crisis' of disconnection between its politicians and the public? Secondly, what impact did the availability of postal voting on demand have in 2005? How far did people avail themselves of the facility, and what contribution, if any, did it make to the increase in turnout which occurred?

Turnout before 2005

There are two main kinds of explanation for declining turnout. One account argues that voters are no longer as strongly motivated to go to the polling station as they once were. Fewer have a strong emotional attachment to a political party.[2] More are cynical about politics and distrustful of politicians.[3] A better educated electorate finds that putting a cross on the ballot box is an inadequate means of expressing its political views and no longer feels the obligation to do so. And a more affluent public with a diversity of leisure opportunities apparently has less time for, or interest in, politics.

An alternative explanation, however, argues that the key to the low turnout in 2001 was a failure by parties to mobilise voters.[4] The election offered the electorate little choice. First, fewer people than ever before thought there was a great deal of difference between the Conservative and Labour parties. Meanwhile, apart from one very brief spell during the 'fuel crisis' of September 2000, the Labour party had enjoyed an unprecedented near ten year period of continuous double digit leads in the opinion polls. Voters were told that the outcome of the election was a foregone conclusion, and in any event they felt there was not much difference between the principal contenders for power anyway.[5] In those circumstances, while those citizens who did have a strong motivation to participate largely still turned out, those with a weaker commitment to voting or little interest in politics, the kind of elector who always has to be mobilised to go to the polls, stayed at home.

The pattern of turnout in mid-term elections held during the course of the last parliament offered some support to this latter interpretation. By 2003, Labour's dominance of the electoral landscape was under challenge. Even if the ideological distance between Labour and the Conservatives remained narrow, other political parties such as the United Kingdom Independence Party, the British National Party, and Respect were offering distinct platforms on issues with substantial emotional resonance, such as Europe, immigration, and Iraq. In these circumstances, turnout showed signs of recovery. Turnout in five English by-elections held in hitherto safe Labour seats – but ones where in many cases Labour now faced a serious challenge from the Liberal Democrats—averaged 40.1%, well above the 24.9% recorded in by-elections held in such seats in the 1997–2001 parliament and even the 37.8% in the 1992–97 parliament. A record high turnout of 38.2% was recorded in the 2004 European elections. While this figure was boosted by the use of all-postal ballots in some areas and by holding the election on the same day as local elections in others, it still appears that turnout would have been close to the level of the 1979 and 1984 European elections even if those measures had not been in place.[6] In any event, turnout in the contemporaneous 2004 local elections was above the norm for such elections in recent years.[7]

Turnout in 2005

After these indications that perhaps the British electorate might be returning to the ballot box, albeit in mid-term elections that usually fail to command the participation of as many as half of voters anyway, the low turnout in the 2005 election could be regarded as something of a disappointment. Perhaps voters have lost the motivation to vote after all? Or can we demonstrate that the election might still have seemed a rather dull one to many voters?

One piece of evidence collected during the election campaign suggests that voters were indeed no less motivated in 2005 than they had been previously. During the middle of the election campaign MORI asked about how much interest people have in politics, a question that it has administered on a number of occasions over the last thirty years. As Table 1 shows, in fact slightly more people than ever before said they were 'very' or 'fairly' interested in politics. As many as 61% fell into one or the other of these two categories, more than matching the previous all-time high of 60% recorded in 1973 and 1991. On this evidence, at least, it is difficult to argue that the low turnout in 2005 is a reflection of any marked reduction in the willingness of voters to participate.

So were voters once again simply not motivated by parties to vote? Certainly, as Table 2 shows, it remained the case that relatively few felt that there was a great deal of difference between the parties. A NOP poll conducted just before the election campaign in 2005 found that only 21% believed that there was a 'great deal' of difference between the Conservative and Labour parties, up only slightly on the record low of 17% in 2001, and still well short of the previous low before that of 33%. Moreover, those who said that there was a great deal of difference between the parties were 15 points more likely to say they were absolutely certain to vote than were those who did not see such a large difference between the parties.

1. Political Interest 1973–2005

	1973 %	1991 %	1995 %	1997 %	2001 %	2003 %	2004 %	2005 %
How interested would you say you are in politics?								
Very interested	14	13	13	15	14	9	13	16
Fairly interested	46	47	40	44	45	42	37	45
Not very interested	27	26	30	29	29	30	33	28
Not at all interested	13	13	17	11	11	19	17	11

Note: The 2001 figure is for the whole of the United Kingdom; the remainder are for Great Britain only.
Sources: 1973–2004; Extracted from Electoral Commission, *An Audit of Political Engagement 2*, Electoral Commission Hansard Society, 2005; MORI/Financial Times poll April 2005.

2. Indicators of Potential Mobilisation 1945–2005

	% Feel a Great Deal of Difference between Con and Lab	Average Lead in Final Polls
1945	na	6
1950	na	1
1951	na	5
1955	na	4
1959	na	3
1964	48	2
1966	44	10
1970	33	3
Feb. 1974	34	4
Oct. 1974	40	9
1979	48	5
1983	88	20
1987	85	8
1992	56	1
1997	33	16
2001	17	14
2005	21	5

na: not available.
Sources: A. Heath and B. Taylor, 'New Sources of Abstention?' in G. Evans and P. Norris (eds), *Critical Elections: British Parties and Voters in Long-Term Perspective,* Sage, 1999; C. Bromley and J. Curtice, 'Where Have All the Voters Gone?' in A. Park, J. Curtice, K. Thomson, L. Jarvis and C. Bromley (eds), *British Social Attitudes: The 19th Report.* Sage, 2002; NOP/Independent poll February 2005.

On the other hand the opinion polls suggested a much closer contest than they did in either 1997 or 2001. No longer was the message one of double digit leads but rather of a more modest lead that averaged just five points in the final polls. While this still meant that the contest looked less close than the majority of elections held in the 1950s and 1960s, at least the election no longer appeared to be a walkover. Thanks to the pro-Labour bias in the electoral system,[8] however, when the findings of the polls were projected into seats, they were typically represented as pointing to a third three-figure Labour majority in a row. The prospect of a Conservative victory appeared to be utterly remote. Thus arguably the message of the polls was still one that suggested little doubt about the outcome.[9]

So it appears that while citizens might have seen slightly more reason to vote than they did in 2001—a somewhat closer contest and perhaps a slightly bigger gap between the two main parties—for the most part the stimulus to vote was probably still relatively weak in 2005, and it was certainly insufficient to generate anything more than the most modest of increases in turnout. But if the closeness of an election makes a difference to voters, then we should find that not only does it affect the total number of people who vote but also where people vote. Those living in marginal constituencies would appear to have more reason to participate than those who live in safe constituencies. Parties have more incentive to campaign heavily in these areas too.

3. Turnout by Marginality and Winning Party 2001

(a) Average % Turnout 2005

% Majority 2001	Winning Party 2001		All Seats
	Conservative	Labour	
0 to 5	66.2	65.9	66.7
5 to 10	65.5	64.6	64.9
10 to 20	65.0	63.1	64.1
20+	65.2	55.7	57.4
All	65.2	58.6	60.9

(b) Average Change in % Turnout 2001–05

% Majority 2001	Winning Party 2001		All Seats
	Conservative	Labour	
0 to 5	+3.2	+2.2	+2.7
5 to 10	+1.9	+2.6	+2.1
10 to 20	+2.2	+1.9	+2.0
20+	+2.3	+1.8	+1.8
All	+2.3	+1.9	+2.0

Source: Author's calculations from checked and corrected version of BBC Election Results database.

Table 3 indicates that those living in marginal constituencies were indeed more likely to vote. On average the turnout was nine points higher in the most marginal constituencies (where the lead of the winning party over the second party was less than 5% in 2001) than it was in the safest constituencies (where the winning party had a lead of 20% or more). Furthermore, despite the fact that many of the marginal constituencies had also been close prior to the 2001 election and had therefore experienced below-average drops in turnout between 1997 and 2001,[10] the increase in turnout was also nearly one-point greater in the most marginal seats than it was in the safest.

It is not clear though that we can ascribe all of these differences between marginal and safe seats to the closeness of the contest. For Table 3 also indicates that the picture in safe Conservative seats is very different from that in Labour ones. Turnout was, at 65.2% , well above the national average in safe Conservative seats while the increase in turnout, +2.3%, was also a little above average too. Neither of these figures quite matches that in the most marginal Conservative seats, but the gap in both cases is only of the order of one point. It was exclusively in safe Labour seats that turnout was particularly low and increased less compared with 2001.

This suggests that perhaps it is something about the type of people living in safe Labour constituencies that also helps to account for the low turnout in these seats, and not simply the apparent inevitability of the local outcome. One possibility is that these seats include a relatively large proportion of disaffected Labour voters who are persistently and increasingly opting to stay at home—the gap between the turnout in safe Labour seats and that in the rest of the country has grown at each and every election since 1992.[11] However, there is no consistent evidence in this election that Labour's vote fell most where turnout fell most. But, equally as likely, it may also be the case that those living in more socially deprived neighbourhoods, neighbourhoods that are most commonly found in safe Labour constituencies, may have been particularly affected by the lack of stimulus to vote at the last two general elections. Certainly those in working class occupations, those who have few educational qualifications, and those who are unemployed are all more likely to evince relatively low levels of interest in politics, and are less likely to feel they have a duty to vote, the very characteristics that we saw earlier were associated with falling levels of turnout in 2001.

These alternative possibilities are difficult to disentangle. But multivariate analysis indicates that even after we take into account Labour's share of the vote in a constituency, there remains a relationship between both the level of turnout in 2005 and the change in the level of turnout since 2001, and indicators of the social characteristics of a constituency, such as the percentage who say they are in good health or the percentage who are routine manual workers. We illustrate this in Table 4 which shows that even if we confine our attention to safe Labour constituencies, turnout was both higher and increased more in seats with relatively high proportions of people in good health and with relatively few routine manual workers. So it may well be the case that the reason why turnout is so low in safe Labour seats is not simply because they are safe but also because they contain a disproportionate number of people who need to be mobilised to go to the polls, and for whom nether the local nor the national political contest provided much incentive to vote in 2005.

The 2005 election appears then to have been similar to 2001 in its failure to provide voters with a stimulus to vote. As in 2001, few saw much difference between the parties, while in practice the message of the opinion polls was still that only one party appeared to have a chance of winning. This lack of mobilisation may have had a particularly strong impact in safe Labour constituencies, not just because they are safe, but also because voters in such seats are particularly likely to require some stimulus to vote. Certainly, as in 2001, there is little evidence that the low turnout is simply or even primarily an indication of a new disinclination on the part of voters to vote.

4. Turnout in safe Labour seats by the social character of the constituency

| | % in good health | | % routine manual workers | |
	Low	High	Low	High
Turnout 2005	53.7	57.0	56.2	55.2
Change in turnout since 2001	+1.5	+2.0	+2.2	+1.4

Note: Based only on safe Labour constituencies, defined as those won by Labour in 2001 with majorities of 20% or more. Percent in good health: Low—Less than 65% of adults in good health (2001 Census); High—more than 65% in good health. Percent routine manual workers: Low—Less than 11% of those aged 16–74 employed in routine manual occupations (2001 Census); High—more than 11%. Source: Author's calculations from checked and corrected version of BBC Election Results database.

Postal voting

But perhaps even the two-point increase in turnout overestimates the degree to which there was any greater interest in this election than there was in its predecessor. Maybe the increase is simply accounted for by the easier availability of postal voting. After all, being able to vote at home and then to put one's ballot in the nearest post box certainly reduces the time and effort involved in voting, and any reduction in the 'costs' of voting should make it more likely that people actually cast a ballot.

Full details of how many people voted by post are not available at the time of writing; however, we do have access to information collected by the BBC on the number of postal votes issued for 594 of the 627 constituencies in Great Britain where an election was held. Meanwhile, by modelling these data we have been able to impute the likely figures in the remaining 33 constituencies. We also have information collected by the Electoral Commission for each constituency on the number of postal votes issued and the number validly returned at the last election. This means we can also examine how the increase in postal voting varied from constituency.

As we anticipated, there was a substantial increase in the number of people opting to vote by post. Just under 12% of the electorate in Great Britain were issued with a postal vote, treble the proportion who were issued with such a vote in 2001. Given that those who opt to vote by post are more likely to actually cast a vote, this suggests that around 15% of all valid votes cast were cast by post.[12]

Just as we might expect turnout to be higher in marginal constituencies, so we might imagine that postal voting would be higher in such seats too. Voters would appear to have more incentive to ensure that they did not miss out on the chance to vote should they be unable to reach the polling station on election day. More importantly, perhaps, political parties, aware that those registered for a postal ballot are more likely to vote, have a particular incentive to encourage their supporters to apply for a postal ballot. Indeed the role of political parties in encouraging and enabling people to apply for postal votes became the subject of some controversy after the 2004 local and European elections, most notably following a well publicised case of electoral fraud in Birmingham, and this has since led to the government proposing that political parties should not handle such applications on behalf of voters.[13]

There is, however, little evidence that postal voting was more common in marginal constituencies. The proportion of the electorate issued with a postal vote in the average marginal constituency (one with a 2001 majority of five points or less) was 11.8%, slightly below the equivalent figure, 12.0%, for the average safe seat (one with a 2001 majority of 20 points or more). Meanwhile the latter figure for safe seats also represented a rather larger increase on 2001 (+8.3%) than the

5. Postal Voting by Government Region

Region	% electorate issued with postal vote	Increase in % since 2001
All-Postal Ballot 2004		
North East	19.3	+13.5
Yorkshire & Humber	13.9	+10.2
North West	12.4	+8.8
Conventional Ballot 2004		
East Midlands	12.9	+9.1
South West	12.5	+7.7
Wales	12.0	+7.1
South East	11.3	+7.2
Eastern	11.2	+6.3
West Midlands	10.7	+7.4
London	10.6	+7.0
Scotland	7.8	+5.0

Source: Author's calculations from checked and corrected version of BBC Election Results database.

former figure for marginal seats (+7.6%). If political parties were attempting to encourage people to vote by post in marginal seats they appear, collectively at least, to have been remarkably unsuccessful.

What does appear to have made a difference to the incidence of postal voting is familiarity. Applications to vote by post were notably higher in those parts of the country with previous experience of voting by post. This can be seen in Table 5 which shows the average proportion of the electorate registered to vote by post in each of the eleven government regions, and the increase this represented on 2001. Postal voting was by far the highest and increased most in the North East. This was not only one of the regions which had undertaken an all-postal ballot in both the 2004 Euro elections, but it also conducted a further such ballot in the regional referendum that autumn, and it was an area in which a relatively large proportion of local authorities had undertaken all-postal ballots in local elections prior to 2004. Requests for postal ballots were second highest in another region where an all postal ballot was held in 2004, Yorkshire & Humberside. Although the increase in postal voting was lower in the North West, the third region to have an all-postal ballot in 2004, than it was in the East Midlands, the latter is a region where local authorities appear to be particularly keen to promote postal voting.[14] The Electoral Commission has now lost its former enthusiasm for all-postal ballots on the grounds that the system denies voters the opportunity to choose how they would like to vote. Nevertheless it appears that electors, encouraged perhaps by local authority administrators, are in fact more likely to opt to vote by post once they have had experience of doing so.

But did this increased take-up of the facility to vote by post have any impact on the overall level of turnout? Did the ease of voting by post mean that those who might not otherwise have voted did so? Or was it simply the case that those who chose to vote by post were for the most part the relatively interested and engaged who would have voted anyway?

If the increased use of postal voting helped to increase turnout then we should find that turnout rose most in those constituencies where postal voting increased most. This is the analysis performed in Table 6, which shows how much turnout increased since 2001 according to how much the proportion of the electorate issued with a postal vote increased.

This analysis suggests that the wider availability of postal voting had, at most, a small impact on turnout in the 2005 election. Turnout did rise least in those seats with the lowest increase in postal voting over the previous four years and most in those seats where the increase was biggest. But the difference between them was little more than half a point. Making it easier for people to vote by post may give people the right to choose how they vote but it evidently does not, unlike all postal ballots,[15] make them significantly more likely actually to cast a ballot. Meanwhile the fact that turnout increased by at least one and a half points in those constituencies which had had only modest increases in postal voting certainly suggests that the overall increase in turnout since 2001 cannot simply be accounted for by the wider availability of postal voting.

Conclusion

In the event the political circumstances in which the 2005 election was fought were too similar to that of 2001 to engender anything more than a modest increase on the record low turnout of that year. Voters were as interested in politics as ever, but they continued to feel there was little choice between the parties, while the opinion polls appeared to point once again to a comfortable if somewhat narrower Labour victory. Lacking any stimulus to vote, many again stayed at home. Not even the prospect of being able to avoid the journey to the polling station enticed many voters to exercise their franchise. Turnout depends not on giving people a choice about how to vote but rather on what they are voting about.

But does this mean that we can be sanguine about the prospects of turnout eventually returning to its previous levels once political circumstances change? Not necessarily. One long run change that affects voters' likelihood of going to the polls has occurred over the last forty years: a decline in party identification. Now in more recent years sections of the British electorate have begun to lose the habit of voting. Indeed in the case of some younger voters, they have not had the chance to develop the habit in the first place. Together these developments probably mean

6. Postal Voting and Turnout

Increase in % voting by post since 2001	Change in % turnout since 2001
Less than 4%	+1.6
4 to 6%	+2.0
6 to 8%	+1.9
8 to 10%	+2.2
10% or more	+2.2

Source: Author's calculations from checked and corrected version of BBC Election Results database. Notes

that the degree of stimulus required to produce a turnout of 70% or more is now rather greater than it was ten years ago. Unless that stimulus comes soon, perhaps too many people will have lost the habit of voting entirely.

1   All references in this chapter are to Great Britain excluding Northern Ireland, unless otherwise stated. The recent history of turnout in Northern Ireland has been very different from that in the rest of Great Britain. Turnout actually rose slightly to 68.0% in 2001, when the election took place in the midst of a major debate about the future of devolution in the province. In 2005, however, by which time there seemed to be no immediate prospect of restoring devolved political institutions, turnout fell by 5.1 points to 62.9%, the lowest ever in a Westminster election since partition in 1922.

2   I. Crewe and K. Thomson, 'Party Loyalties: Dealignment or Realignment?' in G. Evans and P. Norris (eds), *Critical Elections: British Parties and Voters in Long-Term Perspective*, Sage, 1999.

3   P. Norris (ed.), *Critical Citizens: Global Support for Democratic Governance*, Oxford University Press, 1998; C. Bromley, J. Curtice and B. Seyd, 'Political Engagement, Trust and Constitutional Reform' in A. Park, J. Curtice, K. Thomson, L. Jarvis and C. Bromley (eds), *British Social Attitudes: The 18th Report—Public Policy, Social Ties*, Sage, 2004; R. Dalton, *Democratic Challenges, Democratic Choices*, Oxford University Press, 2004.

4   C. Bromley and J. Curtice, 'Where Have All the Voters Gone?' in A. Park, J. Curtice, K. Thomson, L. Jarvis and C. Bromley (eds), *British Social Attitudes: the 19th Report*, Sage, 2002; M. Franklin, *Voter Turnout and the Dynamics of Electoral Competition in Established Democracies since 1945*, Cambridge University Press, 2004.

5   See the argument developed in A. Heath and B. Taylor, 'New Sources of Abstention?' in G. Evans and P. Norris (eds), *Critical Elections: British Parties and Voters in Long-Term Perspective*, Sage, 1999.

6   J. Curtice, S. Fisher and M. Steed, 'Appendix: Analysis of the Results' in D. Butler and M. Westlake, *British Elections and European Politics 2004*, Palgrave, 2004.

7   C. Rallings and M. Thrasher, *Local Elections Handbook 2004*, Local Government Chronicle Elections Centre, 2004.

8   R.J. Johnston, C.J. Pattie, D.F.L. Dorling and D.J. Rossiter, *From Votes to Seats: The Operation of the UK Electoral System since 1945*, Manchester University Press, 2001.

9   Indeed, a poll conducted just before polling day by Populus for *The Times* found that no less than 78% thought that Labour would win an overall majority, with nearly one in three of this group anticipating a Labour majority of more than 100.

10 J. Curtice and M. Steed, 'Appendix 2; The Results Analysed' in D. Butler and D. Kavanagh, *The British General Election of 2001*, Palgrave, 2001.

11 J. Curtice and M. Steed, 'Appendix 2; The Results Analysed' in D. Butler and D. Kavanagh, *The British General Election of 1997*, Macmillan, 1997.

12 In the average constituency in 2001, the proportion of votes cast by post was 1.286 times the proportion of voters issued with a ballot paper.

13 A number of the allegations about the possible abuse of postal voting, including the case in Birmingham, have involved areas with high Asian populations. On average, however, the proportion of the electorate registered to vote by post was not particularly high in constituencies with relatively high Asian populations. On average, in those constituencies where according to the 2001 Census more than 10% of adults are from an Asian background, just over 11% were registered to vote by post. For details of the government's proposals on postal voting, see Department for Constitutional Affairs, *Electoral Administration: A Policy Paper for Discussion,* Department for Constitutional Affairs, 2005; Electoral Commission, *Securing the Vote,* Electoral Commission, 2005.

14 Electoral Commission, *Electoral Pilots at the June 2004 Elections*, Electoral Commission, 2003.

15 J. Curtice, S. Fisher and M. Steed, 'Appendix: Analysis of the Results' in D. Butler and M. Westlake, *British Elections and European Politics 2004*, Palgrave, 2004.

RON JOHNSTON, CHARLES PATTIE AND DAVID ROSSITER

The Election Results in the UK Regions

Regional variations are frequently highlighted in discussions of voting at UK general elections and in the consequent patterns of Parliamentary representation. With regard to voting patterns, the implication is of inter-regional differences in the propensity of voters to support the various political parties because of differences in local 'political culture'—as exemplified by relatively high levels of support for the Liberal Democrats in Devon and Cornwall which cannot apparently be 'accounted for' by the characteristics and experiences of people who live there. It is thus assumed that such regional divergences from a hypothetical national pattern reflect spatial differences in the political parties' ability to mobilise support across the country. This is not surprising in Scotland, Wales and Northern Ireland, the first two of which have nationalist parties contesting with the three parties that field candidates in all British constituencies (Conservative, Labour and Liberal Democrat) whereas Northern Ireland has a totally separate party system reflecting its distinct 'political culture'. Within England, however, there is little evidence of separate and distinct regional political cultures, save in a few areas such as the Southwest.

As a consequence, electoral analysts have debated not only the extent but also the significance of apparent regional variation in voting at recent UK general elections. The evidence of such variation was especially strong in the 1980s when a clear north-south divide was identified, associated by many with the industrial and social changes stimulated by the economic policies of successive Conservative governments: Labour (at the nadir of its post-second world war fortunes) gained much of its support in the northern regions of England, Scotland and Wales which suffered most from the unemployment and social ills concentrated there, whereas the Conservatives were particularly strong in the southern regions that largely prospered at the same time. Curtice and Steed also identified an urban-rural split cross-cutting this regional divide, with Labour strongest in the towns and the Conservatives in the countryside.[1] For some, these two splits accentuated patterns established throughout

© Oxford University Press 2005
doi: 10.1093/pa/gsi061

much of the twentieth century, whereas critics suggested that closer examination of voting patterns showed that the region in which people lived had at best a small impact on how they voted.[2] That division of opinion forms the foundation of this analysis of regional variations in voting across the UK.

Whatever the debate about regional variations in voting support for the political parties, one unquestionable pattern concerned parallel variations in party representation in the House of Commons. In the 1980s, for example, many of the country's eleven regions were predominantly represented by MPs from a single party only. Regional polarisation in voting was much exaggerated in the patterns of representation.

Did Labour's mid-1990s electoral resurgence narrow the regional gap, as substantial numbers of voters were converted to the party's cause in the southern regions and many more seats were won there?[3] To address that question, we report analyses of both votes and seats won across the last four general elections—1992–2005—and also address the critics' contention that observed regional variations simply reflect the generalisation that different types of people—who tend to live in different regions—vote for different parties.

Our data for these analyses use a standard set of constituencies for all four elections in England and Wales. New constituencies were introduced for the 1997 election, and were used again in 2001 and 2005, except in Scotland where, as part of the 1998 devolution settlement, its Boundary Commission was instructed to use the same quota for its next review as that deployed by the English Commission. This resulted in a reduction of Scottish MPs from 72 to 59 (Scotland had been significantly over-represented in the House of Commons since the 1944 Act).[4] These new seats were approved by Parliament on 1 February 2005, and used in the May 2005 general election. The pre-existing constituencies were used in the other three countries of the UK, however.[5] The 1992 election was fought in an earlier set of constituencies, first deployed in 1983. For comparative purposes, we use the likely 1992 result estimated as if that election had been fought in the new constituencies introduced three years later.[6] For Northern Ireland, which has a separate party system, we report on the results for the province as a whole: it had 17 MPs in 1992, and 18 at the next three contests.

The pattern of voting

The percentage of voters who supported each of the three main parties in Great Britain's eleven regions across the four elections is shown in Table 1, along with the percentage of the electorate who turned out. In addition, the table includes a summary statistic—RV (regional variation)—which is the difference between the maximum and minimum value in the relevant column.

1. Voting by Region, 1992–2005

Region	Conservative				Labour			
	92	97	01	05	92	97	01	05
Southeast	55	41	43	45	21	32	32	26
East Anglia	51	39	42	42	28	38	36	29
Greater London	45	31	30	32	37	49	47	39
Southwest	48	37	39	39	19	26	26	23
West Midlands	45	34	35	35	39	48	45	39
East Midlands	47	35	38	38	37	48	45	39
Yorkshire/Humberside	38	28	30	29	44	52	49	44
Northwest	37	27	28	27	45	54	52	46
North	33	22	25	23	51	61	56	50
Wales	29	20	21	21	50	55	49	39
Scotland	26	18	16	16	39	46	44	39
TOTAL	43	31	33	33	35	44	42	36
RV	29	23	27	29	32	35	30	27

Region	Liberal Democrat				Turnout			
	92	97	01	05	92	97	01	05
Southeast	23	22	21	24	80	74	61	64
East Anglia	20	18	19	24	80	75	64	64
Greater London	16	15	17	22	73	68	55	58
Southwest	31	31	31	33	81	75	65	66
West Midlands	15	14	15	19	77	71	68	61
East Midlands	15	13	15	18	80	73	61	63
Yorkshire/Humberside	17	16	17	21	75	68	57	59
Northwest	16	15	17	22	76	70	55	57
North	16	13	17	23	76	69	58	58
Wales	12	12	14	18	79	74	62	62
Scotland	13	13	16	22	75	71	58	61
TOTAL	18	17	19	23	77	72	59	61
RV	19	19	17	15	7	6	10	9

Note: Percentage of votes cast for the three main British parties and turnout (percentage of registered electors who voted). Source: Calculated from data in the British Parliamentary Constituency Database 1992–2005.

These values show that regional variation was greatest for Labour at each of the first three elections and least for the Liberal Democrats, with the Conservative party occupying a central position—closer to Labour in 1992 and 2001 but closer to the Liberal Democrats in 1997. The variations suggest a continuing split within the country after Labour's post-1992 surge in support and the consequent Conservative decline. For Labour and the Conservatives, those variations were entirely consistent with the notion of a north-south divide. The Conservatives never obtained more than 40% of the votes in the five 'northern' regions of Yorkshire/Humberside, Northwest, North, Wales and Scotland, whereas Labour failed to win support from half of those who voted in any of the six 'southern' regions. [7] For the Liberal Democrats, the Southwest stands out as providing much greater support than any other part of the country.

Between 2001 and 2005 Labour's overall decline of 6 percentage points in the poll was reflected in nearly every region. Labour's vote share fell by five to seven points across all of Great Britain except in two regions—the Southwest, where it won only just over one-quarter of the votes in 2001, and Wales, where it suffered a major haemorrhage to an independent candidate in Blaenau Gwent. The Conservative share, which remained at 33% nationally, changed very little in most regions: a slight increase in the Southeast and Greater London was compensated by falls in England's three northernmost regions. For the Liberal Democrats, too, the 4% increase in their national share of the vote was virtually uniform across all regions. Reflecting this consistency, the RV values changed only slightly between the two elections, increasing by two points for the Conservatives but declining by three and two points respectively for Labour and the Liberal Democrats. The extent of regional differentiation remained largely constant across the four elections.

There was less regional variation in turnout, though it grew as abstentions increased overall in 2001. Each election displays a north-south split, with slightly lower turnouts in the north of England and in Greater London. Turnout in Wales was slightly above the national average at all four contests, but in Scotland it was either below or the same as the national figure.

Regions: or people in places?

Table 1 indicates a continuing regional divide to British voting behaviour. Is that divide 'real', however, or is it simply a reflection of the geographies of class and prosperity which have also characterised Great Britain for many decades? Many analyses show two consistent patterns of voting behaviour. The first relates to social class, broadly defined. Those in manual occupations and living in rented housing tend to support Labour, whereas the Conservatives win most support among non-manual workers and owner-occupiers: the Liberal Democrats have a less clear-cut social base to their support. Secondly, there have been strong—though disputed—arguments that over recent decades people have increasingly voted according to their perceptions of both the national and their own economic situation: those feeling well-off and optimistic about the future tend to vote for the government to be returned to power on the basis of its economic management record, whereas those feeling less well-off and/or pessimistic about the future tend to vote for opposition parties. In 2005, whereas Labour sought to focus the campaign on its economic record and delivery of public service reform, its opponents pressed arguments regarding issues such as participation in the Iraq war, trust in the Prime Minister (notably over the war), and specific concerns regarding public services such as university fees and cleanliness in hospitals.

Class and relative prosperity have their own geographies within Britain. People from different class backgrounds and occupying different positions within the labour and housing markets are concentrated into different types of area. Similarly, relative prosperity is unevenly distributed: different places have experienced varying impacts on levels of living and life chances over recent decades. These two geographies do not map directly into the country's regional divisions: pockets of both prosperity and depression can be found in most regions, for example, even if some regions have more prosperity and others have more depression. It may well be, therefore, that once these geographies have been taken into account, the regional variations in voting described above substantially disappear. Work on the north-south divide in the 1980s found clear evidence supporting this claim. Constituencies were classified according to their population and housing characteristics, and voting variations across the types were shown to be greater than those across the country's regions.[8]

To address that issue for recent elections we use a classification of the new constituencies introduced in 1997. Twelve variables derived from 1991 census data were deployed to identify twenty separate constituency types.[9] Their brief titles are given in the relevant tables: most are self-explanatory, with the names reflecting the particular characteristics of each type: thus, for example, 'Manufacturing' constituencies have relatively high proportions of their workforce employed in manufacturing industries, and the 'Middle Britain' type comprises constituencies whose socio-demographic profiles are close to that of the country as a whole.[10] Allocation of the new Scottish constituencies in 2005 to these types was based on the characteristics of the former seats from which they were comprised.[11]

Table 2 shows voting patterns by constituency type using that classification. Variations across the twenty types are as expected. The Conservatives received least support in the deprived inner city areas, for example, and their greatest in rural areas, among constituencies with a strong military presence, and in white-collar towns—with their fall in support between 1992 and 1997 relatively consistent across all types. Labour's strongest support was in the deprived areas, as well as in constituencies with high unemployment levels. The white-collar areas, the rural constituencies and those with a substantial military presence provided above average support for the Liberal Democrats.

Each column in Table 2 has a summary statistic (TV—variation across types) showing the difference between the largest and smallest value. These are all substantially larger than the comparable Regional Variation values, especially for turnout—more than double that across regions, with the lowest turnout in the deprived areas and highest in the areas with above average white-collar components within their populations. The TV values fell markedly for the Conservatives between 1992 and 1997 and increased slightly thereafter, but there was a continuous decline for Labour: there was a slight decrease for the Liberal Democrat share of the vote after 1997, but at a much lower average level than for the other two parties, and a comparable slight increase for turnout.

Of the three parties, Labour experienced the main changes in the geography of support by constituency type between 2001 and 2005. Its overall vote share fell by six points, but by 13 in the 'Deprived/Immigrant'

2. Voting by Constituency Type, 1992–2005

	Conservative				Labour			
	92	97	01	05	92	97	01	05
Cities with Immigrants	35	23	25	22	50	59	56	49
Deprived Inner City	17	11	10	10	64	70	67	58
Manufacturing	37	27	28	27	47	56	53	47
Middle Britain	48	35	35	37	35	48	46	39
Higher Status	52	41	42	44	26	37	37	32
White-Collar	54	41	41	43	20	29	29	23
Low Status	28	18	18	17	55	63	59	52
Inner London High Status	48	34	32	34	35	47	43	35
White-Collar Towns	57	44	45	47	17	26	25	21
Slightly Deprived	31	20	19	17	47	57	54	46
Rural	50	40	43	43	19	28	27	23
Military	54	42	44	48	20	30	29	22
Retirement	50	38	40	41	22	31	30	27
Deprived/Immigrant	26	16	15	15	54	63	60	47
Rural/Military	39	27	30	29	22	29	27	25
Major Military	49	37	41	41	23	36	36	28
Energy Producing	34	24	26	27	47	55	51	46
London Suburbs	46	31	27	28	40	56	56	46
Energy/Unemployment	30	20	23	21	56	64	59	54
Rural/Energy	39	27	26	27	20	25	26	23
TOTAL	43	31	33	33	35	44	42	36
TV	40	33	35	38	47	44	42	37

	Liberal Democrat				Turnout			
	92	97	01	05	92	97	01	05
Cities with Immigrants	12	12	13	19	73	65	53	56
Deprived Inner City	11	10	12	18	65	58	44	46
Manufacturing	13	12	14	17	78	72	57	60
Middle Britain	15	12	13	17	79	73	60	61
Higher Status	21	18	18	20	82	76	64	66
White-Collar	23	23	25	28	79	75	63	66
Low Status	12	11	13	19	75	68	55	56
Inner London High Status	15	16	20	26	74	68	56	60
White-Collar Towns	25	25	27	28	82	76	64	67
Slightly Deprived	14	13	16	24	73	67	53	55
Rural	29	27	26	28	80	75	65	66
Military	23	22	22	26	80	74	63	64
Retirement	26	25	24	26	79	74	63	65
Deprived/Immigrant	17	13	17	22	64	59	48	51
Rural/Military	27	26	27	31	77	73	63	65
Major Military	19	14	14	18	77	71	60	60
Energy Producing	14	13	16	20	79	72	59	60
London Suburbs	12	9	12	21	73	68	55	60
Energy/Unemployment	12	11	14	17	76	70	56	57
Rural/Energy	23	25	26	32	73	71	59	61
TOTAL	18	17	19	23	77	72	59	61
TV	18	18	15	15	18	18	21	21

Notes: Percentage of votes cast for the three main British parties and turnout (percentage of registered electors who voted). The constituency types are defined and listed in the paper referred to in endnote 10. Source: Calculated from data in the British Parliamentary Constituency Database 1992–2005.

areas (possibly reflecting a fall in support among Muslim communities because of their opposition to the Iraq war), by ten points in 'London Suburbs', and by nine in 'Deprived Inner City' areas. The Liberal Democrats, on the other hand, obtained a nine-point increase in their share in the 'London Suburbs', compared to four points overall, and an eight-point increase in 'Slightly Deprived' areas (where Labour experienced an 8-point drop). There was much less variation around the Conservatives' static situation across Britain as a whole, on the other hand, with 11 of the 20 constituency types showing either no change or a one-point shift only: the largest increase was four points in the 'Military' group and the largest decline three points in the 'Cities with Immigrants' category. The small increase in turnout was similar across most types, with none experiencing a decline: the largest increase was five points in the 'London Suburbs' where, as discussed below, a considerable number of seats changed hands.

Table 2 shows greater variation across constituency types than does Table 1 for regions. The types are not evenly distributed across the regions, however. At the first three of the elections, of the 18 'Deprived, Inner City', constituencies, for example, eight were in the Northwest region and six in Scotland,[12] with six regions having none of that type at all; similarly, of the 54 'Retirement' constituencies, 19 were in the Southeast, 14 in the Southwest, and eight in Wales. Given this uneven distribution, do the variations in Table 1 merely reflect differences in the types of constituencies found in each region?

To answer this question, we undertook statistical analyses which separated out the relative importance of constituency type and regional location in accounting for variations across constituencies in support for the three main parties and turnout.[13] The first analysis identified the amount of variation accountable by the constituency classification alone; the second added the regional division. The difference between the two is the independent 'Regional Effect'.

Although there is always a regional effect, it is small relative to the classification effect at all four elections (Table 3). Regional variations in British voting behaviour are largely the consequence of different types of places—and hence different types of people—being concentrated in different parts of the country. This is especially the case for Labour voting, turnout and, to a lesser extent, Liberal Democrat voting. Only the

3. Percentage of Variation in Votes and Turnout Accounted for by the Classification of Constituencies into Types and by Region, 1992–2005

	Conservative				Labour			
	92	97	01	05	92	97	01	05
Classification Alone	58	59	54	59	67	62	60	61
Classification and Region	74	73	71	71	73	68	64	65
Regional Effect	16	14	17	12	6	6	4	4

	Liberal Democrat				Turnout			
	92	97	01	05	92	97	01	05
Classification Alone	33	29	21	16	53	55	55	55
Classification and Region	46	39	29	24	59	60	61	59
Regional Effect	7	10	8	8	6	5	6	4

Note: The constituency types are defined and listed in the paper referred to in endnote 10. Source: Calculated from data in the British Parliamentary Constituency Database 1992–2005.

pattern of Conservative voting shows a substantial independent regional effect, which declined considerably between 2001 and 2005: the party is somewhat stronger in some regions than others, irrespective of the type of places there. Even so, the regional effect is less than one-third of the classification effect.

Regions, places and the geography of representation

A substantial body of research has shown very significant disproportionality in the translation of votes into seats at UK general elections, with the largest party almost invariably getting a disproportionate share of the seats.[14] Given the observed variations in support for the various parties, such disproportionality can be identified in each region and constituency type.

Table 4 shows that in 1992 the Conservative party predominated by winning the great majority of seats in three regions (Southeast, East Anglia and Southwest), even though it only won a bare majority of the votes cast in the first two and less than half in the third. Conversely, a further three regions (North, Wales and Scotland) sent a predominance of Labour MPs to Westminster. The other five regions had more 'balanced' delegations.

4. The Distribution of Seats Won by Political Parties, by Region, 1992–2005

Region	1992 C	1992 L	1992 LD	1997 C	1997 L	1997 LD
Southeast	112	5	0	73	36	8
East Anglia	19	3	0	14	8	0
Greater London	41	32	1	11	57	6
Southwest	39	6	6	22	15	14
West Midlands	31	28	0	14	43	1
East Midlands	30	14	0	14	30	0
Yorkshire/Humberside	22	34	0	7	47	2
Northwest	24	45	1	7	60	2
North	6	29	1	3	32	1
Wales	8	27	1	0	34	2
Scotland	10	50	9	0	56	10
TOTAL	342	273	19	165	418	46

Region	2001 C	2001 L	2001 LD	2005 C	2005 L	2005 LD
Southeast	73	35	9	83	27	7
East Anglia	14	7	1	15	5	2
Greater London	13	55	6	21	44	8
Southwest	20	16	15	22	13	16
West Midlands	13	43	2	15	39	3
East Midlands	15	29	0	18	26	0
Yorkshire/Humberside	7	47	2	9	44	3
Northwest	7	59	4	8	56	6
North	3	32	1	2	32	2
Wales	0	34	2	3	29	4
Scotland	1	56	10	1	40	11
TOTAL	166	413	52	197	355	62

Source: Calculated from data in the British Parliamentary Constituency Database 1992–2005.

Five years later, the regional imbalance was much greater. Only three regions (Southeast, East Anglia and Southwest) sent more Conservative than Labour MPs to Westminster, although each had a substantial increase in the size of its Labour delegation. Labour, meanwhile, predominated in the five northern regions, in only one of which it gained more than 55% of the votes cast (Table 1), and it had a substantial majority of MPs from the Midlands' regions and Greater London. Indeed, whereas its share of the votes in London increased from 37% to 49%, its share of the 74 seats went from 43% to 77%: an 8 percentage points increase in vote share was translated into a 34 point increase in seats won. There was virtually no change between 1997 and 2001.

The greatest changes in seat shares between 2001 and 2005 were in the Southeast and Greater London, where Labour support was substantially eroded and the Conservative vote share increased slightly. In Greater London, for example, a drop of seven points in Labour's vote share produced a net loss of 11 of the region's 74 seats (15% of the total): the Conservatives, on the other hand, had a net increase of eight seats (11% of the total) with only a 2 percentage point increase in their vote share. Similar exaggerated change occurred in the Southeast region, with the Conservatives increasing their vote share by two percentage points but gaining a net increase of ten seats (8.5% of the total of 117). Elsewhere, with the exception of the North, Labour suffered net losses of two to five seats in each region and the Conservatives had net gains of one to three seats. The Liberal Democrats increased their tally in all but two regions—the East Midlands, where they still have no representatives, and the Southeast, where they suffered a net loss of two. Their main gains were in their 'heartland' region of the Southwest, where all six of Cornwall's constituencies now return a Liberal Democrat MP.

In Wales, the Conservatives won three seats, having held none there since 1997, despite no increase in their vote share. Plaid Cymru lost one and Labour's five losses included one to an independent. In Scotland, Labour's share of the new set of 59 constituencies fell to 68% of the total, compared to 78% of the 72 contested in 2001: both the Liberal Democrats and the SNP increased their absolute as well as relative seat shares, despite the overall reduction in numbers. Comparison of the 2005 results with the estimated 2001 outcome in the new constituencies shows that Labour 'lost' five of the 45 it was expected to win, one to the Conservatives and two each to the Liberal Democrats and the SNP.[15] Northern Scotland is now dominated by the Liberal Democrats and the SNP, with Labour holding just three of the seats—two in Aberdeen and one in Dundee. (The Liberal Democrats' extra Scottish seats were won on the back of a rise in their vote share—up by 6.3 points to 22.6% in 2005, making them Scotland's second party—whereas the SNP increased its representation despite a fall in support—down 2.4 points to 17.7%.) In Wales, too, Labour is being pushed back into the old industrial areas of the south and northeast, with the more rural areas returning either Plaid Cymru, Liberal Democrat or Conservative MPs (with the three Tories representing more 'English' parts of the country).

Table 5 shows representation by constituency type rather than region and again suggests much greater polarisation by the former than the latter. In 1992, for example, only five types sent a delegation to the House of Commons which was not dominated by a single party—the 'Manufac-

5. The Distribution of Seats Won by Political Parties, by Constituency, 1992–2005

	1992			1997		
	C	L	LD	C	L	LD
Cities with Immigrants	0	23	1	0	23	0
Deprived Inner City	0	18	0	0	18	0
Manufacturing	23	55	0	3	75	0
Middle Britain	47	9	0	11	45	0
Higher Status	38	1	1	16	21	3
White-Collar	59	5	1	39	18	7
Low Status	2	73	0	0	75	0
Inner London High Status	9	6	0	2	12	1
White-Collar Towns	28	0	0	23	1	4
Slightly Deprived	2	15	0	0	17	0
Rural	33	0	0	27	5	10
Military	15	2	0	14	2	1
Retirement	49	4	1	25	23	6
Deprived/Immigrant	0	17	1	0	17	1
Rural/Military	14	4	7	5	8	10
Major Military	3	1	0	3	1	0
Energy Producing	9	25	0	2	32	0
London Suburbs	8	4	0	0	12	0
Energy/Unemployment	1	10	0	0	11	0
Rural/Energy	2	1	2	0	2	3
TOTAL	342	273	19	165	418	46
	2001			2005		
	C	L	LD	C	L	LD
Cities with Immigrants	0	24	0	0	24	1
Deprived Inner City	0	18	0	0	15	0
Manufacturing	3	75	0	3	76	0
Middle Britain	11	44	0	16	36	1
Higher Status	17	19	4	25	11	4
White-Collar	39	17	9	42	10	12
Low Status	0	75	0	0	69	1
Inner London High Status	2	12	1	5	7	3
White-Collar Towns	22	1	5	24	0	4
Slightly Deprived	0	17	0	0	16	1
Rural	23	4	10	27	2	8
Military	14	2	1	14	0	1
Retirement	25	23	6	30	16	7
Deprived/Immigrant	0	17	1	0	16	1
Rural/Military	4	9	11	4	7	13
Major Military	3	1	0	3	1	0
Energy Producing	3	30	1	3	27	1
London Suburbs	0	12	0	1	10	1
Energy/Unemployment	0	11	0	0	11	0
Rural/Energy	0	2	3	0	1	3
TOTAL	166	413	52	197	355	62

Note: The constituency types are defined and listed in the paper referred to in endnote 10. Source: Calculated from data in the British Parliamentary Constituency Database 1992–2005.

turing', 'Inner London High Status', 'London Suburbs', 'Rural/Military', and 'Rural/Energy' types. (In the last two this was largely because they returned either Liberal Democrat and/or Plaid Cymru or SNP MPs.) Five years later, this polarisation was even more pronounced in most types, in several because of a massive switch of seats from Conservative to Labour. The 'Manufacturing' category, for example, experienced a net switch of 20 seats to Labour, consequent on a net nine percentage point increase in its vote share. In other types, the delegation became more 'balanced' as a result of shifts to Labour: in 1992, for example, the Conservatives won 38 of the 40 'High Status' seats, but lost 22 of them to either Labour or the Liberal Democrats in 1997; similarly the Conservatives won 49 of the 54 'Retirement' constituencies in 1992, but only 25 at the next election. As with the regional distribution, the pattern in 2001 was virtually the same.

The 2005 election saw substantial changes to the delegations from some constituency types. (Recall that the number of constituencies in several of the types changed because of the reduction in Scotland's seats.) Five types experienced most change: the 'Middle Britain', 'Higher Status', 'White Collar', 'Inner London High Status', and 'Retirement' categories, where Labour won 115 seats in 2001 but only 80 four years later. (The Conservatives won 94 and 118 seats there at the two elections respectively.) The Conservatives won back seats in many of their traditional 'heartlands', therefore, but not to the level of 1992 when they won 202 seats in those five types and Labour only 25. Further, all of the Conservatives' lost ground was not partially recovered in every type: in 1992, for example, they won 23 of the 78 'Manufacturing' seats, but only three of them in 2005; they also won 14 of the 'Rural/Military' seats at the first of the four elections, but only four of them in 2001 and 2005, with the Liberal Democrats becoming the dominant party in that type.

Tables 4–5 suggest much greater polarisation of representation by constituency type than by region, which can be evaluated as with the tests for voting polarisation.[16] For all three parties, the independent regional effect is small relative to that for constituency classification (Table 6). Once constituency type is known, the additional information

6. Percentage of Variation in Representation Accounted for by the Classification of Constituencies into Types and by Region

	Conservative				Labour			
	92	97	01	05	92	97	01	05
Classification Alone	56	37	36	43	61	50	51	54
Classification and Region	62	43	43	48	64	53	53	55
Regional Effect	6	6	10	5	3	3	2	1

	Liberal Democrat			
	92	97	01	05
Classification Alone	12	13	13	13
Classification and Region	15	17	16	16
Regional Effect	5	4	3	3

Note: The constituency types are defined and listed in the paper referred to in endnote 10. Source: Calculated from data in the British Parliamentary Constituency Database 1992–2005.

provided by knowledge of regional location has very little impact on predicting whether a seat has a Conservative, Labour or Liberal Democrat MP at any election. In general terms constituency type is best at predicting whether a seat returns a Labour MP—i.e. they are most polarised in terms of the types of constituencies they represent—and least successful at predicting whether it has a Liberal Democrat MP.

Northern Ireland

The predominant determinant of voting behaviour in Northern Ireland is culture, with the main split between those of Roman Catholic background who tend to support 'Nationalist' parties, which favour association with the Republic of Ireland, and Protestants, who back the 'Loyalist' parties committed to membership of the United Kingdom. Geographically, this split is reflected by a northeast-southwest divide: the Nationalist parties are strongest in the dominantly Roman Catholic areas of the west and south, as well as in west and south Belfast, whereas Loyalist parties gain most support in the north and east.

These two blocks are deeply entrenched in Northern Ireland voting behaviour. The Loyalist block—dominated by the two Unionist parties (Democratic Unionist—DUP—and Ulster Unionist—UUP)—gained just under half of the votes cast at each of the four elections (Table 7). The Nationalist block (the Social Democratic and Labour Party—SDLP— and Sinn Féin) increased their support between 1992 and 1997 and have since obtained a little over 40% of the votes cast.

There have been considerable changes within the two party groups over the period, however, notably after 1997. Within the Loyalist block, the DUP vote has increased very substantially. At the 2001 general election it obtained 21% of the votes, as against the UUP's 23%; it overtook the UUP in the voting for the Northern Ireland Assembly in 2003 (winning 26% to the UUP's 23%) and in 2004 won almost twice as many votes as its opponent in the European Parliament Election (32% as against 17% for the UUP). The Nationalist block has seen a similar switch, with Sinn Féin overtaking the SDLP at the 2001 general election, obtaining a 6.5 percentage point advantage in the 2003

7. Percentage of Total Votes Cast and Seats Won at General Elections in Northern Ireland, 1992–2005

		DUP	UUP	All	SDLP	SF
1992	Votes	13.1	34.5	8.7	23.5	10.0
	Seats	3	9	0	4	0
1997	Votes	13.6	32.7	8.0	24.1	16.1
	Seats	2	10	0	3	2
2001	Votes	22.5	26.8	3.6	21.0	21.7
	Seats	5	6	0	3	4
2005	Votes	33.7	17.7	3.9	17.5	24.3
	Seats	9	1	0	3	5

Note: DUP—Democratic Unionist Party; UUP—Ulster Unionist Party; All—Alliance; SDLP—Social Democratic and Labour Party; SF—Sinn Féin. Source: Calculated from data available on http://www.ark.ac.uk/elections/.

Assembly elections and a lead of 10.4 points a year later at the European election. (At the 1999 European election, the SDLP had a similar lead over Sinn Féin.) At the 2005 election, Sinn Féin had a 7-point lead over the SDLP.

These shifts in support within each of the two blocks are reflected in the pattern of representation. The extra seat created before the 1997 election went to the Nationalists, and in 2001 Sinn Féin won an additional two, giving it a majority within that community which it sustained in 2005. Within the Loyalist camp there was a very significant shift away from the UUP, which lost five of the six seats it won in 2001. Four went to the DUP (including Lagan Valley, where the UUP MP defected to the DUP in 2004), which also experienced large increases in electoral support in the five seats that it already held—in all but one case at the UUP's expense (both experienced an increase in East Belfast).

The UUP's fifth loss, in South Belfast, went to the SDLP. The UUP and DUP together won 51% of the votes cast there, but these were split relatively evenly between the two, allowing the SDLP candidate to win with less than one-third of the votes: the Sinn Féin candidate finished a poor fourth. Given the geography of religious affiliation in Northern Ireland, most of the constituencies have such a large majority from one side only of the Protestant/Roman Catholic divide that a victory for a candidate from the other block is very unlikely, however.

From disproportionality to bias

As discussed in the book's introduction, and in Chapter 13, British general elections invariably produce disproportional outcomes, with each party's share of the seats incommensurate with its share of the votes; the 2005 election was no different with Labour having a three percentage point lead over the Conservatives in vote share but a 25-point lead in the allocation of seats. The elections also tend to produce biased outcomes, with the degree of disproportion varying between the two main parties. The degree of bias, measured as the difference in the number of seats the two main parties would obtain if they had equal shares of the votes, has increasingly favoured Labour. If it and the Conservatives had obtained equal vote shares in 2001, Labour would have had 140 more seats than its opponent.[17] In 2005 that was reduced somewhat: if Labour and the Conservatives had each won 34.7% of the votes cast, with Labour 'losing' 1.5 percentage points of its votes in each constituency and these being 're-allocated' to the Conservatives, Labour would have won 334 seats and the Conservatives only 222—a difference (or bias) of 112 seats with equal shares of the votes.[18] Much of that bias is the result of Labour winning in constituencies with fewer registered voters and, especially, lower turnouts than the Conservatives—those with relatively small electorates and relatively large abstention rates. In addition it is a consequence of its votes being more efficiently distributed: Labour has fewer surplus votes (i.e. more than the number needed for victory over the second-placed party) in the constituencies that it wins than does the Conservative party.

Conclusion

Great Britain has a long-established regional geography to its voting patterns—the 'north-south divide': the 'north' is more pro-Labour and the 'south' more pro-Conservative. Each party gets around 30% more of the votes in its favoured regions than it does elsewhere. This was the case at each of the last four elections, despite considerable shifts in the two parties' relative popularity. As their support has waxed and waned, regional variation has remained constant.

The divide's existence suggests important inter-regional differences in political cultures, with similar types of people voting differently in different regions because of socialisation into local attitudes and values and the strength of the parties' mobilising activities. If we look at constituency types defined according to population characteristics, however, we find much greater variations in support for the main political parties. Furthermore, analysis of constituency type and regional variations together finds that the former accounts for much more of the variation than the latter. The observed regional variation in voting for Great Britain's three main political parties is very much a function of different types of constituency being concentrated in different regions. Some of those types have been the main battlegrounds between the parties, especially at the 2005 election when most of the Conservative gains at Labour's expense occurred in just five types, and thus in the regions where they were concentrated—Southeast and Greater London.

Different types of constituency, concentrated in different regions, return MPs from different parties, producing polarised geographies of representation. Labour won all of the seats in four of the types in 1997, for example, despite winning only between 59% and 70% of the votes there. As discussed by Dunleavy and Margetts in this volume, this disproportionality in representation relative to voter support has been accentuated at each of the 1997, 2001 and 2005 elections: Labour won many more seats than the Conservatives would have done with the same vote share.

Although consistency is the major characteristic of the overall pattern of regional and constituency type variation in voting and representation across the four most recent general elections, there have been changes within that pattern, mainly associated with the Liberal Democrats. Outside their southwest England heartland, where they won about a third of the votes at each election, there was a clear north-south divide in support in 1992 and 1997. This closed somewhat over the subsequent two elections, as the party increased its vote share and representation in several northern regions, including Scotland: by 2005, only the two Midlands regions provided the party with substantially lower levels of support—and just one seat.

The main change in political complexion for a UK region occurred in Northern Ireland. The southwest-northeast regional divide in support for and representation by Nationalist and Loyalist parties remained in place, but within each there was a major shift. Sinn Féin more than doubled its share of the votes cast across the four elections within the Nationalist block, gaining five seats in 2005 as against none in 1992. The SDLP lost votes as a consequence, but only one seat. Within the Loyalist block, the DUP increased its share of the vote to the same extent as Sinn Féin and tripled its number of MPs: the UUP, on the other hand, saw its share of the votes halved and its Parliamentary delegation reduced from nine to one. Within the continuity of a fixed regional pattern—as in Great Britain—there was much more variability in the fortunes of individual parties.

1   R.J. Johnston, C.J. Pattie and J.G. Allsopp, *A Nation Dividing?*, Longman, 1988; J. Curtice and M. Steed, 'Electoral Choice and the Production of Government: The Changing Operation of the Electoral System in the United Kingdom since 1955', 12 *British Journal of Political Science* 1982, 249–98. See also W.H. Field, *Regional Dynamics: the Basis of Electoral Support in Britain*, Frank Cass, 1997.
2   I. McAllister and D.T. Studlar, 'Region and Voting in Britain 1979–87: Territorial Polarization or Artifact?', 36 *American Journal of Political Science*, 1992, 168–99.
3   J. Curtice and A. Park, 'Region: New Labour, New Geography?' in G. Evans and P. Norris (eds), *Critical Elections: British Parties and Voters in Long-Term Perspective*, Sage, 1988, pp. 124–47.
4   D.J. Rossiter, R.J. Johnston and C.J. Pattie, *The Boundary Commissions*, Manchester University Press, 1999.
5   The Boundary Commissions for England and Northern Ireland had not completed their work in time for their recommendations to be delivered to the relevant Secretary of State. The Welsh Commission delivered its recommendations to the Deputy Prime Minister on 31 January 2005, but they were not presented to Parliament before it was prorogued and so the 2005 general election was fought in the same constituencies as 2001.
6   C. Rallings and M. Thrasher, *Media Guide to the New Parliamentary Constituencies*, Local Government Chronicle Elections Centre, University of Plymouth, 2005.
7   The percentages for Wales and Scotland are lower than for the other 'northern' regions because of the successes of Plaid Cymru and the SNP, who won 2.2–2.5% of all votes cast at each of the three elections: the SNP won 21.5, 22.1, 20.1 and 17.6% of the votes in Scotland in 1992, 1997, 2001 and 2005 respectively, with Plaid Cymru gaining 8.9, 9.9, 14.3 and 12.6% of the Welsh votes at the four contests respectively.
8   Johnston, Pattie and Allsopp, op. cit.
9   If this study was of the 2005 election alone, then it would have been desirable to produce a new classification using data from the 2001 census. We did not do this for three reasons: (1) at the macro spatial scale of Parliamentary constituencies their relative characteristics change very little over time—the categories will be the same and the membership of each virtually so also; (2) as we are analysing data for four elections stretching back to 1992, the charge of analysing 1992 results using 2001 data could have been levelled just as strongly as that of analysing 2005 results with 1991 data; and (3) because of changes in the available variables an exactly matching data set for the two censuses—allowing two classifications—was not feasible. We believe that the results produced here—in a very short time after the election—are robust.
10 For full details of the classification, see R.J. Johnston, D.J. Rossiter and C.J. Pattie, 'Three Classifications of Great Britain's New Parliamentary Constituencies', *Essex Papers in Politics and Government*, 1997, p. 117. The original research produced three separate classifications: we have chosen that which had the greatest average differentiation between types in the percentages voting for the main parties at each of the elections studied here.
11 For this we used the data in D.T. Denver, C. Rallings and M. Thrasher, *Media Guide to the New Scottish Westminster Parliamentary Constituencies*, Local Government Chronicle Elections Centre, University of Plymouth, 2004. Where all parts of the new constituency were drawn from previous constituencies of the same type, the allocation was clear. For the remainder, we placed them in the type associated with the constituency forming the largest part of the new one.

12 The number in Scotland of this type was reduced to four after the constituency changes.
13 These were Analyses of Variance (ANOVAs). The dependent variables were the percentage support for each party at each election in each constituency and the independents were the two classifications—constituency type and regional location. The statistics reported in Table 3 are the R^2 values modified for degrees of freedom.
14 R.J. Johnston, C.J. Pattie, D.F.L. Dorling and D.J. Rossiter, *From Votes to Seats: The Operation of the UK Electoral System since 1945*, Manchester University Press, 2001.
15 The estimated results of the 2001 election for the new constituencies were produced by Denver, Rallings and Thrasher (see footnote 11).
16 The dependent variable was binary—whether or not the constituency returned an MP from the defined party—and the ANOVA evaluated how well a constituency's representation (whether it had a Conservative MP or not, for example) could be predicted by knowledge of its type and region.
17 R.J. Johnston, D.J. Rossiter, C.J. Pattie and D.F.L. Dorling, 'Labour Electoral Landslides and the Changing Efficiency of Voting Distributions', *Transactions of the Institute of British Geographers*, NS27, 2002, pp. 336–61.
18 After the delayed contest in Staffordshire South (held on 23 June) the bias fell to 111 seats.

PAUL WHITELEY, MARIANNE C. STEWART, DAVID SANDERS
AND HAROLD D. CLARKE

The Issue Agenda and Voting in 2005

The 2005 British general election was a competitive contest. In the preceding 2001 election, Labour had held 'all of the cards'. Presiding over a robust economy, it had the most party identifiers, the most popular leader, and it was judged best on issues deemed important by many voters. Four years later, Labour had been dealt a new, very different hand—Tony Blair's approval ratings had plummeted in the wake of the Iraq war, the number of Labour partisans had fallen substantially, and the Conservatives and Liberal Democrats were poised to challenge Labour on issues that many people thought had been mishandled or neglected. In the event, Labour did secure a third consecutive victory, but a significant loss of votes and seats gave the party faithful little cause for celebration.

In this chapter, we investigate how issues affected electoral choice in 2005. Although issues are at the centre of general election campaigns, there is longstanding disagreement about how they influence voting. Academics, journalists and assorted political pundits frequently adopt a particular view of how issues work. Parties are seen as staking out 'for' and 'against' positions on issues such as Britain's adoption of the Euro, the invasion of Iraq or the trade-off between tax relief and public services spending, and often are criticised for failing to 'capture the middle ground' or 'shift to the centre'. Thus, a common explanation of the Conservatives' electoral misfortunes since 1997 is that they have adopted extremist positions—travelling too far to the right on the ideological spectrum.[1] Now there is a debate about how far the Liberal Democrats are to the left of New Labour.[2]

Despite the popularity of this positional or spatial model in media commentary and academic research, it failed to provide a convincing account of voting in the 2001 general election.[3] There are also grounds for thinking that the positional model fared poorly again in 2005, particularly for explaining support for Labour and the Conservatives. Accordingly, we first examine reasons why an alternative 'valence'

© Oxford University Press 2005
doi: 10.1093/pa/gsi062

model may tell a better story of issue effects on political choice. After discussing the position and valence models, we investigate how they worked in 2005 using data from the British Election Study's (BES) Rolling Campaign Panel Survey (RCPS).[4] The conclusion reprises the major findings and briefly reconsiders how issues affected the election outcome.

Rival models of issue voting

In Anthony Downs' path-breaking study, the basic idea underlying the spatial model of party competition is that voters choose the party closest to them on policies that reflect positions on a left-right ideological continuum.[5] In this way, voters rationally maximise their utility, i.e. the benefits or income that they expect to receive from one party being in government as opposed to another. Downs' best-known theoretical result was that, in a two-party system with a normal distribution of voters along an underlying ideological continuum, parties will locate themselves at the position of the median or 'middlemost' elector to maximise the votes that they receive. Much subsequent research has examined this result and its extensions to multi-party competition in multi-dimensional ideological spaces.

The valence model, originally introduced by Donald Stokes, constitutes the major rival perspective. According to Stokes: 'valence-issues [are] those that merely involve the linking of the parties with some condition that is positively or negatively valued by the electorate'.[6] The key point is that party competition and public issue concerns typically are not about the ends of government action. Rather, they involve competing claims about which party has the means—who is best able to deliver what (virtually) everybody wants. In Britain, voters have been consistently concerned about valence issues. A healthy economy is the classic example, with the vast majority of voters demanding strong economic performance as indexed by high rates of growth coupled with low interest rates, in addition to low inflation and unemployment rates. Non-economic valence issues are also important, and parties are judged by their ability to deliver highly valued public services in areas such as crime, education, health care, and national security.

The valence model contains an important submodel—the issue-priority model—that claims parties benefit differentially from the salience of particular issues. The importance of issue salience may be understood with reference to theories about how parties use issues in elections. As argued by Budge and others, party competition involves attempts to impose rival issue agendas.[7] Parties concentrate on promoting a subset of valence issues that they 'own', or have a marked advantage on, and they ignore other issues, particularly those 'owned' by their rivals. Theoretically, this can be done both with position and valence issues, but the evidence below shows that in practice it done almost entirely with the latter. This is because parties have an advantage if they can get the electorate to concentrate on consensus issues which favour them, rather than position issues over which they may have only a marginal advantage. If a party can pre-empt the issue agenda, it gains a strategic advantage. Because the issues involved typically are valence issues, that advantage can be decisive.

There are several reasons why the valence model may provide a better explanation of issue voting than the spatial model. In his critique of the spatial model, Stokes criticised all of the assumptions underlying the model which he thought were inconsistent with evidence about how voters behave. These assumptions underpin the argument that there is a single, unchanging, ordered left-right dimension along which the parties manoeuvre. In the valence model, there is no ordered, unchanging dimension but, rather, a single point in issue space where the voters want to locate, since that provides the optimal outcome. Thus, the theoretical apparatus defining the valence model is much simpler than the spatial model and really reduces to the question: 'which party will deliver on a consensually valued policy outcome?'

There is an important theoretical connection between the valence and spatial models that is particularly relevant to the 2005 British election. If the Downsian median voter theorem applies to *party strategy*, then the spatial model turns into the valence model. When parties locate themselves at an equilibrium point they, by definition, eliminate any spatial distances between themselves, so voters can no longer choose between them on spatial grounds. In that case, electoral choice becomes a decision about which party can best deliver the equilibrium policy. Thus, in an election in which policy distances between the parties are modest, or one where valence issues dominate, we should observe much more valence voting than spatial voting.

Another important point is Stokes' argument that parties compete in a highly variable, multidimensional and potentially mutable issue space. He writes, '[j]ust as the parties may be perceived and evaluated on several dimensions, so the dimensions that are salient to the electorate may change widely over time'.[8] In essence, Stokes observed that the issue/ideological space becomes contested, rather than being a stable framework within which competition occurs. This insight accords well with the idea of issue priorities: parties try to compete on dimensions most favourable to them and to ignore those that are unfavourable.

In sum, the suggestion is that the spatial model might be less important than the valence model in influencing electoral choice in a variety of contexts. In Britain, there are reasons why the importance of the spatial model has declined over the past decade. One is that policy distances between the main parties have narrowed. Budge *et al.*'s 'Manifesto Project' data document that the three main parties were closer together in their manifesto promises in 2001 than at any other time since 1945.[9] This situation did not change appreciably in 2005. Consequently, one would expect the spatial model to become less relevant over time as 'position politics' is being transformed into 'valence politics' by a lack of spatial variation in the policies offered. If differences between the main parties on a classic position issue like taxation versus public service spending have become relatively trivial, then it would not surprise that the voters do not judge these parties on these issues.

A second consideration involves the possibility that valence issues have more retrospective than prospective content, whereas spatial issues have more of the latter than the former. Valence is about performance; although voters may evaluate valence issues both prospectively and retrospectively, they are likely to put more emphasis on retrospection (performance) rather than prospective thinking (promise) because retrospective thinking enables them to use 'hard' information about parties' (and party leaders') track records. In contrast, spatial issues are about promises and, when deciding how to vote, people must take into account their uncertainties about whether parties and politicians can and will deliver.

This reasoning suggests that spatial issues may become increasingly irrelevant when a governing party has been in power for several years, such as Labour in 2005, since voters can judge it on its record. Is the economy robust? Are cherished public services being delivered? Are the streets safe? Is national security at risk? For opposition parties in this situation, there is no recent track record to go on, and so spatial issues will continue to play a role when people think about voting for them. This is particularly the case for smaller parties such as the Liberal Democrats or the Greens that may not have a national-level government record by which they can be judged.

It is not hard to find examples of valence issues and issue-priority strategies operating in the 2005 election campaign. In his first campaign speech, Michael Howard spoke of 'the smirking politics of Mr. Blair and the woolly thinking of the Liberal Democrats'.[10] This is not the language of spatial issues, but rather an attempt to focus public attention on the untrustworthiness of an unpopular prime minister while branding a rival opposition party as unfit for national power. In response, Tony Blair countered by challenging that the aim of the election was 'to build on the progress made, to accelerate the changes, to widen still further the opportunities available to the British people and above all else to take that hard-worn economic stability, the investment in our public services, and entrench it' (*Guardian*, 6.4.05). Blair's emphasis was entirely on selected aspects of his government's record—on key valence issues relating to economic performance and public service delivery.

The Conservatives also recognised the importance of valence issues and issue-priorities. Accordingly, they concentrated on what they defined as security issues, principally crime, asylum-seekers, and immigration, and largely avoided Labour's strong card, the economy (*Guardian*, 11.4.05). Before the campaign began, it appeared that

Labour might play into the Tories' hand by marginalising Chancellor of the Exchequer Gordon Brown, widely lionised as the architect of Britain's economic prosperity. With polls showing their party's support flagging, however, Labour strategists decided to 'bring Gordon back'. By putting Brown in the spotlight beside Tony Blair, Labour dramatised its 'ace' issue priority—the economy. The Conservative and Labour campaign strategies thus provide excellent examples of issue-priority politics—where the contest involves trying to set the content of a valence politics agenda rather than debating the pros and cons of contentious position issues.

Issues and voting in 2005

To evaluate the role of issues in 2005, we specify indicators of the spatial and valence models and estimate their effects in multivariate models of electoral choice for the three main British parties. For this purpose, we use data from the British Election Study Rolling Campaign Panel Survey. The first wave of this survey was conducted just before the campaign began; the second, during the campaign; and the third, immediately after polling day. In the following analyses, the dependent variable—vote choice for the three main parties—is measured using the post-election data, and independent variables are measured using pre-election data.[11]

The spatial model is tested using three position issues: Britain's relationship with the European Union, taxation versus public spending, and combating crime versus defending the rights of the accused. Regarding the former, although Britain's relationship with the EU was not prominent in the election, the parties nonetheless took distinctive stances on the issue. For the most part, these were extensions of longstanding positions and should have been readily apparent to voters. The Conservatives were committed to rejecting the European constitution outright in the referendum promised by Labour. The Liberal Democrats and Labour favoured the constitution, although the former party has been consistently more supportive of European integration than the latter. Clearly, 'Europe' had potential to be an important position issue since it divided the government and the main opposition parties.

Positions on the issue are measured using an 11-point scale anchored at zero by the phrase '*Britain should definitely get out of the EU*', and at ten by the phrase '*Britain should definitely stay in the EU*'. Respondents were requested to locate themselves on the scale. Their average score was 5.2. When asked to score the three major parties, they assigned average scores to Labour, the Conservatives, and Liberal Democrats of 7.6, 4.3, and 6.9, respectively. Thus, Labour was viewed as slightly more supportive of the European Union than the Liberal Democrats, and a great deal more supportive than the Conservatives.

The second position issue was taxation versus public spending as measured by a similar question. The zero point of the scale was labelled as '*government should cut taxes a lot and spend much less on health and social services*', and the ten point was labelled as '*government should raise taxes a lot and spend much more on health and social services*'. The average self-assigned score was 5.5, and average scores for Labour, the Conservatives, and Liberal Democrats were 6.6, 4.1, and 6.7, respectively. These numbers suggest that, in the public mind, real policy differences existed between the governing and the main opposition party. Interestingly, the Liberal Democrats' widely publicised policy of raising income tax for affluent tax-payers did not separate them significantly from Labour.

The third position issue was combating crime versus defending the rights of the accused. Respondents were presented with a zero to ten scale and asked: '*Some people think that reducing crime is more important than protecting the rights of people accused of committing crimes. Other people think that protecting the rights of the accused is more important than reducing crime. On the 0–10 scale below, where would you place your own view?*' In this case, respondents gave themselves an average score of 2.3, and Labour, the Conservatives, and the Liberal Democrats average scores of 5.4, 3.2, and 5.6, respectively. Like Europe, but unlike taxation, the Conservatives were closer to the position of the average voter than Labour or the Liberal Democrats.

These position issues were incorporated into the voting models by combining them into three additive indices—one for Labour, one for the Conservatives, and one for the Liberal Democrats. Each of these indices measures how close a respondent is to the party in question on each of the three position issue scales (stay in-get out of EU, decrease taxes-spend more, fight crime-rights of accused). Since each issue-position scale ranges from zero to ten, each index ranges from zero to 30. Smaller scores on an index indicate respondents are positioned close to a party and larger ones indicate respondents are positioned distant from a party.[12]

Turning to valence issues, these were measured with three sets of items. First are voters' evaluations of national and personal economic performance. As shown in Table 1, substantial minorities offered negative evaluations, and in no case did more than one-quarter indicate that they thought conditions would improve in the future. There were also sizable minorities, however, ranging from 33 to 40%, who believed that things would remain the same. In the context of a relatively buoyant economy

1. Economic Evaluations, 2005

Economic Evaluations	Lot Worse	Little Worse	Same	Little Better	Lot Better
Personal economic conditions over past year	13	32	33	19	3
National economic conditions over past year	8	33	37	21	2
Personal economic conditions over next year	10	31	34	22	3
National economic conditions over next year	8	31	40	21	1

Note: Horizontal percentages. Source: 2005 BES Rolling Campaign Panel Survey, pre-campaign wave (weighted N = 7862)

such as Britain enjoyed in 2005, these latter responses can be interpreted as indicators of economic optimism.

The economic evaluations were supplemented by a measure of emotional reactions to the economy. Respondents were asked to select from a list of eight words to describe how they felt. As Figure 1 indicates, the most frequently reported feeling (45%) was uneasiness, but another large group (38%) described themselves as hopeful. Approximately 20% said they were confident or afraid, and from 7 to 13% indicated they were proud, disgusted, happy, or angry. Creating two summary indices by counting positive feelings (proud, confident, hopeful, happy) and negative ones (afraid, uneasy, disgusted, angry) reveals a virtually even balance of emotional reactions. Overall, 48% selected one or more positive words to describe their feelings about the economy, and 50% chose one or more negative words.

A third measure of valence issues uses questions about government performance in several policy areas. These include the economy, the NHS, asylum seekers, crime, education, railways, pensions and terrorism. Figure 2 displays percentages judging that the Labour government had handled each of these issues 'very' or 'fairly' well and percentages who thought a Conservative government would perform 'very' or 'fairly' well. Labour had an edge on five of the seven issues, although apart from the economy, the advantages were not large. For their part, the Conservatives had a substantial lead on asylum-seekers and modest ones on crime and pensions. Perhaps the larger story is the strong tendency

1. Emotional Reactions to the Economy in 2005

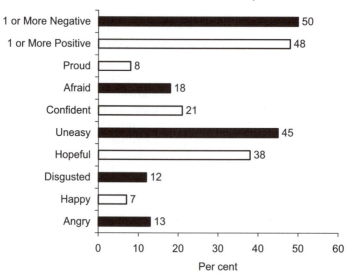

(weighted N=7862)
Source: 2005 BES Rolling Campaign Panel Survey, pre-campaign wave.

2. **Issue Performance Evaluations of Labour and the Conservatives in 2005**

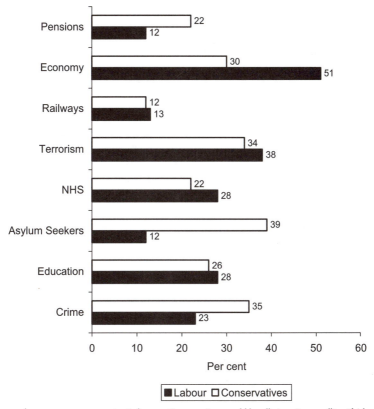

Note: numbers are percentages saying Labour or Conservatives would handle issue 'very well' or 'fairly well'.
(weighted N = 7862)
Source: 2005 BES Rolling Campaign Panel Survey, pre-campaign wave.

to report uncertainty about issue performance or to claim that neither party would do a good job. Only on the economy does even a slight majority (51%) state that a party (Labour) would perform well. Overall, the average percentage offering a positive endorsement is only 27%.

To measure issue salience, we use an open-ended question about the most important issue facing the country. A follow-up question asked which party was best able to handle this issue. The results are summarised in Table 2. Responses to the first question were diverse, with only one issue (asylum seekers/immigration) being mentioned by more than 20% and only two others (crime, NHS) being mentioned by more than 10%. Two more general points are noteworthy. First, a complex of issues that had been largely absent in 2001 was prominent in 2005. Altogether, 41% mentioned asylum/immigration, crime, or terrorism. Second, valence, not position, issues dominated the issue agenda. Position issues that have occasioned sharp debate among parties, pundits,

2. Most Important Issue Facing Country and Party Best Able to Handle It, 2005

Party Best Able to Handle Issue †

Most Important Issue	Labour	Conservatives	Liberal Democrats	Other	D.K. None	Total Citing Issue‡
Asylum Seekers/ Immigration	10	**42**	3	19	27	23
Crime	20	35	6	2	37	14
National Health Service	36	15	10	2	37	14
Economy General/ Unemployment	54	18	5	3	21	9
Education	31	11	25	1	32	4
Taxation	9	39	18	4	30	4
Terrorism	43	15	2	3	38	4
Political Pathologies	2	27	20	10	41	3
Europe/Euro	13	34	8	33	13	2
Environment	9	0	9	62	18	2
Housing Prices/Cost of Living	22	6	12	3	57	2
Iraq War	10	13	35	7	35	2
Social Pathologies	27	14	17	7	35	2
Public Services	35	22	12	4	27	2
Tony Blair's Leadership	8	45	19	5	24	2
Civil Liberties	3	20	53	5	20	1
Values/Morality	6	16	13	9	56	1
Miscellaneous Other Issues	27	15	12	7	40	8
Not Sure/Don't Know	9	4	3	2	82	2
Party Preference All Most Important Issues	23	26	9	9	33	

Note: †—horizontal percentages; ‡—vertical percentages; Boldface percentages indicate party favoured by plurality of electorate on an issue. Source: 2005 BES Rolling Campaign Panel Survey, campaign wave (weighted N = 6119).

and public, such as Europe, the Iraq War, taxation, and civil liberties, were seldom top priorities. Altogether, less than 10% cited any of these issues as most important.

When interpreting Table 2, it bears emphasis that simply because voters cite an issue as 'most important' does not mean that they believe all other issues are *unimportant*. Data gathered in national monthly surveys conducted between April 2004 and March 2005 make the point.[13] For example, in the March survey, mean scores on zero (low importance) to ten (high importance) scales for the economy, asylum seekers, terrorism, and the NHS were very similar—7.8, 7.6, 8.3, and 8.6, respectively. Parties thus had good reason to emphasise one or more of these issues if they thought the issue(s) would work to their advantage. The economy, which Labour believed was likely to be the party's strongest card, is a case in point. Although Table 2 reveals that only 11% cited unemployment, inflation, or the economy generally as the most important issue facing the country, 61% of people interviewed in the March 2005 survey ranked the economy as equally important as or more important than crime, and 65% did so for asylum seekers. Taken together with the data in Table 2, these numbers from earlier surveys suggest that the economy had strong, but not fully realised, potential to shape the 2005 issue agenda.

In this regard, Table 2 shows the party the BES survey respondents judged to be best able to handle various most important issues. Labour did indeed have a large edge on the economy as well as on public services, particularly the NHS. Perhaps less predictable was the party's lead among those citing terrorism. As for the Conservatives, in addition to being favoured by people dissatisfied with Tony Blair's performance, the Tories had large leads on two issues—immigration and crime. They also had advantages on two other issues—Europe and taxation. Again, the April 2004-March 2005 survey data show that the Conservatives had enjoyed advantages on these four issues for several months before the campaign began. Emphasising them during the campaign thus made good sense for Mr. Howard and his colleagues—these issues were ones on which the party was likely to attract voters. For their part, the Liberal Democrats enjoyed strong support on civil liberties and the Iraq War. Unfortunately for them, these issues were chosen as most important by only 3% of the electorate, although, as discussed below, Iraq did become quite salient in the latter part of the campaign.

Overall, no party had a commanding lead on the most important issues, with 26% favouring the Conservatives, 23% favouring Labour, and 9% favouring the Liberal Democrats. This was a very different distribution than in 2001, when fully 39% of the BES respondents chose Labour, and only 14% and 7%, respectively, supported the Conservatives and Liberal Democrats. What *was* similar to 2001 was the fact that no party was able to dominate the issue agenda. In 2001, fully 38% had said that no party was best equipped to handle the most important issue or that there were no important issues. The 2001 figure was only slightly less, at 33%.

The different issue variables are used to investigate how position and valence issues affected voting in 2005. As indicated, the effects of position issues are assessed using three summary indices that measure the proximity of voters to the three main political parties on the issues of membership in the EU, taxation-public spending, and crime-rights of accused dimensions. We also include a variable measuring support for or opposition to Britain's involvement in Iraq.[14] Although Iraq was cited as most important by relatively few respondents, the Blair government's decision to join the US-led invasion was a classic, and highly contentious, position issue that had received enormous publicity throughout much of the 2001–05 period. During the election campaign, the issue was revived when Howard openly accused Blair of lying to the British public and, after several leaks on the matter had occurred, Downing Street was forced to publish advice it had received on the legality of the war.

Assessments of Labour's performance on valence issues are measured with a factor-score variable generated by a principal components analysis of economic evaluations, emotional reactions to the economy, and judgments about how the party had handled several other issues.[15] This analysis produced two factors—one for the economy and one for public services. Similarly, a factor-score variable is generated to measure assessments of how the Conservatives would handle various valence issues.[16] Issue-priority effects are assessed using dummy variables that delineate the party best able to handle most important issues.

We specify a multivariate model that includes the issue variables just described. To evaluate accurately the relative importance of position and valence issues, the model includes controls for leader images, partisanship, and socio-demographic characteristics. Partisanship is measured using dummy variables based on responses to the standard BES party identification question. Party leader images are summarised using eleven-point dislike-like scales. Socio-demographic variables include age, education, ethnicity, gender, home ownership, occupational status, and work sector. Two variants of the model are analysed. In the first, voting for the governing Labour Party is contrasted with voting for the opposition parties. In the second, voting for the Conservatives, Liberal Democrats, or all other parties is considered, with Labour voting treated as a reference category.

Models of electoral choice

Binomial logistic regression estimates of the Labour versus other party voting model reveal that partisanship and leader affect have highly significant effects and that all coefficients are correctly signed (see Table 3, Panel A). Regarding valence issues, the variables measuring economic evaluations-emotional reactions to the economy and Labour's handling of non-economic policy areas have expected positive effects. As also anticipated, evaluations of how the Conservatives would handle various policy areas have significant negative effects. Again, all issue-priority variables measuring party preferred on most important (largely valence) issues are statistically significant and properly signed. Only one of the three position-issue indices achieves significance, namely perceptions of proximity to Labour influences the likelihood of casting a ballot for the party. Similarly, opinions about British involvement in Iraq did not have a significant effect.

Table 3, Panel B contains multinomial logistic regression estimates for the opposition party voting model. Leader and partisanship variables again are important, although there are some interesting differences between the parties. Feelings about Charles Kennedy have no impact on Conservative voting, and feelings about Michael Howard have no effect on the Liberal Democrat voting. In contrast, feelings about Tony Blair influence voting for all opposition parties.

Regarding issues, opinions about Iraq influence Liberal Democrat voting in a predictable way (opponents of involvement were more likely to vote for the party) but do not affect Conservative or 'other' party voting. Also, spatial variables have some significant effects. Proximities to the Conservative and Liberal Democrat parties influence Conservative

3. Models of Electoral Choice

Predictor Variables	Panel A Labour v. non-Labour vote	s.e.	Conservative	s.e	Panel B Liberal Democrat	s.e.	Other	s.e.
Party Identification:								
Conservative	−1.09***	.21	1.05***	.23	0.03	.25	0.47	.29
Labour	1.28***	.12	−2.16***	.22	−1.10***	.13	−1.20***	.21
Liberal-Democrat	−0.96***	.18	−0.08	.26	1.19***	.18	−0.35	.31
Other Party	−0.82***	.21	−0.58*	.29	0.26	.23	1.90***	.24
Party Leader Affect:								
Blair	0.25***	.02	−0.31***	.03	−0.22***	.02	−0.25***	.03
Howard	−0.07**	.03	0.29***	.04	−0.01	.03	0.08*	.04
Kennedy	−0.15***	.02	−0.02	.03	0.24***	.03	0.06	.03
Party Handle Most Important Issue:								
Conservative	−0.86***	.18	1.18***	.21	0.11	.20	0.52*	.25
Labour	0.41***	.13	−0.17**	.30	−0.58***	.14	−0.40*	.24
Liberal-Democrat	−0.67***	.19	0.22	.29	0.59***	.19	0.16	.30
Other Party	−0.58***	.01	0.61**	.26	0.07	.22	1.05***	.22
Party-Issue Proximity:								
Conservative	0.01	.01	0.05**	.02	−0.01	.01	−0.00	.02
Labour	0.03*	.01	−0.02	.02	−0.03*	.02	−0.04*	.02
Liberal-Democrat	−0.01	.01	−0.05**	.02	0.05***	.02	−0.02	.02
Performance Evaluations:								
Labour Economy	0.24***	.06	−0.35***	.08	−0.26***	.06	−0.09	.08
Labour Services	0.43***	.08	−0.59***	.12	−0.38***	.08	−0.54***	.11
Conservative Services	−0.28***	.08	0.84***	.13	0.24**	.09	−0.00	.12
(Dis)Approve Iraq War	0.05	.04	.01	.06	−0.08*	.05	−0.04	.06
Constant	0.48	.45	−1.50*	.65	−1.26**	.49	−1.49*	.65
McFadden R^2	.55				.54			
% correctly classified	88.0				78.1			
Lambda	.67				.66			

Notes: The results of two analyses are presented. Panel A: binomial logit analysis of voting for Labour (the governing party) v. voting for any of the opposition parties. Panel B: multinomial logit analysis of Conservative, Liberal Democrat and other party voting, with Labour voting as the reference category. Analyses include controls for age, education, ethnicity, gender, home ownership, occupational status and work sector. $*-p \leq .05$; $**-p \leq .01$; $***-p \leq .00$.
(weighted N = 5002)
Source: 2005 BES Rolling Campaign Panel Survey, pre-post panel.

voting, and proximities to Labour and Liberal Democrats affect voting for the latter party. Proximity to Labour affects 'other party' voting. Taken together with the findings for the Labour voting model discussed above, it appears that voters do not take into account their evaluations of *all* of the spatial distances between parties, which classic Downsian theory suggests that they should. So the evidence is not fully consistent with the tenets of the spatial model, which requires individuals to evaluate all the choices on offer before reaching a decision.

Table 3, Panel B also documents numerous effects of valence issues on opposition party voting. Conservative support is influenced by all three performance evaluation variables, and three of four issue-priority variables. The story for Liberal Democrat support is similar—two performance evaluations are significant and properly signed, as are two of the issue-priority variables. 'Other' party voting is also affected by several of the valence issue variables.

The next step in the voting analyses involves calibrating the relative importance of valence versus position issues, and the importance of both types of issue compared to party leader images and partisan orientations. To this end, we first set all independent variables at their means. Next, changes in the probability of voting for a party are calculated as the values of variables of interest are varied from their minimum to maximum values. Figures 3, 4 and 5 show the five predictor variables with the largest effects on Labour, Conservative, and Liberal Democrat voting, plus the effects of statistically significant issue-proximity variables.

Figures 3 and 4 tell similar stories. The dominant predictors are leader images and valence issues. Varying feelings about Tony Blair from their minimum to their maximum value increases the probability of a Labour vote by fully 46 points, and varying scores on the Labour public service delivery issue variables increases that probability by 45 points. The comparable figures for Conservative voting are nearly identical. Effects of the issue-proximity variable are much more modest—14 points for Labour and 16 points for the Conservatives. The Liberal Democrat story is different. Figure 5 shows that the top five predictors include the party's issue-proximity variable which can change the probability of a Liberal Democrat vote by fully 41 points—less than the

3. Effects of Selected Predictors on Probability of Voting Labour

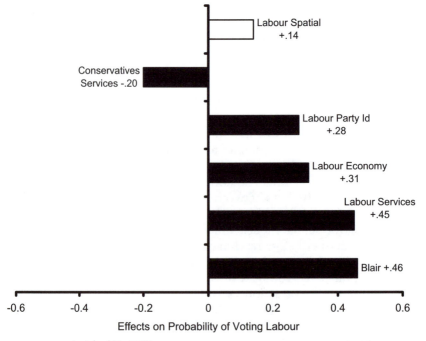

(weighted N = 5002)
Source: 2005 BES Rolling Campaign Panel Survey, pre-post panel.

4. **Effects of Selected Predictors on Probability of Voting Conservative**

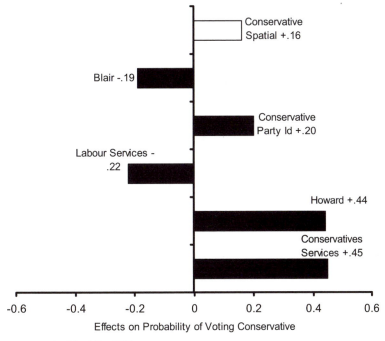

Effects on Probability of Voting Conservative

(weighted N = 5002)

Source: 2005 BES Rolling Campaign Panel Survey, pre-post panel.

49 points associated with changing feelings about Charles Kennedy, but considerably larger than any other significant predictor. Taken together, these findings are consistent with the conjecture that position issues have their strongest effects on support for smaller parties such as the Liberal Democrats. Valence issues dominate for the larger parties.

Conclusion

Valence issues concerning economic performance and public service delivery in several areas joined leader images and partisanship to strongly influence voting for the Labour and Conservative parties in 2005. Effects of spatial issues, although not wholly absent, were much smaller. The situation was different for Liberal Democrat voting, where both valence and position issues, as well as feelings about Charles Kennedy and Liberal Democrat partisanship, were major predictors of party support. Overall, these findings accord well with theoretical expectations, and they indicate that voters' issue orientations played a major role in determining voting in 2005.

The analyses also provide insight regarding the election outcome. The mix of salient issues in 2005 clearly was very different than in 2001. When voters went to the polls in Britain's first 'post-9/11' general elec-

5. **Effects of Selected Predictors on Probability of Voting Liberal Democrat**

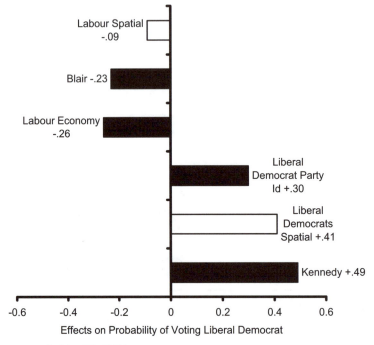

Effects on Probability of Voting Liberal Democrat

(weighted N = 5002)
Source: 2005 BES Rolling Campaign Panel Survey, pre-post panel.

tion, issues such as immigration, crime, and terrorism, which had virtually no play in 2001, were collectively accorded top priority by over
40% of the electorate. Although Labour received relatively good grades
for its performance on the latter issue, it failed miserably on the former
two. More generally, although Labour continued to receive relatively
high marks for its work on the economy, the NHS, and education, the
new issue agenda clearly took its toll. Overall, less than one voter in
four chose Labour as best able to handle their most important issue.
The Conservatives did only slightly better, while the Liberal Democrats
and various other parties remained essentially 'non starters' on the
issues that mattered most to people.

Clearly, even with a strongly biased electoral system, Labour could
not have remained in power had issues, principally valence issues, been
the only thing that mattered in 2005. Other key variables—leader
images and partisanship—provided Tony Blair and his party with the
additional leverage they needed to win again. Although Blair's image
had been severely tarnished by the events precipitated by his decision to
join the United States in invading Iraq, he was fortunate that his principal rival, Michael Howard, was even less warmly received. Labour
also continued to enjoy a substantial, if substantially reduced, edge in

party identifiers. Taken together, a triumvirate of valence issues, leader images, and partisanship gave Mr Blair just enough of what he needed to stay in No.10—at least for now.

 1   See J. Gray and D. Willetts, *Is Conservatism Dead?*, Profile, 1977.
 2   See P. Marshall and D. Laws, *The Orange Book: Reclaiming Liberalism*, Profile, 2004.
 3   H.D. Clarke, D. Sanders, M. Stewart and P. Whiteley, *Political Choice in Britain*, Oxford University Press, 2004.
 4   The 2005 BES survey data and questionnaires are available at www.essex.ac.uk/bes.
 5   A. Downs, *An Economic Theory of Democracy*, Harper and Row, 1957.
 6   D. Stokes, 'Spatial Models of Party Competition', 57 *American Political Science Review*, 1963, 368–77.
 7   I. Budge and D. Farlie, *Explaining and Predicting Elections*, George Allen and Unwin, 1983.
 8   D. Stokes, op cit., p. 371.
 9   I. Budge *et al.*, *Mapping Policy Preferences*, Oxford University Press, 2001.
10   *Guardian*, 6.4.05.
11   Details regarding the measurement of variables used in the voting analyses are available at the 2005 BES website. See note 4 above.
12   Index scores are multiplied by −1 so that coefficients in the voting models will have intuitively plausible signs, i.e. close proximity to a party on position issues increases the likelihood of voting for that party.
13   These data were gathered as part of the authors' research project: 'Government Performance, Valence Judgments and The Dynamics of Party Support'. The project (funded by the National Science Foundation (US)) involves 48 consecutive monthly cross-sectional and panel surveys of national samples of the British electorate. The fieldwork is conducted by YouGov.
14   The variable is based on the following question: 'Please tell me whether you strongly approve, approve, disapprove or strongly disapprove of Britain's involvement in Iraq?' RCPS campaign-wave data indicate that 36% favour Britain's involvement in Iraq, and 64% oppose it.
15   The measure relies on responses to the items listed in Table 2, minus the economy, which we enter separately. The issues include asylum seekers, crime, education, the NHS, pensions, railways, and terrorism.
16   Issues include the economy plus those mentioned in note 15 above.

GEOFFREY EVANS AND ROBERT ANDERSEN

The Impact of Party Leaders: How Blair Lost Labour Votes

Since the 2001 election there have been stark changes in the fortunes of the leader of the Labour Party and in the personnel leading the Conservatives. Of the main national parties only the leadership of the Liberal Democrats was relatively stable in terms of public perceptions and occupancy, and even Charles Kennedy had his share of negative publicity relating primarily to his social life and political commitment. Yet has this leadership flux made a difference? Can we say that the electorate's voting preferences in 2005 were affected by the varying fates of the party leaderships over the electoral cycle? The goal of this chapter is to examine the influence of the electorate's evaluations of the main party leaders on voting in the 2005 election. We start by examining public opinion polls showing some of the main features of the changing appraisals of party leaders. We then examine the impact of leader images on voting intentions in 2005 using the British Election Study. We do this by estimating a model of influences on voting decisions that includes enduring values, election-specific issues and assessments of the government's record, social background variables, various indicators of partisanship, and, of course, perceptions of the party leaders. Though cautioning against making strong causal interpretations based on estimates of leadership effects using cross-sectional evidence, we conclude that appraisals of Blair, Howard, and Kennedy were indeed significantly and strongly related to vote in 2005. Blair's decline in popularity appears to have cost Labour a substantial number of votes, but Howard's appeal was too lukewarm for the Conservatives to benefit fully.

2001–05: swings and roundabouts for party leaders

The last electoral cycle saw a period of considerable change in one way or another for the party leaders. In 2001 Mr Blair contributed positively and substantially to his party's repeated massacre of the opposition.[1]

© Oxford University Press 2005
doi: 10.1093/pa/gsi065

The well-known story since is that it has been anything but easy for Blair, with the Iraq war and its cover-ups, David Kelly's suicide, and the PM's tactical evasions proving to be a geopolitical escapade that was taken too far in the eyes of much of the electorate.

By comparison with the position of strength occupied by Labour at the start of the electoral cycle, the attempt by the Conservative Party to renew its prospects under Michael Howard was a matter of some urgency given the parlous state of Iain Duncan Smith's occupancy of the leadership. It seems unlikely that the selection of a figure with such resonant connections to the Conservative Party so roundly beaten in 1997 was the magic bullet the party needed. Even the Liberal Democrats were not immune to leadership *faux pas*: 'chat show Charlie', 'good time Charlie', 'champagne Charlie'—all nicknames given to the Liberal Democrat leader Charles Kennedy. Questions about his commitment to the role of leader surfaced in 2002 along with discussions of his 'health'. His appearances on programmes such as *Have I Got News for You* were at times mocked. On the other hand, the performance of the Liberal Democrats in 2005 was not at all bad, so all these soubriquets could simply indicate that Kennedy is perceived as a rather interesting person with a sense of humour and a life outside of the unhealthy confines of party politics.[2]

In Figure 1 we show evidence of how public evaluations of the leaders of the three major parties changed between the 2001 and 2005 using polling estimates by MORI, the most extensive time series measures of public opinion on this question (other polls do not differ dramatically). The evidence reveals a clear decline in evaluations of Blair, whose prime ministerial approval rating declined from a peak in the mid-60s in late 2001 to a stable and considerably lower level at about 40% by mid-2003. So Teflon Tony, so long an asset, had perhaps became more of a liability. He was not, however, such a liability that his party was seriously challenged in 2005 despite all of the misplaced journalistic enthusiasm for every minor bump and grind of the polls.[3] The inequities in the distribution of votes by seats certainly helped turn a slim popular endorsement into a substantial mandate in Westminster, but even without this the conditions for a severe negative Blair effect on voting are not as evident as some commentators might have thought. Moreover, the idea that a change in leadership could be sufficient to restore Conservative fortunes was unfounded: Howard to a large degree found himself facing the same difficulties as his predecessor so that he had, at best, brought a small increment in Prime Ministerial approval over Duncan Smith, and his popularity was almost always below that of Blair throughout the cycle.[4] Finally Kennedy does not appear to have suffered unduly from publicity with respect to his perceived job performance. There was a decline from an average satisfaction rating in the mid-40s in 2002 to one in the late 30s from 2004 onwards, but from mid-2003 onwards he was always given higher ratings than Blair.

1. Satisfaction with How Party Leaders are Doing Their Jobs, 2001–05

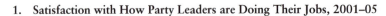

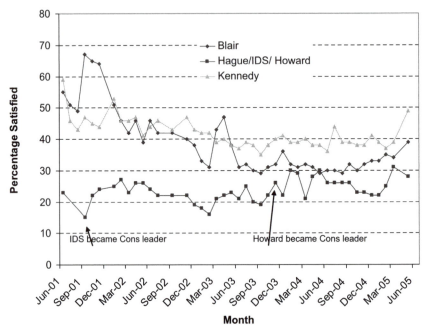

Source: MORI polls www.MORI.com.

Each of the above questions asks about the leaders in isolation—there is no direct comparison required by respondents. In Figure 2, however, we present responses to a YouGov question on which of the three 'would make the best Prime Minister', thus forcing the issue. Although not directly comparable to the Mori poll time series, because they only commence in 2003, answers to this question raise further doubts about the extent of Blair's demise and Kennedy's apparent rise in the popularity stakes. Blair goes almost unchallenged as the best Prime Minister, while Howard improves his position to displace Kennedy for the number two slot. We must conclude therefore that the changing fortunes of the party leaders do not point to a clear reversal of fortune for their parties.[5] Whether we take Mori's separate Prime Ministerial approval question as our benchmark or the forced choice option used by YouGov, Blair is consistently ahead of Howard in 2005.

The radical drop in relative Prime Ministerial approval for Kennedy in the forced choice format might well reflect the more obvious partisan biases that come to the fore when explicit trade-offs have to be made between leaders of the parties. This is a general problem when examining responses to party-laden questions which are likely to reflect partisanship—when asked who would be the best PM, a Labour, Conservative or Liberal Democrat, it is not surprising if people who

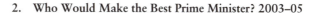

2. **Who Would Make the Best Prime Minister? 2003–05**

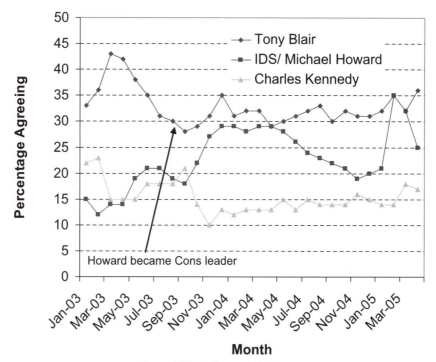

Source: MORI polls www.MORI.com.

support those parties tend to affirm their own. This raises the question, then, of how much of an effect leadership actually has on voting: Is the leadership factor swamped by party preference? Can we say with confidence that Blair has become a liability in that his attempts to be a player in geopolitics have cost him dearly at home; that Howard probably did help shore up the Conservatives when compared to their likely fate under IDS; that the image of champagne Charlie was benign for the relatively successful Liberal Democrat outcome?

How to estimate leadership effects

Political parties market their leaders to mass appeal. Telegenic presentation and carefully planned sound-bites designed to make leaders appear as though they can relate to voters are now common practices of party strategists. The growing worldwide emphasis on leaders rather than parties is also evident in the vast number of countries that now have leaders' debates during election campaigns. Even in a parliamentary system like Britain's where the party is elected, not the Prime Minister, appraisals of leaders have long been argued to matter.[6] Thus, in 2001 it was widely thought that the Conservative Party suffered because of Hague's leadership. Hague was attacked for his apparent uncertainty, lack of clarity, and general lack of personal appeal which allegedly resulted in a lack of support from voters. By comparison Blair was favourably perceived by most voters, which in turn contributed to the success of the Labour Party.[7]

But other scholars have disagreed. Bartle and Crewe argue that leadership effects in the 2001 election were small.[8] Indeed, with respect to Hague's apparent unpopularity, Bartle writes: 'To be sure, voters thought that Tony Blair would make a better prime minister than William Hague, but these evaluations are almost entirely predictable on the basis of voter predispositions, policy preferences and evaluations of party competence. William Hague was not the Conservative Party's problem. Quite the reverse: the Conservative Party was William Hague's'.[9]

These differences of opinion reflect the problems faced in identifying what should count as leadership 'effects'.[10] Clearly, the separation of partisanship from leader appraisal is necessary if one is to identify their distinct impact. Moreover, it is important to control for a range of other influences that can condition voting. Even with such controls, the inference of any causal impact is open to question, as Bartle and Crewe have observed.[11] Nonetheless, it is still possible to provide evidence that rigorously assesses whether there is an association between perceptions of leaders and voting that *might* indicate a causal connection. For such a task, reliable data, appropriate indicators, and careful model specification are of paramount importance.

Data and measures

We use the 2005 BES pre-campaign data. These data were gathered by in-person CAPI interviews carried out in February and March 2005. Survey fieldwork was conducted by the National Centre for Social Research. We include the boosted samples for Scotland and Wales, with dummy variables to control for their effects. The total sample size is 3589 respondents, though after removing missing data our analytical sample size is 2252. The dependent variable—vote—is divided into three separate variables: (1) Labour versus all others (including non-voters), (2) Conservative versus all others, and (3) Liberal Democrat versus all others.

To measure evaluations of leaders we use four scales for each of the leaders of the three major parties. These are designed to capture like-dislike, competence, responsiveness, and trust. For full wording see Table 1. Responses to the questions are very strongly inter-connected, and when responses to the four questions for each leader are combined to form a summated rating scale they produce exceptionally high Cronbach alphas: Blair (.927), Howard (.904), and Kennedy (.900). Given this redundancy it makes no sense to include the scales as separate variables in our models—essentially they are indexing one negative/positive dimension for each leader evaluated. We thus employ the summated scales in our analyses.

1. Summary of Indicators Used in the Analysis

Leadership Perceptions

(1) **Like/dislike** 'Using a scale that runs from 0 to 10, where 0 means strongly dislike and 10 means strongly like, how do you feel about Tony Blair . . . Michael Howard . . . Charles Kennedy?'

(2) **Competence.** 'Using a scale that runs from 0 to 10, where 0 means a very incompetent leader and 10 means a very competent leader, how would you describe Tony Blair . . . Michael Howard . . . Charles Kennedy?'

(3) **Responsiveness** 'Use the 0 to 10 scale to indicate the extent to which the different leaders respond to voters' concerns' (0=Does not respond at all to voters' concerns; 10 = Responds fully to voters' concerns).

(4) **Trust** 'Use the 0 to 10 scale to indicate how much trust you have for each of the party leaders, where 0 means no trust and 10 means a great deal of trust'.

Control Variables:

(1) Social Background:
  a. Gender
  b. Age—continuous variable (tested for nonlinearity but not significant)
  c. Education—degree, other qualification, no qualifications
  d. Religion—Anglican, other, none
  e. Minority—all minorities, white
  f. Social Class—(1) professional & managerial, (2) self-employed, (3) routine non-manual, (4) skilled working class, (5) unskilled working class, (6) other (no job, housewives, etc.).
  g. Public sector versus other

(2) Party identification—(1) Labour, (2) Conservative, (3) Libral Democrat, (4) other, (5) none.

(3) Issues:

  a. Economic perceptions (four 5-point scales for retrospective and prospective, egocentric, and sociotropic perceptions)
  b. Euro—respondent feels should join Euro (coded 1) else = 0.
  c. Tax/spend (10-point scale)
  d. Iraq (10-point scale)
  e. Immigrants take jobs (5-point scale)

Dependent Variables:

(1) Labour Vote intention versus all others (including nonvoters);
(2) Conservative Vote intention versus all others (including nonvoters);
(3) Liberal Vote intention versus all others (including nonvoters).

The BES data also allow for thorough controls of partisan orientations, which are typically intertwined with views of leaders.[12] As a result, our models represent demanding tests of the robustness of leadership effects. Not only do they include measures of partisanship that are closely related to vote and are relatively stable, long-term aspects of political belief systems, but they also include variables such as perceptions of the economy that are arguably more strongly influenced by political support than *vice versa* and that therefore could be quite reasonably not included as independent variables.[13] We do this so that we can claim to have tested the leadership effects hypothesis as rigorously as possible given the data at our disposal. For the analysis presented here we use party identity measured concurrently. In other analyses we have also controlled for the effects of reported 2001 vote and party like-dislike scales. The findings are substantively equivalent regardless of how we control for partisan orientations.

The economy is given attention both through measures of valence issues—economic expectations and retrospective appraisals—and measures of issues where there are social and political divisions in orientations—respondents' positions on the theme of reducing taxation versus increasing public spending. Following the established literature on economic perceptions,[14] we include four measures of economic perceptions: (1) retrospective egocentric perceptions; (2) retrospective sociotropic perceptions; (3) prospective egocentric perceptions; (4) prospective sociotropic perceptions. Sociotropic perceptions were measured by a question asking respondents how well they thought the British economy was performing or would perform. The egocentric perception items asked respondents how they felt their own personal household income had been affected in the past year or would be affected in the coming year. Each of these is coded so that high values indicate positive perceptions, i.e. the perception that the economic situation was or would be better. The taxation-versus-spending issue is central to the established left-right division in British politics and therefore captures this key dimension of non-valence economic issues.[15] We also include in our models attitudes towards politically salient issues which are to some degree distinct from the traditional left-right division, such as the Euro, which was an issue that the Conservatives emphasised in 2001 with some success,[16] immigration, which the Conservatives placed more weight on in this campaign, and, of course, the war in Iraq.

Finally, we also include social structural variables as controls. While social characteristics have been thought to be in decline as influences on political preferences they are certainly not negligible, with class, ethnicity, and education in particular continuing to provide significant bases of party support, while the salience of the war in Iraq makes it likely that religion might also influence voters' decisions.[17] All of the control variables used in this analysis are summarised in Table 1.

Statistical methods

The statistical analysis has three main goals: (1) to determine the relative importance of leadership perceptions compared with other important variables in predicting vote for each of the major parties; (2) to assess the importance of the three leaders relative to each other; and (3) to determine how leaders affected vote for each of the parties—i.e. to explore the functional form of the relationship between attitudes towards leaders and vote choice.

We began by fitting Generalised Additive Models in order to explore for possible nonlinearities in the effects of leaders on vote choice.[18] Although it was discovered that several of the leadership effects were nonlinear, these nonlinearities were relatively simple and could be adequately modelled using polynomial regression.[19] As a result, the final estimates reported in this article are from three binomial logit models, one for each of the three major parties: Labour, Conservative, and Liberal Democrat. The fact that we could model the trends using parametric regression allowed us to compare the relative importance of sets of predictors. We do so using the measure of relative importance proposed by Silber *et al.*, which is a generalisation of standardised variables to non-quantitative regressors or sets of regressors.[20] Finally, since we are interested in understanding the nature of the effects of leaders on vote choice, and the effects are nonlinear, it is important to graph them. We do so using effect displays.[21]

Findings

Figure 3 displays the density estimates of the distributions (i.e. smoothed histograms), the means, and the standard deviations of the leader evaluation scales for Blair, Howard, and Kennedy. We see that on average Blair is rated more positively than Howard but slightly less so than Kennedy. These patterns are consistent with the decline in Blair's popularity between 2001 and 2005 shown in Figure 1. Importantly, however, we can see from the density curves that perceptions of Blair are more polarised than are perceptions of the other two leaders. Not only is the distribution of perceptions of Blair flatter and wider, but there is distinct bulge at the very bottom of the scale—i.e. those with a very negative view of him across all four measures that form the scale. Perceptions of Howard and Kennedy have a closer to normal distribution,

3.   **The Distribution of the Leadership Scales, 2005, All Respondents**

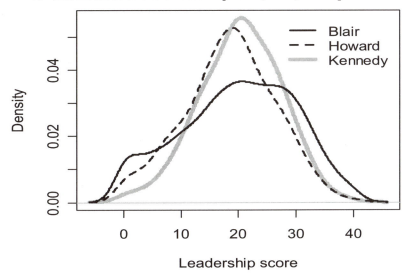

Descriptive Statistics:	Mean	Standard deviation
Blair	19.8	9.8
Howard	18.4	7.9
Kennedy	20.3	7.1

Source: British Election Study 2005 Pre-campaign Survey.

possibly reflecting a lesser degree of knowledge of these leaders and lower intensity of feelings towards them. On this basis alone we would expect perceptions of Blair to have more impact on voting than perceptions of the other two leaders.

Figure 4 below uses box plots to display how perceptions of the three leaders differ by vote intention. This provides some initial evidence of a leadership effect. In each case, the opinions of the relevant leader are clearly more positive among people who intend to vote for the party in question. Evidence for this is seen both in the higher medians and inter-quartile ranges. All other groups—other, undecided, abstain, and those who intend to vote for other parties—have similarly less positive views. The one instance where this does not appear to hold is with respect to opinions of Blair, where evaluations are lower among non-supporters, but not equally so. Specifically, evaluations are especially low among those who intended to vote Conservative. This again demonstrates the

4. **Box Plots Showing the Distribution of the Leadership Scale for Each Leader, by Vote Intention**

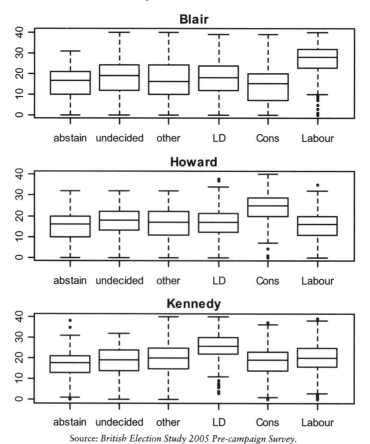

Source: *British Election Study 2005 Pre-campaign Survey.*

polarised nature of perceptions of Blair and of his potentially stronger effect on vote.

We now turn to the logit analysis. Various models were run initially with different types of predictors or blocks of predictors—social structure, partisanship, issues, and leadership perceptions. Although all of these types of predictors were significantly related to vote intention when examined alone, in this presentation we focus on their effects in the fully-specified models. Table 2 presents an Analysis of Deviance of each of the predictors in the full models. The differences in deviance between the full model (including all predictors) and models excluding particular terms but including all others provides Type II Chi-square tests for the impact of those terms on model fit.[22] In other words, the figures in Table 2 tell us how each of the independent variables in our models improved the fit of the model, controlling for all other predictors.

Although variables such as class, ethnicity, employment sector, and education have significant effects in less heavily specified models of vote intention (these are available from the authors), these indicators of 'objective' social characteristics are to a large degree unimportant in determining vote intention when leadership effects, partisanship, and issues are included in the model—only education retains any substantial predictive effect. This should not be taken to indicate the irrelevance of

2. The Impact of Leadership on Voting Intentions, Spring 2005

	Labour			Voting intentions Conservative			Lib Dem		
Demographics									
Gender (male)	.04	(1)		.15	(1)		.33	(1)	
Age	2.10	(1)		1.14	(1)		.96	(1)	
Religion	.38	(2)		7.85	(2)	*	1.46	(2)	
Minority	3.56	(1)		2.04	(1)		.00	(1)	
Education	12.38	(2)	**	4.30	(2)		7.12	(2)	*
Social Class	8.22	(5)		6.73	(5)		7.38	(5)	
Public Sector	2.15	(1)		1.54	(1)		0.31	(1)	
Partisanship									
Party identity	483.54	(4)	***	402.08	(4)	***	343.19	(4)	***
Issues & economic perceptions									
Euro	2.20	(1)		.33	(1)		.07	(1)	
Tax/Spend	7.77	(1)	**	.08	(1)		.53	(1)	
Iraq	.30	(1)		.28	(1)		1.87	(1)	
Immigration	2.46	(1)		.04	(1)		.02	(1)	
Retro. egocentric	.79	(1)		1.15	(1)		3.51	(1)	
Prosp. egocentric	.42	(1)		.02	(1)		.43	(1)	
Retro. sociotropic	.98	(1)		4.82	(1)	*	.65	(1)	
Prosp. sociotropic	.03	(1)		.34	(1)		.11	(1)	
Leaders									
Evaluation of Blair	258.99	(1)	***	54.09	(2)	***	38.47	(2)	***
Evaluation of Howard	61.91	(2)	***	275.18	(1)	***	33.47	(2)	***
Evaluation of Kennedy	17.85	(1)	***	59.27	(2)	***	133.25	(3)	***

Note: Analysis of deviance with Type II chi-square tests * $p < .05$; ** $p < .01$; *** $p < .001$; Degrees of freedom are in parentheses. Source: British Election Study 2005 Pre-campaign Survey.

social structure, but rather that their direct effects are small. Clearly social structure is likely to influence many of the other predictors in the model, whereas they in turn cannot plausibly be argued to influence social structure. On the other hand, the direction of influence of subjective perceptions, attitudes, and orientations of one form or another to and from partisanship when measured concurrently is always open to question.

Moving down the table, we see that party identification is a massively significant predictor of vote intention, despite the large number of controls. This is not a surprise, of course—party identification and vote intention measured at the same point in time just before an election should be very strongly related to each other. (Similar relations with vote intention are found for reported 2001 vote and the party like/dislike measures.) When we examine the issue positions, however, we see almost no such effects. Tax/spend retains a significant impact on labour voting (pro-tax = pro-Labour), and retrospective sociotropic perceptions have a barely significant impact on Conservative voting (negative perceptions = pro-Conservative). Nonetheless, as with social structure, issues generally fail to predict voting once partisanship and leadership perceptions are included in the models.

The main question is: are leadership effects removed when partisanship and issues are included in the analysis? The final rows of the table show, dramatically, that this is not the case. All three leaders have highly significant effects on voting for all three main parties. As we would expect, perceptions of Blair improve the model fit to a much greater extent than perceptions of the other two leaders for Labour voting; Howard has greater predictive strength for Conservative voting; and to a lesser degree Kennedy improves predictions of Liberal Democrat voting. The most important finding, however, is that all of these leadership effects are highly statistically significant despite the inclusion of a vast number of controls, including other partisanship measures not included here such as reported past vote and the party like/dislike scales.

Assessing relative importance

As the relative nature and magnitude of the leadership effects cannot easily be observed from the deviance analysis presented in Table 2, we next present comparisons of the relative importance of blocks of variables in terms of the strength of their effects. We do so using the measure of relative importance proposed by Silber, *et al.* referred to above.[23]

The relative importance of leadership perceptions compared with other sets of variables in the final models is displayed in Table 3. Each of the columns in the table displays the ratio for each vote choice. Positive values indicate that leadership perceptions are of more importance; negative numbers indicate that the other variables are of more importance. The main finding is that leader evaluations are *far* more important than either social structure or issues in determining vote intention for

3. The Relative Importance of Leaders Compared with Other Sets of Influences on Voting Intentions, Spring 2005

	Labour			Vote Intention Conservative			Lib Dem		
		se	Sig		se	Sig		se	Sig
Leaders/Demographics	1.76	(.23)	***	1.71	(.22)	***	1.25	(.28)	***
Leaders/Party id.	.19	(.10)		.38	(.10)	**	.06	(.11)	
Leaders/Issues	1.74	(.25)	***	2.42	(.42)	***	1.77	(.42)	**
Leaders/All others	.11	(.10)		.26	(.09)	*	−.02	(.12)	

Note: * p < .05; ** p < .01; *** p < .001; Standard errors in parentheses; Relative importance of leaders measured by the log of the standard deviation ratio. Source: British Election Study 2005 Pre-campaign Survey.

all three parties (all of the ratios are positive and statistically significant). When compared with the effects of party identification, however, there is a far more even picture: there is only one significant difference in the relative importance of leadership compared to party identification, which occurs for Conservative voting, though the effect for Labour voting is also marginally significant. Both of these differences are positive, which indicates leadership perceptions are slightly more important for vote intention than even party identification.

Table 4 extends the relative importance of analysis by comparing the strength of perceptions of the three leaders on each voting outcome. Here positive values indicate that the first named leader in the comparison has stronger effects; conversely, negative values indicate that the second leader has stronger effects.

The top half of the table shows that perceptions of Blair have far stronger effects on voting for Labour than perceptions of either of the two other leaders, particularly Kennedy. Howard has far stronger effects than either of the other two leaders on voting Conservative; Kennedy has stronger effects—though less so—than the other two on voting for the Liberal Democrats. In the bottom half of the table we summarise the strength of effects for each of the leaders compared with both others. This tells us that perceptions of Blair counted for far more than perceptions of other leaders for Labour voting; Howard was

4. Relative Importance of Leaders

	Labour			Vote intention Conservative			Lib Dem		
		se	Sig		se	Sig		se	Sig
Blair/Howard	.72	(.14)	***	−.69	(.14)	***	.10	(.25)	
Blair/Kennedy	1.60	(.23)	***	.18	(.20)		−.37	(.18)	*
Howard/Kennedy	.88	(.29)	***	.87	(.12)	***	−.46	(.18)	*
Blair/Others	.61	(.12)	***	−.70	(.14)	***	−.46	(.19)	***
Howard/Others	−.72	(.14)	***	.34	(.09)	***	−.58	(.19)	***
Kennedy/Others	−1.74	(.24)	***	−1.00	(.13)	***	.10	(.14)	

Note: * *p* < .05; ** *p* < .01; *** *p* < .001; Standard errors in parentheses. Source: British Election Study 2005 Pre-campaign Survey.

also more important for Conservative voting, though not by the same degree; but Kennedy had no dominant effect on Liberal Democrat voting, having a similar weight to the combined perceptions of the other leaders.

The shape and magnitude of leadership effects

Let us now turn to the effect displays for leader evaluations. Figure 5 shows displays for the effects of evaluations of each leader on the probability of voting Labour. Although the effect of appraisals of Blair is strong and linear on the logit scale, the line is curved slightly because it has been plotted on the probability scale. We notice clearly that those with a very negative appraisal of Blair have a probability very close to 0 of voting Labour, while those who gave Blair a very high rating (i.e. near the top of the scale) were almost certain to vote Labour. By contrast, perceptions of Howard and Kennedy have non-linear effect patterns indicating that only the more positive appraisals affect the likelihood of voting Labour. In other words, up to a certain level of approval there is no discernable effect of variations in approval. It is only when appraisals of these other party leaders are markedly positive that the odds of voting Labour decrease noticeably.

In Figures 6 and 7, we can see a similar though more muted pattern for Conservative and Liberal Democrat voting. In Figure 6, appraisals of Howard clearly have a much stronger effect than appraisals of other leaders on the likelihood of voting Conservative across most of the range of opinion. As was the case with Blair for the Labour vote, the effect of appraisals of Howard on Conservative voting are strong and

5.   **The Effect of Leaders' Evaluations on the Probability of Voting Labour**

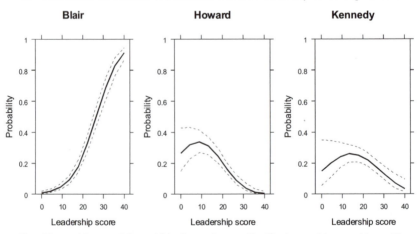

Note: The models control for social background, party identification, and issue positions. All control variables are set to their means (quantitative variables) or proportions (categorical variables) when calculating the effects. Source: British Election Study 2005 Pre-campaign Survey

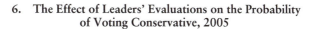

6.   The Effect of Leaders' Evaluations on the Probability
of Voting Conservative, 2005

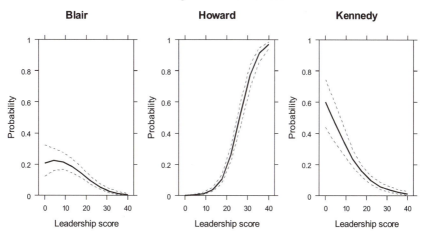

Note: The models control for social background, party identification, and issue positions. All control variables are set to their means (quantitative variables) or proportions (categorical variables) when calculating the effects. Source: British Election Study 2005 Pre-campaign Survey.

7.   The Effect of Leaders' Evaluations on the Probability of Voting Liberal
Democrat, 2005

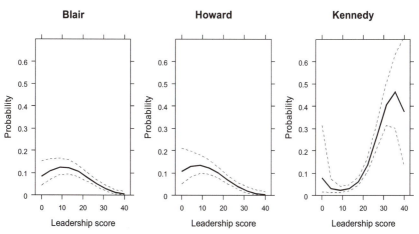

Note: The models control for social background, party identification, and issue positions. All control variables are set to their means (quantitative variables) or proportions (categorical variables) when calculating the effects. Source: British Election Study 2005 Pre-campaign Survey.

linear on the logit scale, and the effects of appraisals of the leaders of other parties matter only at higher levels of approval.

Finally, the results in Figure 7 indicate that appraisals of Kennedy are an important predictor of the Liberal Democrat vote, though they matter to a lesser degree than do appraisals of the other leaders for the popularity of their parties. Appraisals of Kennedy are strong in the mid-range and non-linear at the tails, reflecting the smaller number of cases in the tails (see Figure 3). Much as we saw for Labour and Conservative vote choice, the effects of appraisals of other leaders are only observable towards the high end of the range of opinion.

In general, then, appraisals of a party leader are very strong predictors of voting for that party. It is clear, too, that appraisals of all leaders matter for all three parties. The effect of the leader of the party in question is, of course, most important, and this importance is seen throughout the range of opinion of the leader. On the other hand, though the other leaders matter, it is generally only when levels of approval of these leaders is very high, at which point there is a strong pull factor towards the party of that leader.

Using the fitted curves, we can also assess how voting might have differed if the popularity of the three leaders had differed. Of course, this counterfactual exercise must be interpreted cautiously because the model from which these fitted values were drawn may change significantly if opinions of leaders were radically shifted. Nonetheless, it illustrates the possible impact of leaders in this election.

We start by considering how Blair's decline in popularity might have hurt his party in the 2005 election. In the middle of the probability scale, an increase in one point on the leadership scale for Blair with opinions of the other leaders remaining unchanged is associated with an increase in support for the Labour Party of about four percentage points. If we consider that the actual popular support for the Labour Party was 36.2%, this suggests that Labour would have obtained around 40% of the popular vote if Blair were only moderately more popular (one point is not a massive change given that the difference in the mean scores of Howard and Kennedy was around two points). In other words, the decline in Blair's popularity appears to have cost the party many potential votes. The impact is not quite as strong for Howard, but it is still substantial. If Howard's popularity had been only one point higher, and Blair and Kennedy's popularity did not change, it would translate into a gain of about three percentage points for the Conservatives, meaning that they would have gone from 33.2 to around 36.2% in popular support. In other words, they would have equalled Labour. By marked comparison, an increase in one point in Kennedy's popularity would have translated into an increase of about only 0.7 percentage points, suggesting that the party's vote would have only risen minimally from 22.6 to 23.3%. This suggests that Kennedy's leadership performance is simply far less important to the Liberal Democrat's fortunes in terms of vote share.

Discussion and conclusion

This paper has set out to test the importance of leader appraisals on voting in the 2005 British election. Having first established that the

Prime Minister's standing with the electorate had declined over the 2001–05 electoral cycle, we estimate whether such changes in perceptions influence vote intentions. To ensure that we did not mistakenly interpret spurious relationships our analysis controls for other factors commonly used to predict vote. We find that appraisals of Blair, Howard, and Kennedy are significantly and strongly related to vote in 2005. These results persist even after controlling for many other predictors of vote: party identification, past vote, party like/dislike issues, and social structure. We also show that these leader effects are far more important than a wide range of issues, social background, and even, though to a far lesser degree, party identification.

Simply put, these findings suggest that Blair's decline in popularity lost the Labour Party votes and seats. It probably cost them more votes than anything else at this election. Yet as we know, this was not enough to endanger the Labour Party's control of Westminster. Howard's modest popularity contributed only slightly to the fortunes of the Conservatives, while the more positive evaluations of Charles Kennedy had somewhat weaker effects than the other two leaders on voting. Although approval of Kennedy was relatively high, not many people voted for the Liberal Democrats, which suggests that differences in public support between the Liberal Democrats and the other main parties are perhaps largely related to long-term party attachments. While our findings do not address this directly, it is also likely that the Liberal Democrats receive less support simply because they are not seen as likely winners of the election. One could speculate that this is why so many people took a relatively benign view of Kennedy—he was not a serious contender.

There are some qualifications that are worth briefly considering. For example, it is possible that some voters might simply be more 'leader centred' than others—'the effect of leadership traits may well vary between, say, those with high and low levels of political awareness or between those with "extreme" and "moderate" ideological positions'.[24] In analyses of these data, however, we find no evidence of such heterogeneity: leadership impacts equivalently across all levels of attention to politics, as we also found in the 2001 election.[25]

Similarly there are unanswered questions concerning both model specification and the endogeneity of leader effects.[26] With respect to model specification, there are clearly more issues that could be included in our analyses. More thorough examination of the government's record, for example, might chip away at the effect of leaders, but the granite-like resoluteness of the leader effects in the face of contemporaneously measured partisan controls that are so similar to vote—almost raising questions of tautology—suggests that they will not be removed by dredging up a few more sets of responses to questions about performance for inclusion in the models.

But what if the endogeneity problem remains, if, for example, opinions on the issues themselves affect leadership perceptions? Questions of endogeneity bedevil all of these sorts of political measures, and more than likely issues affect perceptions of leaders and thus account for voting indirectly. For example, other analyses not presented here indicated that attitudes towards the Iraq war were indeed strongly and positively correlated to appraisals of Blair, both when controlling for party identity and when not, i.e. respondents who thought that the war was successful were more likely to approve of Blair. Nevertheless, even if issues influenced perceptions of Blair and other party leaders, a wide range of issues are included in the model as controls (including Iraq), and even then the partial effects of leaders are very strong. In other words, the indirect effects of these issues are likely to be very small compared to the sheer size of the direct net effects of leadership perceptions on voting. And of course, perceptions of party leaders are not, of course, the only variables typically employed in models of voting behaviour that might be 'contaminated' by prior influences—economic perceptions, party images, and even positions on election issues could also be strongly influenced by, among other things, previous partisanship.[27]

To conclude, even in a model that contains indicators of party identification, political issues, economic perceptions, and social structure we find robust leadership effects. Taken at face value these results confirm commonsense rather than some of the more sceptical interpretations taken by survey analysts. All of the main party leaders would appear to have played their role, for good or ill, in the relative electoral fates of their parties, and, unlike in 1997 and 2001, the Prime Minister was clearly a source of weakness for Labour. Though the immediacy of this analysis undertaken with the very first wave of election data from the 2005 BES suggests that some caution is advisable when making such claims, other more demanding tests of the endogeneity of leader effects and of many other favoured explanatory candidates of political popularity and voting indicate that leadership is exogenous, far more so than many political issues, ideological orientations, and perceptions of the economy. We therefore feel some confidence that these conclusions will withstand further, more leisurely analysis.

*   We would like to thank the BES team for making their 2005 Pre-Campaign Survey available so swiftly and Sonia Exley for research assistance.
1   R. Andersen and G. Evans, 'Who Blairs Wins? Leadership and Voting in the 2001 Election', 13 *British Elections & Parties Review*, 2003, pp. 229–47; H.D. Clarke, D. Sanders, M. Stewart and P.F. Whiteley, *Political Choice in Britain*, Oxford University Press, 2004.
2   N. Assinder, BBC News Online, 17.9.03, http://news.bbc.co.uk/1/hi/uk_politics/3096172.stm.
3   See A. Cooper's question-and-answer session in *The Times Online*, 6.5.05, for a more balanced view, http://www.timesonline.co.uk/article/0,,616-1600904,00.html.
4   See P. Cowley and J. Green, 'New leaders, same problems: The Conservatives' in A. Geddes and J. Tonge (eds), *The British General Election of 2005* , Palgrave Macmillan, 2005, forthcoming.
5   Note also that Mori polls (on Bob Worcester's Weblog) indicate that although Mr Blair's perceived trustworthiness declined over time, so did that of the Conservative leadership. Moreover, despite much chest-beating about the recent demise of political trust, levels of public trust in 'politicians generally' (18%) and in 'government ministers' (20%) to 'tell the truth' were no lower in 2005 than they were in the early-1980s (18% and 16% in 1983) and higher than in the early-1990s (14% and 11% in 1993).

6   A. Mughan, *Media and the Presidentialization of Parliamentary Elections*, Palgrave, 2000; C. Bean and A. Mughan, 'Leadership Effects in Parliamentary Elections in Australia and Britain', 83 *American Political Science Review*, 1989, pp. 1165–79; I. Crewe and A. King, 'Did Major win? Did Kinnock Lose? Leadership Effects in the 1992 election' in A. Heath, R. Jowell and J. Curtice with B. Taylor (eds), *Labour's Last Chance? The 1992 Election and Beyond*, Dartmouth, 1984; J. Curtice and S. Holmberg, 'Leaders' in Jacques Thomassen (ed.), *The European Voter*, Oxford University Press, forthcoming.

7   Andersen and Evans, 'Who Blairs Wins?', op. cit.; Clarke, *et al.*, *Political Choice in Britain*, op. cit.; J. Bartle, 'Partisanship, Performance and Personality: Competing and Complementary Characterisations of the 2001 British General Election', 9 *Party Politics*, 2003, pp. 317–45. A. King (ed.), *Leaders' Personalities and the Outcomes of Democratic Elections*, Oxford University Press, 2002; D. Butler and D. Kavanagh, *The British General Election of 2001*, Palgrave, 2001; P. Norton, 'The Conservative Party: Is There Anyone Out There?' in A. King (ed.), *Britain at the Polls, 2001*, Chatham House, 2002; C. Seymour-Ure, 'New Labour and the Media' in Anthony King (ed.), *Britain at the Polls, 2001*, Chatham House, 2002.

8   J. Bartle and I. Crewe, 'The Impact of Party Leaders in Britain: Strong Assumptions, Weak Evidence' in A. King (ed.), *Leaders' Personalities and the Outcomes of Democratic Elections*, Oxford University Press, 2002.

9   J. Bartle 'Why Labour Won: Again' in Anthony King (ed.), *Britain at the Polls 2001*, Chatham House, 2002, p. 192.

10 King, *Leaders' Personalities and the Outcomes of Democratic Election*, op. cit.; Curtice and Holmberg, 'Leaders', op. cit.

11 'The Impact of Party Leaders in Britain', op. cit.; see also King and Crewe, 'Did Major Win?, op. cit.; R.M. Worcester and R. Mortimore, *Explaining Labour's Landslide*, Politico's, 1999.

12 Andersen and Evans, 'Who Blairs Wins?', op. cit.; Bartle, 'Why Labour Won?', op. cit.

13 G. Evans and R. Andersen, 'Endogenizing the Economy: Political Preferences and Economic Perceptions across the Electoral Cycle', 1 *Revue do la Maison Francaise d'Oxford*, 2003, pp. 117–44; G. Evans and R. Andersen, 'The Political Conditioning of Economic Perceptions', *Journal of Politics*, forthcoming; C. Wlezien, M.N. Franklin and D. Twiggs, 'Economic Perceptions and Vote Choice: Disentangling the Endogeneity', 19 *Political Behavior*, 1997, pp. 7–17.

14 See, e.g. M. Fiorina, *Retrospective Voting in American National Elections*, Yale University Press, 1981.

15 G. Evans, A. Heath and M. Lalljee, 'Measuring Left-Right and Libertarian–Authoritarian Values in the British Electorate', 47 *British Journal of Sociology*, 1996, pp. 93–112.

16 G. Evans, 'European Integration, Party Politics and Voting in the 2001 Election',12 *British Elections & Parties Review*, 2002, pp. 95–110.

17 We also included 'attention to politics' in preliminary models and tested for interactions with leadership perceptions on vote choice, but none of these effects were significant so we exclude them from the models reported here.

18 T. Hastie and R. Tibshirani, *Generalized Additive Models*, Chapman and Hall, 2002.

19 For the Labour vote, it was determined that the influences of appraisals of Blair were linear, but for Howard and Kennedy quadratic polynomials were necessary to capture the nonlinear trend. For the Conservative Party, the effect of Howard and Kennedy was adequately modelled with a linear trend, but a quadratic polynomial was necessary for Blair. The effects of leaders on vote for the Liberal Democrats were slightly more complicated, requiring quadratic polynomials for Blair and Howard and a cubic polynomial for Kennedy.

20 J.H. Silber, P.R. Rosenbaum and R.N. Ross, 'Comparing the Contributions of Groups of Predictors: Which Outcomes Vary with Hospital Rather than Patient Characteristics?', 90 *Journal of the American Statistical Association*, 1995, pp. 7–18. The measure compares the ratio of the overall contribution to the dependent variable of two sets of variables through the log of the standard deviation ratio between the two sets. In other words, the ratio of the overall contribution of a particular set of variables, X, compared with that of another set of variables, Z, should equal 0 (i.e. X/Z = 1) if the two variables have equal importance in terms of their effects on Y. If the ratio is less than 0 (i.e. it is a negative number) then Z is more important than X. On the other hand, if the ratio is larger than 0 (i.e. a positive number), X is more important than Z. We use the David Firth's relimp package for R to implement the relative importance measure (http://www.warwick.ac.uk/go/relimp).

21 J. Fox, 'Effect Displays for Generalized Linear Models', 17 *Sociological Methodology*, 1987, pp. 347–61; J. Fox, 'Effect Displays in R for Generalised Linear Models', 15 *Journal of Statistical Software*, 2003, pp. 1–27. Effects are calculated by finding fitted values for a set of contrived observations for all values through the range of the leadership variable in question with all control variables (including the leadership variables not being examined) set to typical values (means for quantitative variables and proportions for categories of categorical variables). We then transform the fitted values from the logit scale to

the scale of the response, i.e. to the probability scale, and plot them against the leadership variable under examination.

22 See J. Fox, *Applied Regression Analysis*, Sage, 1997, Chapter 15.

23 Silber, Rosenbaum and Ross, 'Comparing the Contributions of Groups of Predictors', op. cit. This measure compares the overall contribution to the dependent variable of two sets of variables through the log of the standard deviation ratio between the two sets.

24 Bartle and Crewe, 'The Impact of Party Leaders in Britain', op. cit., p. 82; see also J. Bartle, 'Homogenous Models and Heterogeneous Voters', *Political Studies*, forthcoming.

25 Anderson and Evans, 'Who Blairs Wins?', op. cit.

26 For previous disputes on such matters, see G. Evans, 'Economics and Politics Revisited: Exploring the Decline in Conservative Support, 1992–95', 47 *Political Studies* 1999, pp. 139–51; G. Evans, 'Economics, Politics and the Pursuit of Exogeneity: Why Pattie, Johnston and Sanders are Wrong', 47 *Political Studies*, 1999, pp. 933–8; and C. Pattie, R. Johnston and D. Sanders, 'On Babies and Bathwater: A Comment on Evans' "Economics and Politics Revisited"', 47 *Political Studies* 1999, pp. 918–32.

27 For an elaboration of this argument with respect to economic perceptions, see Evans and Andersen, 'Endogenizing the Economy', op. cit. Evans and Anderson, 'The Political Conditioning of Economic Perceptions', op. cit; Wlezien, Franklin and Twiggs, 'Economic Perceptions and Vote Choice', op. cit. On issues, see G. Evans and R. Andersen, 'Do Issues Decide? Partisan Conditioning and Perceptions of Party Issue Positions across the Electoral Cycle', 14 *British Elections and Parties Review*, 2004, pp. 18–39.

ROSIE CAMPBELL AND JONI LOVENDUSKI

Winning Women's Votes? The Incremental Track to Equality

In the incremental track to equality for women, small and gradual improvements to their position in politics, at work, and in their pay and benefits may lead, eventually, to parity between women and men. In this conceptualisation women are content to wait for equality through decades of gradual change until a new equilibrium between the sexes is achieved. The alternative fast track strategy uses affirmative action to jump-start the equality process by placing women in positions of power and authority, altering recruitment mechanisms accordingly. Throughout the world, the use of fast track strategies has increased in politics since the 1980s, and measures such as quotas have now been used in more than 90 countries.[1] Britain is a puzzling case as it has the mechanisms for the fast track strategy, but its progress suggests it is firmly on an incremental track. Slow progress results partly from the limited opportunities provided by the Westminster election system and, as a consequence, partly from the failure of all but one of the major political parties to select women for winnable seats.

The 2005 general election saw a return to the small increases of women MPs characteristic of Westminster elections during the 1980s and early 1990s. In 2005, ten more women were returned to the 646-member House of Commons than in 2001, bringing their numbers up to 128 or 19.8% of all members. At 45th place in the Inter-parliamentary Union ranking of women in legislatures, this is above the world average for women in the lower house (16%), but it remains far lower than the 28% which is the West European average.[2] The British figures are also disappointing because parliament approved the Sex Discrimination (Election Candidates) Act (SDCA) in 2001. The act is permissive: it allows, but does not require, political parties to implement quotas of women. Only the Labour Party took advantage of its provisions by reintroducing All Women Shortlists (AWS) in its candidate selection for the 2005 general election. Each of the three main parties increased their

© Oxford University Press 2005
doi: 10.1093/pa/gsi072

numbers of women MPs. The apparently similar small increases in the numbers of women MPs for each party conceal substantial differences in the measures adopted to increase the representation of women, raising questions about the complex patterns of women's equality strategies in British political parties. Such questions are framed by broader issues about the gendered nature of political representation and the relationship between substantive and descriptive political representation.

Representation is a process. In any political system it is more than a simple matter of who is elected. It is also about what happens between elections and may be a matter of considerable public debate before and after elections. Therefore, to assess the quality of women's political representation following the May poll we must consider their part in the processes of candidate selection, manifesto making, and campaigning in the context of assessing the performance of elected women MPs as representatives of women. A focus on women is justified because Westminster politics are overwhelmingly male dominated, meaning that the long campaign for the equality of women and men in parliament is first and foremost about increasing the presence of women. Feminist theory suggests that increasing women's presence brings about a feminisation of politics that affects women and men.[3] These are processes of regendering politics in which change in the numbers of women and men are associated with changes in the behaviour of both sexes, with considerable potential impact on politics. Accordingly, this study offers a gendered account of the 2005 British General Election. We first review the campaign since 2001 to alter the balance of the House of Commons in favour of women. We then discuss the extent to which political parties highlighted women in their campaigns and targeted women voters in their manifestos and assess reactions both in the form of media coverage of the campaign and the response of women voters to the parties. We then describe the outcomes in terms of the position of women in the House of Commons and in government and the gender implications of the government's policy agenda. Finally, the study summarises how well women are represented at Westminster and whether the slowly growing gender balance involves changes in substantive representation.

Women's equality advocacy 2001–05

In 1997 the Labour party returned a record number of women MPs to the House of Commons. This increase was due to the Labour party's implementation of all-women shortlists in the run up to the 1997 general election. However, prior to the election they were declared illegal and abandoned by the party. As a result Labour returned fewer women after the 2001 general election. In order to increase the number of women MPs further, the party introduced the Sex Discrimination (Election Candidates) Act 2002. The bill permitted all-women shortlists for a limited time period. The Labour party committed itself to placing women, through this process, in the majority of its retirement seats (where the Labour MP was standing down).

Renewed activity to increase the presence of women at Westminster in 2005 began before the 2001 election results were declared. Women's advocates at the Fawcett Society and in parliament anticipated the fall in women's representation. One effect was the immediate agreement by government to the legislation described above. Considerable press coverage was devoted to major reports detailing discrimination against women in candidate selection, sexism at Westminster, and the impact of gender on political participation. The Fawcett report found evidence of sex discrimination operating in all of the parties' selection procedures.[4] The study found a 'self-perpetuating male candidate syndrome' and that 'favourite sons' were privileged over other candidates.[5] It concluded with a call for equality guarantees. The report's findings received wide media attention and brought women's representation onto the political agenda. The evidence of institutional sexism within the Labour party gave further force to the long-running demand from feminist members for the legalisation of all-women shortlists.

In 2004 a number of research reports on women and politics were widely reported in the media. The electoral commission's report on political participation demonstrated that women are still less likely than men to be active in formal politics, but this pattern is reversed in constituencies with a woman MP.[6] Although this finding has not been extensively researched, similar conclusions have been made in the United States.[7] At the end of 2004, reports by women MPs of sexual harassment at Westminster generated a media outcry.[8] These events ensured that women's representation remained on the political agenda during the long campaign.

'Gender gaps' in public opinion were a mainstay of political journalism during the period. Surveys reported that women were less satisfied with government than men, less likely to support the Conservatives, and more disaffected by politics. These findings were taken up by journalists who provided a steady stream of commentary on women's issues and women voters. This journalism did not happen by accident. Women MPs were active on the issue throughout the parliament. Together with other party women, they ensured that debates about increasing women's representation took place in the major political parties. During the 1990s, women's advocates became adept at political communications. Fawcett, in particular, operated an effective press strategy in which sympathetic journalists were cultivated and briefed. Research framed in terms of standard political narratives of voter satisfaction and preferences was commissioned, then offered as exclusives to key journalists, and launched at well-publicised press conferences. Sophisticated press releases and statements by the society's director were issued at regular intervals. Fawcett repeatedly used gender gap data to make its case for women's political representation. In short, women's advocates used evidence about an emerging gender gap to place pressure on parties to feminise politics. They made links between substantive and descriptive representation of women; they used pragmatic arguments to suggest that fair representation of women would bring an electoral reward. These interventions were and are clever politics. All of the main political parties responded to the media scrutiny and the potential impact upon women's votes. Teresa May called for the Conservative party's modernisation programme to include equality guarantees for women.[9] The party rejected her demands for all-women shortlists but recognised the need to find other mechanisms to increase the number of women MPs.

Candidate selection changes and diversity issues

The selection of electoral candidates is determined by supply and demand in each political party. On the demand side, selectors must be willing to choose women, and for this to be possible a sufficient supply of qualified aspirant women candidates must be available. The three strategies political parties use to increase the diversity of their candidates operate both on supply and demand. The strategies are *equality rhetoric, equality promotion*, and *equality guarantees*.[10]

Equality rhetoric is the public acceptance of claims for representation. It is found in party campaign platforms and discourse, including the speeches and writings of political leaders. Equality rhetoric may include, for instance, exhortations to women candidates to come forward. Such words and arguments may well influence the attitudes and beliefs of the selectorate and aspirant candidates. For example, Michael Howard stated that 'We must be an inclusive party. We must represent every section of British society' (*Radio 4*, November 2004). Equality promotion goes further, attempting to bring those who are currently under-represented into political competition, for example, by offering special training to candidates and selectors, providing financial assistance, or setting targets. Rhetoric and promotion aim to affect demand and supply. Both Labour and the Liberal Democrats have utilised equality promotion strategies since the 1980s, while the Conservatives first adopted it in the form of training for candidates and equality training for selectors after 2001.

By contrast, equality guarantees are directed at demand. Such guarantees require an increase in the number or proportion of particular types of candidates. In using compulsory quotas, for example, parties make a particular social characteristic a necessary qualification for office. The 2002 Act permits political parties to guarantee the selection of women by including a requirement to select women in their procedures. The Westminster first-past-the-post plurality electoral system leaves parties with few options if they wish to implement equality guarantees. Recruitment procedures for the three main parties involve the sequential stages for nominees of approval, application, nomination,

1. Women Candidates and MPs for the Main Parties, 1979–2005

	Conservative		Labour		Liberal Democrat		Total in All Parties	
	PPC	MPs	PPC	MPs	PPC	MPs	N. of all MPs	% of all MPs
1979	31	13	52	11	52	0	19	3.0
1983	40	13	78	10	75	0	23	3.5
1987	46	17	92	21	106	2	41	6.3
1992	63	20	138	37	143	2	60	9.2
1997	69	13	157	101	140	3	120	18.2
2001	92	14	146	94	135	5	118	17.9
2005	118	17	166	97	142	10	128	19.8

Sources: P. Norris and J. Lovenduski (1995) *Political Recruitment* Cambridge University Press and The British Parliamentary Constituency Database, 1992–2005.

short-listing, and final selection. Although all stages of selection have been subject to procedural change to ensure the selection of women, it is the shortlisting and selection stages that are the most important in all three equality strategies. To encourage women's selection rhetorically it is only necessary to draw the desirability of increasing the number of women candidates to the attention of selectors. To promote their selection, measures to ensure that some women are shortlisted are necessary. To guarantee the *selection* of women, it is necessary to ensure that only women may be chosen and, hence, that only women may be shortlisted. To guarantee their election, women candidates must be selected in winnable seats. The alternative mechanism in plurality electoral systems is the use of reserved seats for women, a constitutional or legal rather than an internal party matter. If demand is *the* problem for women's legislative recruitment, then equality rhetoric and equality promotion are likely to be of limited effect. Equality rhetoric may encourage greater numbers of women to enter the candidate recruitment pool; equality promotion may ensure that women aspirant candidates are better prepared, trained, and resourced. Neither of these, however, is sufficient to guarantee that party selectorates will pick women candidates for winnable seats. Equality rhetoric and equality promotion have been repeatedly tested by political parties and found to have limited, if any, effects. Only the Labour Party used guarantees for Westminster elections—in 1997 and in 2005.

For the 2005 general election, all three major parties selected more women than in 2001, however only Labour placed women and men candidates equally in winnable seats (Table 1).

Labour selections

Following passage of the SDCA, all political parties came under increased pressure to alter nomination procedures to accommodate more women. Labour, however, was faced with the problem of managing different kinds of diversity. It adopted three selection goals: (1) increasing the numbers of women elected; (2) avoiding the perception that 'no men need apply'; and (3) increasing the numbers of ethnic minority candidates and MPs. In practice he third goal meant that seats deemed by the party to be winnable by a minority candidate (i.e. where the constituency had a significant ethnic minority electorate) were less likely to be classified as using an all-women shortlist. Since 2001 Operation Black Vote (OBV), an umbrella organisation of ethnic minority equality advocates, has argued repeatedly that the selection process was a zero sum game in which more women candidates meant fewer selections of ethnic minorities. The organisation called for open short-lists in constituencies with large minority populations. Simon Woolley, OBV's national coordinator, claimed that all-women shortlists yield white candidates (*BBC News website*, 1.12.04). OBV's position was criticised by Hannah Pool of the *Guardian*, who felt that the interests of black women were missing from the debate (*Guardian*, 13.12.04). Thus, to achieve the fair representation of black and Asian women, additional mechanisms to supplement all-women shortlists may be required.

In selection for the May 2005 general election, Labour reintroduced all-women shortlists with a long-term objective of achieving equal numbers of women and men MPs. Accordingly, Labour's National Executive Committee devised a strategy aiming to deliver women as 35% of the Labour MPs in England and Wales.[11] Accordingly, sitting Labour MPs were asked to inform the party of their intention to stand down before December 2002. 50% of these retirement seats were expected to select from all-women shortlists. Later announcements would be classified as 'late retirements' and automatically required to select from an all-women shortlists—with the caveat that the NEC retained the power to authorise exceptions in special circumstances (*Guardian*, 10.1.03 & 29.1.03). All challenger seats would be open shortlists, as would by-elections, reselections, and post-trigger selections.[12] In the event, ten early retirement seats were classified as all-women shortlists, and three were left open, a ratio of 3:1.[13] An all-women shortlist was adopted in twenty-one seats where male Labour MPs were standing down, leaving nine constituencies where an all-women shortlist had been used to replace a woman MP who was retiring. The Labour party was able to increase the number of women MPs despite losing seats because of the reintroduction of all-women shortlists. In fact, had the Labour party retained all of its 2001 seats in 2005, women would have made up 30% of the parliamentary Labour party, still short of its 35% target.

Conservative selections

Conservative strategy stopped at equality promotion but did include major changes to selection procedures. Guided by Teresa May, revisions were made to the criteria and processes of approval, and local constituencies were permitted to vary their selection processes.[14] The party commissioned a recruitment expert to review their selection procedures, which had originally been designed by the army for its officer recruitment and adopted by the party in the 1980s. As a result of the review, selection procedures were changed so that formal approval of candidate qualifications depended upon their demonstration of six core competencies, including: communication and intellectual skill, the ability to relate to different kinds of people, leadership and motivation, resilience, and conviction to conservative ideas. Training of selectors and returning officers in equality selection was intended to ensure that the new criteria were well understood. The aim was to establish procedures according to which decisions would be based on candidate quality. Other changes included the introduction of different selection mechanisms in specific seats, including American-style primaries, and city seats strategies. In the latter case, candidates were nominated for an area, such as Newcastle, and they were only allocated to a specific constituency within the area at the start of the official campaign. These new mechanisms were expected to lead to the selection of more women, a prediction that was borne out when 16 of 30 'city seats' and four of eight primaries selected women candidates. The new mechanisms were applied only in unwinnable seats, however, and hence none of the candidates recruited by these means were elected.

Liberal Democrat selection

The Liberal Democrats also stopped with equality promotion. Their procedures included a sex-balancing rule at shortlisting stage, a requirement that the constituency selection committee be sex balanced, training of returning officers, and diversity monitoring of the selection procedures. The use of all-women shortlists was discussed at their 2001 and 2002 party conferences but rejected when it failed to achieve the required two-thirds majority. Opponents mounted fierce opposition to the proposal. In 2001 young women party members who appeared at conference wearing pink t-shirts bearing the slogan 'I am not a token woman' became a potent symbol of opposition to equality guarantees. In 2002 the pink t-shirts reappeared, the vote was lost again, and the matter has since been dropped.[15] Opponents claimed they were vindicated when ten Liberal Democrat women were elected to parliament in May 2005, twice as many as in 2001. Three of the gains were unexpected—in Solihull, Falmouth and Cambourne, and Hornsey and Wood Green, where Loreley Burt, Julia Goldsworthy, and Lynne Featherstone were elected, respectively.

Race was a selection issue in all the parties but especially in Labour, given their greater strength in minority areas. Labour singularly failed to select ethnic minority women as candidates. None were selected on an all-women shortlist, a reflection of the party's decision to concentrate this strategy in constituencies without significant minority populations. Of nine Labour minority women candidates, only two were elected—Dawn Butler and Diane Abbott. Dawn Butler stood and won in Brent South, having failed to be selected in the All-Women-Shortlist seat of West Ham, a constituency in which nearly 60% of the population are ethnic minorities. Brent South was, by default, the first ever use of an all-minority short-list. The number of minority women MPs did not increase, however, because Labour MP Oona King lost her seat in Bethnal Green and Bow to the Respect candidate, George Galloway. Nor were any of the eight Conservative and nine Liberal Democrat minority women candidates elected.

More nominations of women led to a rise in the number of women MPs in each of the main parties. Both Labour and the Lib Dems also increased their proportion of elected women, but only in the Labour Party were there sufficient numbers of women in winnable seats for nominations to match elections.

Table 2 demonstrates that the Labour party selected most of its women candidates in seats it had won in 2001. The majority of women Conservative party candidates were selected in seats where either the party was third in 2001 or in seats where it was more than 10% behind the winning party. The pattern of selection of women Liberal Democrat candidates is more challenging to interpret. Few women were placed in seats that they won in 2001, but a larger proportion was selected for winnable seats, especially where the vote margin was between 5 and 10%. Although the total number of seats in these categories was small, the Liberal Democrats were more successful at selecting women in marginal seats than the Conservative party. However, the marginality of the seat is not the only indication of it being winnable: specific local circumstances are important, such as nature of the candidate, the campaign, and local politics. Table 3 illustrates that the Conservative party did not substantially increase the number of women elected in any type of seat. A different pattern emerged amongst Liberal Democrat candidates: two new women Liberal Democrat MPs were elected in marginal seats, and four new women MPs were elected in seats that were not categorised as winnable. Thus, the increase in women Liberal Democrat MPs is in a large part due to the party's gains in seats they were not expecting to win.

2. Women Candidates by Type of Seat and Party 2005

Type of Seats	Inheritor Seats (i)		Challenger Targets 5% Maj (ii)		Challenger Targets 10% Maj (iii)		Challenger Unwinnable Seats (iv)		Total	
	N	%	N	%	N	%	N	%	N	%
Conservative	14	8.5	4	13.3	7	18.0	93	24.0	118	19.0
Labour	115	28.5	2	25.0	2	9.5	47	24.0	166	20.0
Liberal Democrat	4	8.0	2	22.0	5	38.5	114	23.5	125	20.0

Note: Seats were classified into the following types. (i) 'Inheritor seats', where the women candidate took over from a retiring incumbent from their own party. (ii) 'Challenger target seats', where the women candidate faced an incumbent MP from another party with a majority of 5% or less. (iii) 'Challenger target seats' where women candidate faced an incumbent MP from another party with a majority of 5 to 10%. (iv) 'Challenger unwinnable seats', where the woman candidate faced an incumbent MP from another party with a majority of 10% or more.

Source: The British Parliamentary Constituency Database, 1992–2005.

3. Women MPs Elected in 2005 by Type of Seat

Party	Inheritor Seat		Challenger Targets 5% Maj (ii)		Challenger targets 10% Maj (iii)		Challenger unwinnable seats (iv)		Total
	N	%	N	%	N	%	N	%	N
Conservative	14	9	1	6	1	8	1	17	17
Labour	98	28	0	0	0	0	0	0	98
Liberal Democrat	4	9	1	33	1	25	4	36	10

Note: Seats were classified into the following types. (i) 'Inheritor seats', where the women candidate took over from a retiring incumbent from their own party. (ii) 'Challenger target seats', where the women candidate faced an incumbent MP from another party with a majority of 5% or less. (iii) 'Challenger target seats' where women candidate faced an incumbent MP from another party with a majority of 5 to 10%. (iv) 'Challenger unwinnable seats', where the woman candidate faced an incumbent MP from another party with a majority of 10% or more.
Source: The British Parliamentary Constituency Database, 1992–2005.

Overall incremental improvements in the number of women as candidates and MPs therefore conceals varying rates of progress since 2001, with Labour running faster than the Liberal Democrats, and with the Conservatives retreating in percentage terms. These rates of progress suggest that, under current policies, it will be a very long time before Westminster is comprised of equal numbers of women and men. The results of the May 2005 election put women's representation at Westminster at 41st place in the world—behind Rwanda, South Africa, Germany, The Netherlands, The Nordic Countries, and Spain. The proportion of women MPs at Westminster also compares unfavourably with the Scottish Parliament and the National Assembly for Wales, where women are 42% and 50%, respectively, of members.

The issues: manifestos

During 2004, Labour women made representations to the leadership about both manifesto contents and the need for a more feminised campaign image. The Labour party also produced a children's mini manifesto which may have been targeted at women. Analysis by Sarah Childs demonstrates that the Labour party and the Liberal Democrats manifestos addressed more women's issues than the Conservative manifesto. Using criteria developed by the Fawcett society Childs concludes that where the Conservative party's manifesto 'does address women it has very little to offer feminists'.[16]

Labour's appeal to women was built on its Third Way conception of employment as the key to citizenship. Its manifesto emphasises pledges to help 'hard-working families' through expanding the tax credit system but generally focuses upon crime, stable taxation, and public services.

As in previous campaigns, the Labour party's policy proposals targeted working women (www.tuc.org.uk, 29.4.05). Working women would be the main beneficiaries of the promised increase in the minimum wage, increase in maternity leave, and extension of childcare provision. They pledged to provide universal affordable childcare for 3–14 year olds by 2010. Lone parents, most likely to be women, were guaranteed £258 per week should they work full-time. The strategy is soft on employers, with many caveats in publications about the needs to balance the concerns of women, parent's carers, with those of business and employers. The same conceptualisation informs the governments Equality Bill, due to be debated in the current parliament.

The Liberal Democrats campaign was not overtly directed at women voters but a number of its key policies would have gender impacts. They claimed that their opposition to tuition fees would benefit women, who tend to spend fewer years in the work force. Free care for the elderly would help would be of particular benefit to women, who make up the majority of caretakers (*Guardian*, 21.2.05). Their pledges on pensions targeted women directly, promising that they would redress the current sex discrimination of the system.

The Conservative party made little direct reference to women in the campaign. They focused on immigration and asylum, lower taxes, crime, school discipline, cleaner hospitals, and accountability. In the area of childcare, they promised to extend formal arrangements to include grandparents in the media presentation, although the details were not included in the written manifesto. The Conservative party manifesto, like its campaign, addressed a small number of themes. This strategy marginalised women's interests, which were not central to the campaign.

The campaign strategy

The consistent activity and publicity for women's representation issues portended a more feminised campaign than in 2001. And in the pre-campaign period it seemed that women's issues were to be foregrounded. Women's magazines including *Vogue, Glamour,* and *Cosmopolitan* interviewed party leaders. An issue of *New Statesman* titled *newstateswoman* was published on the fourth of April with articles about women's voting, the likely manifesto pledges, discussions of key issues such as child care and maternity leave, and an interview with the Minister for Culture and Sport, Tessa Jowell. Harriet Harman was featured in *Hello* magazine, while interviews with other women Ministers appeared in popular magazines and the Labour-supporting press. Signs of a struggle over the place of women in the campaign became apparent in February when Alan Millburn, Labour's campaign manager, briefed journalists that women ministers were 'too posh' for normal Labour voters. Ruth Kelly, graduate of Westminster School, Queens College Oxford and the London School of Economics, was thought by Millburn to have a more classless air than other, more feminist-identified cabinet ministers (*Observer*, 6.2.05, *Guardian*, 22.2.05). This was an example of the invocation of class arguments (by middle class men) to trump gender, a common occurrence in the Labour party during the 1980s.[17] Following interventions by senior Labour women, Millburn was forced to deny being the source of such sentiments. The ineffectiveness of this approach is instructive, marking a possible shift in the strategies available to opponents of the feminisation of politics.

Once the campaign proper began, women were relegated to their traditional places in the background, on the sidelines, and as leaders' wives. Although Ruth Kelly and Patricia Hewitt were prominent in the postponed Labour Manifesto launch on 13 April, and that was the last we saw of them for some while. The main Labour campaign soon became something of a buddy film, an election road movie starring Blair and Brown with a number of minor male characters appearing and reappearing as the journey of the buddies progressed, their strengths were displayed, and their relationship apparently developed. Women politicians were slightly more evident than in 2001, but visible mainly in the background, displayed 'like flowers on a kitchen table' as one commentator put it (*Guardian*, 28.4.05). In this campaign, as in 2001, it was the male party leaders who dominated political communications.

All three parties used the media to engage in direct appeals to women voters, a factor examined in more detail below. Labour produced a magazine '*Family Matters*', and Labour and the Liberal Democrats produced manifestos for women. Labour also maintained a website ' What is Labour doing for women?' Less publicised were the efforts of Labour women to campaign for women. A 'women's bus' filled with women MPs, women ministers, and trade unionists visited marginal constituencies to make direct contact with women voters and to encourage women to vote (*Guardian*, 28.4.05).

Media

Analysis of the National Media by the Communication research Centre at Loughborough University showed that 86.3% of images of political actors were men and that issues designated as 'women's issues' accounted for 0.5% of all the themes coded for their sample.[18] In 2001, 90.2% of images of political actors were of males.[19]

In the run up to the 2005 general election the parties and the media were unusually interested in women voters. Attempts to target or 'woo' women's votes were highlighted by the media coverage and became a central feature of the campaign. The generally high levels of interest in the female electorate were not reflected, however, in discussions of women candidates. The Conservative party was keen to inform the media and the public that they had the highest number of minority candidates, albeit in unwinnable seats, but the issue of women's representation was not high on the political agenda.

The media attempted to pigeonhole women voters by a now familiar process of labelling. 'Worcester woman' returned, accompanied by 'letdown woman' and 'do-it-all woman'. These catch phrases allowed the framing of women as a target group of voters. But there was no 'Mondeo man', and men as a group were generally absent from the parties' campaigns and from the newspaper reporting (*Observer*, 20.2.05; *Telegraph*, 30.3.05; *Independent*, 01.4.05; *Mirror*, 15.4.05).

A story developed by a number of different journalists was that Tony Blair had lost his appeal amongst women. Blair appeared to acknowledge this by referring to his 'relationship' with the electorate, suggesting that he might have taken his voters for granted. The press noted Blair's appearance on daytime television shows and interviews in '*Take-a-break*' magazine as indicative of his attempt to present himself as women-friendly. However, some pollsters suggested that older women in particular were disillusioned with the Labour leadership (*Guardian*, 13.3.05; *Independent*, 24.3.05). Thus, women became a key target group in the press.

It was thought that women were especially unhappy about Britain's involvement in the Iraq war. This was magnified when Tony Blair faced a hostile all-female audience on ITV's Jonathan Dimbleby programme, and it was generally thought that Labour might suffer from lower turn-out amongst women. A widely reported MORI poll commissioned by Fawcett found that 60% of women were unhappy with Tony Blair. Women were also considered more likely to be affected by a lack of trust in Tony Blair in particular, suggesting that they might value integrity above competence.

All three party leaders were present in women's media; all of them were interviewed on the BBC's *Woman's Hour*. They answered questions on work-life balance and women's representation in Parliament. They were also asked about they own family life. Charles Kennedy stressed that he wanted to be a 'hands on' Dad, Michael Howard was pressed into admitting that he did not cook, and Tony Blair made a brief reference to Leo. All three were interviewed by *Cosmopolitan* magazine. Tony Blair gave interviews to a number of other magazines including *Grazia*, *Vogue* and *Glamour*. The rest of the media responded in predictable ways. Thus *Daily Mail* readers saw more of Sandra Howard than Conservative MPs. A possibly ill-judged eve of election interview with the Blairs in the *Sun* (4.5.05) offered hints about the romantic life of the couple.

In Michael Howard's interview with *Cosmopolitan* magazine he stated that he was in favour in a reduction in the time-limit for abortion and that he thought that the current system was tantamount to abortion on demand. Howard claimed to have voted for a 22-week ban in 1990 but this was found by Phillip Cowley to be incorrect; Howard had in fact voted for a 24-week limit. A press furore broke out that culminated in the party leaders saying that the issue was not appropriate for election debate.

Closer to the election it was reported that women were perhaps 'returning to Blair' (*Guardian*, 21.4.05). ICM polls put women's support for Labour one point above men's. Overall the vacillation in women's voting intentions reported in the media was probably a result of poor research methods. Women's 'disillusionment' was most often described without any comparison to men (*Daily Mail*, 28.2.05; *News of the World*, 13.3.05). Reports of poll evidence that women were unhappy with Tony Blair frequently did not offer comparable data on men. This sloppy reporting created the impression that women, as a group, were more likely to switch away from Labour. The aggregate MORI data, made available after the election, indicate that no such switch took place; indeed according to this data, the opposite occurred. Thus media representations of women voters were not straightforward. On one hand, the emphasis on women voters provided a positive voice for an under-represented group. Yet the failure to highlight whether women's perspectives were genuinely different from men's led to stereo-typing and the portrayal of women as simplistic voters whose voting intentions were governed by a personalised reaction to Blair.

Women voters

Traditionally women in Britain have been more likely than men to vote for the Conservative party. In 1997, however, Pippa Norris identified a gender generation gap, where younger women were more likely than younger men to support the Labour party.[20] Norris's evidence of a turn towards Labour amongst young women was also evident in the 2001 election, in which younger women were more left-leaning and slightly more likely to support the Labour party than men.[21] Worldwide, women are apparently also becoming more left-leaning than men.[22] Do the results of the 2005 British General election support the 'gender-gen-eration' gap hypothesis that successive generations of women are mov-ing to the left of men? Or, instead, did women of all ages return to the Conservatives? We can estimate any differences between men and women by looking at pooled MORI campaign opinion polls which pro-vide an exceptionally large sample size suitable for subgroup analysis. In the months preceding the election, MORI data suggested that for the first time in the postwar period, a balance of more women than men were likely to vote Labour.[23]

Table 2 outlines the voting patterns found by MORI among men and women of different ages. Within each age group, a gender gap figure is produced and displayed in the final column; a positive figure indicates that women in that group were more likely to support Labour then men.

Tables 4 and 5 indicate that the traditional gender gap in Britain has indeed reversed and that overall women are now more likely to vote for the Labour party than men. Table 2 shows that women under the age of 54 were more likely than men to vote for the Labour party, a trend that is even stronger in the younger age groups. Older women were more likely than men to say that they were going to vote for the Conservative party. This trend confirms the pattern that was already evident in 1997 and 2001. Table 3 demonstrates that 2005 is the first election in which

4. Voting Preference by Sex and Age, 2005

Age	Sex	Conservative	Labour	Liberal Democrat	Con/Lab Gender Gap
18–24	Men	33	34	25	20
	Women	22	43	26	
25–34	Men	29	33	27	18
	Women	21	43	28	
35–54	Men	31	36	22	8
	Women	27	40	25	
55+	Men	40	33	20	0
	Women	41	34	20	
All	Men	34	34	23	6
	Women	32	38	22	

Notes: The gender gap is calculated as Conservative lead over Labour among men minus Conservative lead over Labour among women (% Con men—% Lab men) minus (% Con women—% Lab women).
Source: MORI Final aggregate analysis from the pooled campaign surveys, 16 May 2005, Total N. 17,595 (www.mori.com).

5. The Con–Lab Gender Gap 1992–2001

Year	Size of the Gender Gap
1992	−5.8
1997	−4.5
2001	−1.1
2005	+6.0

Notes: The figures for 1992–2001 are calculated using the series of British Election Studies, validated voters only. The figure for 2005 is estimated using the MORI Final aggregate analysis from the pooled campaign surveys, 16 May 2005, Total N. 17,595 (www.mori.com).

the gender-generation gap meant that more women than men voted Labour.

Could this gradual change in the gender gap be attributable to a successful effort to target women voters mounted by the Labour party? Certainly since 1997 the Labour party has campaigned on issues that are known to be higher priorities for women voters than for men. Women are more likely than men to say that health and education are the most important election issues, although these issues remain important to both men and women.[24]

If the MORI predictions are validated,[25] then it may be that British elections are moving towards the American model, where a gender gap has been evident at the aggregate level since 1980. The media in the United States often use the gender gap to frame election reporting, for example, in stories referring to 'Soccer Moms' in 1996 and the 'Year of the Woman' in 1992. The 2005 pattern in Britain may suggest that we can expect even more emphasis by parties on targeting women and men separately in future campaigns. However, it is worth noting that the focus on the gender gap in the US has been subject to criticism. It is likely that 'gender gaps probably appear and disappear because some aspect of the electoral context or campaign- e.g. the confluence of issues, personalities or events-cues gender as politically or symbolically important in specific elections'.[26] This cautionary note notwithstanding, it seems possible that 2005 will mark a shift in the way elections are reported in future.

Women MPs, women ministers, and the agenda

In the 2005 parliament 38 new women were elected, and 29 women either stood down or lost their seat. As in 2001, only two minority women MPs were returned—in this case, Dawn Butler and Diane Abbot.

All parties lost women to retirement, including some of their most prominent MPs. Eleven Labour women MPs (25%) stood down, including Estelle Morris, former schools Minister. Three Conservative women retired, including former cabinet members Gillian Shepherd and Virginia Bottomley. Oona King and Anne Campbell were among the Labour MPs who probably lost their seats on anti-war votes. Former Women's Minister Barbara Roche was defeated in Finchley. Feminists Yvonne Fitzsimmons and Melanie Johnson were also defeated. In the Welsh seat of Blaenau Gwen, once a Labour stronghold represented by Nye Bevan and later Michael Foot, an anti-all-women shortlist candidate, Peter Law, defeated Maggie Jones on a 49% swing. Helen Clark, nee Brinton, survived three deselection attempts, only to lose her seat to the Conservative candidate. Jane Griffiths was de-selected in Reading East and replaced by local councillor Tony Page, who then lost to the Conservative, Rob Wilson.

After the election, Blair appointed six women to his cabinet and promoted Patricia Hewitt to the Health Portfolio. Hewitt's promotion is the only visible gain for cabinet women, the remainder of whom were reappointed to their previous positions or to similar posts. Thus Hilary Armstrong is Chief Whip, Margaret Becket leads the Department of the Environment, Valerie Amos, once the Executive Director of the Equal Opportunities Commission, leads the House of Lords, while Tessa Jowell adds the women's portfolio to Culture, Media and Sport. Hewitt had been Minister for Women while at the DTI, where the Women and Equality Unit was developed and extended during the previous government. After considerable discussion, Number Ten announced Tessa Jowell's extended responsibilities. Even later it was announced that Meg Munn would be the unpaid junior minister with day-to-day responsibility for the portfolio. Munn's unpaid status provoked an outcry from women's advocates who perceived it as the demotion of the portfolio that it was and feared a return to 1997, when Joan Ruddock was an unpaid junior Minister who was summarily dismissed after a year in office. The fate of the Women and Equality Unit itself is not yet clear. Its functions will be split between departments. The government's new Equality Bill, announced in the Queen's speech, provides for a reorganisation of equality machinery and policy. Responsible for the lead unit on the bill, Munn's introduction to office will be particularly difficult. Twenty-six women MPs and peers were appointed to other positions in government, and most departments of state have women ministers. Exceptions are the Cabinet Office, the Ministry of Defence, the Foreign and Commonwealth Office, the Department for International Development, the Northern Ireland Office, and the Law officer's Department.

Conclusion

The three main political parties in Britain continue their attempts to increase the number of women MPs. Although only Labour has succeeded in making substantial improvements, all three parties are keen to present a more feminised image. The post-election images of the newly-elected Justine Greening, the Conservative winner in Putney, mask an election result in which the percentage of Conservative women has declined. The Liberal Democrats much trumpeted doubling of their numbers of women MPs conceals a result in which women did not win seats in proportion to their candidacies. The overall increase in the presence of women at Westminster is small: women are still less than one fifth of MPs. Their campaigns found parties making direct appeals to women voters but reluctant to foreground women in the component public events. Despite slowly rising numbers of women representatives, there is considerable evidence that, for many male party leaders and strategists, the presence of women is symbolic, and women politicians are tokens. One answer to the question of why Britain continues on the incremental track to women's representation is probably that their progress continues to be slowed by male resistance.

Even so, women are making progress and they are active in parliament, government, and the cabinet. Does it matter? The question of whether increasing the presence of women at Westminster changes their substantive representation is difficult to answer on the basis of electoral evidence, but some tentative connections are evident. We have described how Labour has, since the mid-1990s, both campaigned on issues that are known to be priorities for women, including education and health, and made specific pledges to particular groups of women— mothers, working women, women candidates, and so on. These campaign pledges have been translated into policies such as improvements in childcare, increases in paid parental leave, improvements in domestic violence policy, and changes in electoral and equality laws.[27] It is not yet possible to say if it is Labour's targeting of women voters that has secured an increase in their share of women's votes, but it is likely that women's advocates inside and outside of parliament will argue that it has. Such arguments will inform debates about political representation, campaign strategies, and policy priorities in the run up to the next general election.

1 D. Dahlerup and L. Freidenvall, 'Quotas as a Fast Track to Equal Political Representation for Women: Why Scandinavia is No Longer the Model'. Paper presented to the 19th International Political Science Association World Congress. Durban, South Africa: 29 June–4 July 2003.
2 Calculated from 'Women in National Parliaments' Inter-parliamentary Union www.ipu.org./wmn-e/ classif.html.
3 J. Lovenduski, *Feminizing Politics*, Polity, 2005.
4 L. Shepherd-Robinson and J. Lovenduski, *Women and Candidate Selection*, Fawcett, 2002.
5 Ibid p. 3.
6 P. Norris, J. Lovenduski and R. Campbell, *Gender and Political Participation*, The Electoral Commission, 2004.
7 V. Sapiro and P. Conover, 'The Variable Gender Basis of Electoral Politics: Gender and Context in the 1992 US Election', *British Journal of Political Science*, 1997/27; N. Burns, K. Schlozman and S. Verba, *The Private Roots of Public Action: Gender, Equality and Political Participation*, Harvard, 2001.
8 *Guardian*, 7.12.04.
9 T. May, 'Women in the House: The Continuing Challenge', *Parliamentary Affairs* 2004/57.
10 J. Lovenduski, *Feminizing Politics*, Polity, 2005.
11 Scotland was excluded from this process because of the impact of the reduction of Scottish Parliamentary seats at the 2005 General Election.
12 There were five open selections caused by the sitting MP losing the trigger: Peterborough (where Helen Clarke was successful in winning the selection), Tooting (where Tom Cox lost), Reading East (where Jane Griffiths lost), Brent East, and Leicester South (which followed by-election defeats).
13 There were also early retirement seats in Scotland (Dundee West (Ernie Ross) and Clydebank and Milngavie (Tony Worthington)) and Wales (Bridgend (Win Griffiths) and Blaenau Gwent (Llewelln Smith)).
14 T. May, 'Women in the House: The Continuing Challenge', *Parliamentary Affairs* 2004/57.
15 J. Lovenduski, *Feminizing Politics*, Polity, 2005, p. 127.
16 S. Childs, 'Feminizing British Politics: Sex and Gender in the 2005 General Election' in A. Geddes and J. Tonge (eds), *Britain Decides: The UK General Election 2005*, Palgrave, 2005.
17 J.Lovenduski and V. Randall, *Contemporary Feminist Politics*, Oxford University Press, 1993.
18 The media sample used by the National Media by the Communication research Centre at Loughborough University was BBC1 News, BBC2 News night, ITV News, C4 News, Sky 9 pm News, R1 Newsbeat, R4 Today, and all daily and weekly newspapers. Women's issues were classified as pay and equality issues, gender discrimination, women's movement campaigning, and women's representation in parliament.
19 J. Lovenduski, 'Gender and Politics: Critical Mass or Minority Representation', *Parliamentary Affairs* 2001/4.
20 P. Norris, 'Gender: A Gender Generation Gap?' in G. Evans and P. Norris (eds), *Critical Elections: British Parties and Voters in Long-Term Perspective*, Sage, 1999.
21 R. Campbell, 'Gender Ideology and Issue Preference', *British Journal of Politics and International Relations* 2004/6.
22 R. Inglehart and P. Norris, 'The Developmental Theory of the Gender Gap', *International Political Science Review* 2000/4.
23 R. Mortimore, P. Baines and T. Huskinson, 'Women's Political Opinions in Britain 2001–2005', Paper for PSA annual conference, University of Leeds, April 2005.
24 R. Campbell, 'Gender Ideology and Issue Preference', *British Journal of Politics and International Relations* 2004/6.
25 MORI data will not provide the last word on the emerging gender gap. The BES data available by 8 June 2005 do not support the MORI findings. However this BES release is neither validated for actual votes nor weighted for sample categories. Replication of the MORI findings must await the release of BES cross sectional data.
26 V. Sapiro and P. Conover, 'The Variable Gender Basis of Electoral Politics: Gender and Context in the 1992 US Election', *British Journal of Political Science*, 1997/27.
27 J. Lovenduski, *Feminizing Politics*, Polity, 2005.

PATRICK DUNLEAVY* AND HELEN MARGETTS⁺

The Impact of UK Electoral Systems

In the immediate aftermath of the general election the *Independent* (10 May 2005) ran a whole-page headline illustrated with contrasting graphics showing 'This is what we voted for' and 'This is what we got'. The paper launched a petition calling for a shift to a system that is fairer and more proportional, which in rapid time attracted tens of thousands of signatories, initially at a rate of more than 500 people a day. These developments highlighted the extent to which the plurality rule voting system for general elections (also still used for council elections in England and Wales) itself became an election issue. During the campaign itself the normal bi-polarising statements from Labour and Conservative politicians proclaiming a 'straight choice' between them were typically no sooner issued that drowned out in a chorus of dissent. The *Guardian* (13 and 29 April 2005) featured a prominent campaign by Polly Toynbee for readers to voter Labour with the aid of a clothes peg symbolised distaste for the Hobson's choice of supporting a government with disliked policies like the invasion of Iraq or voting for other parties and possibly 'letting in' the Conservatives (with more disliked policies, notably on immigration). The corollary of accepting the clothes peg was said to be a vigorous post-election campaign to make 2005 the last plurality rule general election.

The 2005 result offered some further significant pointers also to how the problem of achieving change in the election system might work itself out. Colomer has recently argued that there is no evidence to support Duverger's law that plurality rule systems induce a smaller number of parties. Rather he argues that when the number of parties in a system decisively increases above two or three, so the risks for established parties of power grow that they will do badly under the increasingly chaotic results that plurality rule often generates with multiple parties. At this point, and this point only, when the number of parties in a system has already increased, incumbent major party elites will be willing to move to a more proportional system as a defensive move, to safeguard their position against losing out catastrophically.[1] Thus the number of parties typically shows no further change once PR is introduced,

© Oxford University Press 2005
doi: 10.1093/pa/gsi068

because only the prior decisive advent of multi-party politics can trigger this kind of electoral system being conceded by self-interested elites. We have argued elsewhere that the UK is already in the process of a prolonged transition to PR, marked by the 'coexistence' of PR and plurality rule election systems, within which there has been a gradual transition to proportional systems.[2] (The latest increment in this process is the advent of STV for Scottish local elections and the next increment might well be the concession of PR elections for choosing at least a majority of members of the House of Lords.) To assess how far this process was advanced or not by the general election we focus on three different dimensions of electoral system effects: changes in the number of parties competing; the proportionality of the electoral system; and some continuing strengths of the current system.

Most of the analysis here focuses on the regional level, which may seem a rather strange thing to do, because regions play no formal role in plurality rule elections. However, regional results allow us to explore the diversity of plurality rule operations, which is rarely what is seems from national level data. In particular, from an 'experiential' point of view the most important aspect of electoral systems' operations is how they feel to voters. In this sense an experiential approach contrasts strongly with the more conventional, 'institutionalist' approach.[3] Strictly speaking the optimal way of assessing experiential effects would be to map most individual voters' area of reference, the areas that they consider 'around here' for themselves, and then to assess how the voting system operated within the majority perceptions of this localised 'region', whose extent might vary considerably from one constituency or region to another. The data demands of this approach are heavy, however, and we lack the key data on voters' perceptions needed to operationalise it. The regional data considered here are clunky and inadequate by comparison, but they do at least address important dimensions of variations in how citizens experienced the general election, especially by contrast with some other proportional elections recently analysed, such as the 2004 European Parliament elections where the regions are institutionally important as constituencies. Government data is also increasingly presented and analysed in terms of the standard regions.

The number of parties in competition

When the Treasury building in London was redesigned (in 2001 under a PFI project) the designer called in to handle the atrium decorated it with three large illuminated bars, running from floor to ceiling in blue, red and orange. This perhaps belated acknowledgement of the Liberal Democrats' contemporary importance in party politics was mirrored by all sections of the media, which recognised three major parties in 2005, with the Liberal Democrats' equal time allocations even extending into satirical shows. Yet like much else in British life, no sooner was an updating conceded than it in turn became dated. In 2004 the European Parliament elections showed that the number of 'effective' parties ranged between 4.8 and 5.6 across regions in Great Britain, with Labour and the Conservatives struggling to hang on to just over half the total votes between them.[4] In 2005 the 'two party' share of the vote fell below 70% for the first time, and although Labour once again became the clear majority party in the House of Commons its UK vote share fell to the lowest ever recorded for a majority government in the UK's democratic history.[5]

The roots of these changes clearly lie in first the importance of partisan dealignment, which has gradually produced greater detachment of citizens from parties and more conditional loyalties even where links remain over the last thirty years. Second, the coexistence of PR and plurality voting systems has added additional twists. The transition from the 2004 Euro election patterns, when UKIP polled 17% of the vote in Great Britain, to the general election showed one such notable interaction effect, with UKIP's support falling back sharply to just 2.5%, thanks in part to a different issue mix and partisan context and in part to UKIP's disastrous leadership splits and political finance problems in the interim. But the significance of coexistence is not to be charted in such differences alone so much as the strategy changes imposed on the 'major' parties. Thus the rise of UKIP and BNP voting in 2004 lead the government to make drastic policy changes tightening asylum and immigration rules (helping fuel its loss of support from ethnic minorities).[6] It also lead the Conservatives in 2005 to focus much of their campaign on immigration concerns (including the notorious 'It's not racist to want to limit immigration' poster). This tactic suppressed the UKIP vote and held down the BNP to less than 1% support nationally, so that unlike 2004 the Tories in 2005 had no effective enemies on the right. But the consequence of this damage limitation approach was also important, with less than half of 1% increase in the party's overall support compared with that in 2001, triggering Michael Howard's immediate resignation as leader.

The 2005 election saw a mushrooming of candidacies by UKIP, Greens, the BNP and other newer arrivals, including Respect. The votes gained per constituency by these parties were rarely substantial, but Table 1 shows that eight parties nationwide got into the top four placings across the different regions. All eight of these parties should now be considered permanent additions to the British party system, with substantial numbers of council seats for the BNP and with UKIP and the Greens both winning Euro seats and places in the London Assembly in the June 2004 elections.[7]

Table 2 gives a more detailed picture at the regional level of the new contours of competition in 2005, showing the regional rankings that underpin the scoring system used in Table 1. The Labour plus Conservative share of the vote was below two thirds in Scotland and Wales and elsewhere ranged between 69 and 75%. The largest party share of the votes was above half in only one region, the north east, and elsewhere

1. The Top Eight Parties' Votes and Regional Ranking Scores, Great Britain 2005

Party	GB % Vote Share	Average Regional Ranking Score
Labour	36.4	3.27
Conservative	33.1	2.72
Liberal Democrat	22.6	2.27
UK Independence Party	2.5	0.64
Scottish National Party	1.5	0.16
Greens	1.0	0.09
British National Party	0.7	0.09
Plaid Cymru	0.6	0.09

Note: The regional ranking scores derive from the fourth column of Table 2 below. We assign 4 points for a regional first place, 3 points for second place, 2 points for third place and 1 point for coming fourth.

lay in the range from 39 to 45%. Support for fourth or subsequent parties in England was generally 5 to 6%, but in the west midlands nearly touched 8%, thanks to stronger performances there by UKIP, the BNP and a local independent.

Table 2 also shows some indications of the parties that were 'bubbling under' in 2005, of which Respect had the most spectacular campaign with George Galloway capturing the Bethnall Green seat from Labour and two other Respect candidates (one in London and one in the west midlands) achieving around a fifth of the vote in their constituencies. The number of parties winning at least 1% support was generally either 5 or 6, outside the north east and east midlands where it was still just 4. In most regions at least 11 parties gained at least 0.1% of the vote, a generous 'bubbling under' sign. Some of these show signs of endurance, such as the Christian People's Alliance in London, which does better in the Assembly elections there. There was also no shortage of candidates for people to vote for, with at least 17 named and registered parties standing in every region of the country, adding up to more than 30 parties in London and the south east.

The indicator most widely used to capture the weighted importance of different parties in competition is ENP, the effective number of parties. The core idea here is simply explained, namely to take account of all the parties in competition, but weighting them in relation to their size, so that in arriving at an overall number of parties estimate we weight larger parties more than smaller ones. To compute ENP we take the decimal vote shares of all the parties, square them and then add up the sum of the squared numbers. We then divide one by the resulting number to get the ENP score. In fact, ENP is a much more complex index in its mathematical operations than this sounds, since it behaves in a non-linear way around certain key 'whole point' scores.[8] These complications need not detain us long here, but Figure 1 shows as a background grid the underlying shape of the areas that are feasible for ENP scores of different magnitudes. Here the horizontal axis shows the vote share of the largest party, and the vertical axis shows the ENP score for votes, that is the weighted number of parties that voters chose to support. The curvy areas marked show the spaces where ENP scores of a certain magnitude could be. For example, the area marked (5)

2. Patterns of Multi-party Competition across Regions

Region	Lab + Con vote share (%)	Top party vote share (%)	Ranking of top four parties	Vote share of fourth and subsequent parties (%)	No. of parties above 1% support	No. of parties above 0.1 % support	Number of named parties competing
North East	76.2	52.9	L > LD > C > U	5.0	4	10	20
East Midlands	75.6	38.6	L > C > LD > U	5.3	4	11	17
North West	73.7	45.0	L > C > LD > U	5.0	5	13	27
West Midlands	73.7	38.9	L > C > LD > U	7.7	5	12	21
Eastern	73.1	43.3	C > L > LD > U	6.6	5	9	17
Yorkshire and Humberside	72.7	43.6	L > C > LD > B	5.1	6	12	23
South West	71.2	38.6	C > LD > L > U	6.0	5	9	22
London	70.8	38.9	L > C > LD > Gr	6.3	6	12	32
South East	69.4	45.0	C > L > LD > U	5.2	5	9	33
Wales	64.1	42.7	L > C > LD > PC	17.5	5	11	17
Scotland	63.1	41.7	L > LD > SNP > C	20.2	6	11	22
England	*71.1*	*35.7*	*C > L > LD > U*	*6.0*	*5*	*7*	*79*
Great Britain	**69.5**	**36.4**	**L > C > LD > U**	**8.0**	**6**	**10**	**93**
UK (incl NI)	67.6	35.4	L > C > LD > U	10.4	5	12	101

Notes: L Labour; C Conservative; LD Liberal Democrat; U UK Independence Party; SNP Scottish National Party; PC Plaid Cymru; Gr Greens; B British National Party. Number of parties above 1% or 0.1% *includes* independents if they meet the criterion in question. Number of 'named parties' *excludes* independents without party names.

1. **How the Effective Number of Parties Compared in the European Election of 2004 and the General Election of 2005**

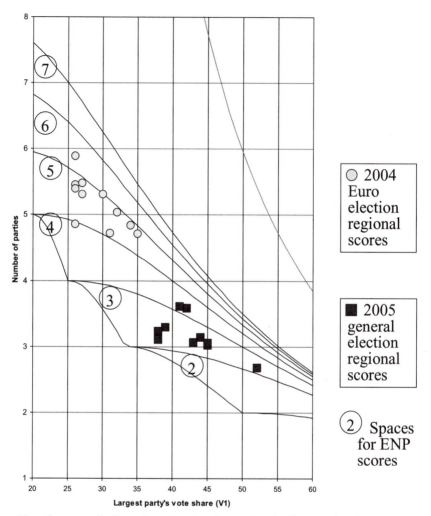

Note: The pattern of background zones here show the area where the effective number of parties score can lie. The area marked 2 shows where ENP scores of 2.0 to 2.99 can lie. The area marked 3 shows the *additional* area where scores of 3.0 to 3.99 can lie: these 3 scores can also occur in virtually all of the 2 area, save for a small strip at the bottom too small to show visually. This pattern of including the zone(s) below then repeats for higher ENP scores. For a fuller explanation see P. Dunleavy and F. Boucek, 'Constructing the Number of Parties', 9 *Party Politics* 3, 2003, pp. 291–315. The data for 2004 are computed from the Electoral Commission's excellent and comprehensive volume, *The 2004 European Parliamentary Elections in the United Kingdom*, Electoral Commission, 2004.

shows where ENP scores from 5.0 up to 5.99 may occur, although (slightly confusingly perhaps) such scores may also occur anywhere in the lower regions below 5, those for 4, 3 or even 2 parties.

The nub of Figure 1 though is to compare the regional ENP for votes scores in the 2005 general election (shown as round dots) with those for the same regions in the 2004 European election less than a year earlier (shown as squares). The two sets of results are completely different, with the 2004 Euro scores more akin to the results of general elections in Italy than they are to the 2005 ENP numbers. Nor is there the same pattern within each of the two data clusters here, with different regions located in different parts of the distribution. Figure 1 summarises visually the importance of coexistence between PR and plurality rule systems. It shows the large gaps in voters' behaviour that separate the two different electoral contexts, in part due to different issue mixes and voter preference patterns across different institutional contexts, but also equally in part because of voters' awareness of the different electoral systems being used to count their votes.

The ENP score can also be computed not just for the votes allocated by citizens across the parties (ENP votes) but also for the MPs allocated by the electoral system across the parties (ENP seats). Figure 2 shows that as ever with plurality rule under multi-party conditions there is a stark contrast between these two scores. The diagonal line up the centre of the Figure shows where a system operating proportionately would be, one where the number of parties winning seats approximates the number winning votes. Only one region (the south west) is anywhere near the line, with most of the rest clustered in the square showing 3 to 3.5 parties in terms of votes, but only 1.5 to 2.0 parties winning representation. The mismatches are especially marked for Scotland, Wales and the north east.

2. The Effective Number of Parties (ENP) for Votes and for Seats Across the Regions, Great Britain 2005

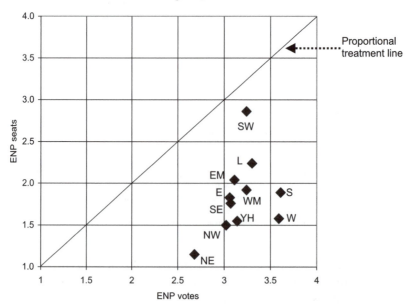

Key: E Eastern; EM East Midlands; L London; NE North East; NW North West; S Scotland; SE South East; SW South West; W Wales; WM West Midlands; YH Yorkshire and Humberside.

3. The Relative Reduction in Parties (RRP) Across Regions, Great Britain 2005

	ENP Votes	ENP Seats	RRP%
North East	2.7	1.2	57
Wales	3.6	1.6	56
Yorkshire and Humberside	3.1	1.6	51
North West	3.0	1.5	50
Scotland	3.6	1.9	48
Eastern	3.1	1.8	43
West Midlands	3.2	1.9	41
South East	3.1	1.8	40
East Midlands	3.1	2.0	34
London	3.3	2.2	32
South West	3.2	2.9	12
Great Britain	3.4	2.3	31
United Kingdom	3.6	2.5	31

Table 3 shows the same results but additionally computes a measure recommended by Taagepera and Shugart known as the relative reduction in parties (RRP).[9] This measure is simply computed as the difference between the two scores times 100, divided by the ENP votes—that is, [(ENPvotes −ENPseats)*100]/ENPvotes. RRP shows how much of the voters' choice set is ignored by the voting system in allocating seats, and for Britain as a whole ran at a high level of 31%—broadly consistent with past elections. This national score is misleading, however, because the picture at individual region level is much worse, and some of these differences are blurred by aggregation to national level. All but three regions (the south west, London and east midlands) have RRP scores above two fifths, and the top four regions in Table 3 have astonishingly high levels above 50%—which means that more than half the voters' choice set in these areas is ignored in allocating seats.

The disproportionality of the voting system

The main measure of disproportionality has been to compute measures of deviation from pure proportionality in the allocation of seats to parties. Figure 3 shows two measures of disproportionality across the regions of Great Britain in 2005. The first and best known is the deviation from proportionality (DV) score. To compute it we first find the differences (deviations) between percentage votes shares and percentage seats shares for each party in a region (or the country at large). We then add up these differences counting the minus scores as positive (or otherwise the deviations will sum to zero), and then because we have double-counted deviations we divide the sum by two.[10] The resulting measure shows the proportion of members of a legislature who hold seats which they are not entitled to by virtue of their party's overall vote share in the elections—that is, what percentage of MPs would be replaced by representatives of different parties under a pure proportional system. The DV measure in theory has a floor of zero but in fact the practicable minimum level is around 4%. (This is because even the purest PR system will have difficulty in giving any representation to votes which are split across many very small parties or independent candidates.)

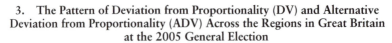

3. The Pattern of Deviation from Proportionality (DV) and Alternative Deviation from Proportionality (ADV) Across the Regions in Great Britain at the 2005 General Election

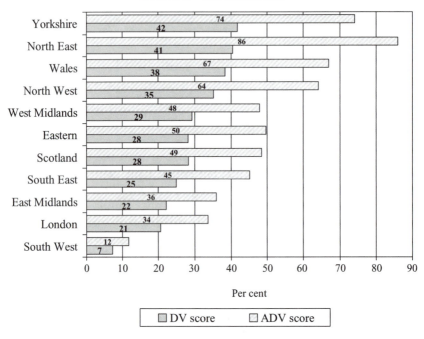

Per cent

☐ DV score   ☐ ADV score

As in previous general elections, the DV scores in Figure 3 demonstrate clearly that national general election DV numbers mask much greater regional disparities in seats and votes under the plurality system. Strong pro-Labour biases in its areas of strength (central Scotland, Wales, the industrial north and inner conurbations) are partly offset in national DV scores by pro-Tory biases elsewhere (such as the outer suburbs, south-east and eastern England and more rural areas).[11] Figure 1 shows instead the levels of disproportionality as they are experienced by voters in the election results *within* the regional areas where they live. The regional DV scores in 2005 were as high as 42% in Yorkshire, 41% in the north east and 38% in Wales. In these areas around two in every five votes found no expression at all in the make-up of the legislature, a staggeringly high level for any liberal democracy. However, there were reductions in DV elsewhere compared with 2001, notably in Scotland.

One of the major problems in interpreting the conventional DV score is that although it has a theoretical floor of zero, there is no relevant upper ceiling. (The DV score will reach 100 only when *none* of the parties winning votes in an election are awarded any of the seats, which is clearly a nonsensical measure to think about in relation to liberal democracies.) To cope with this problem Figure 1 also shows a measure called 'alternative deviation from proportionality' (or ADV score). It is calculated by multiplying the DV score by 100 and then dividing it by the share of the votes going to the second and subsequent parties (which is most easily operationalised as 100 minus the vote of the largest party).[12] The reasoning here is that the larger the initial size of the largest party's vote, the less scope inherently exists for deviations from proportionality to occur through 'leader's bias'. The ADV measure starts at zero but reaches 100 when the largest party wins all the seats available, whatever vote share it obtains. This is a relevant point to define a ceiling because if a polity goes across this line (for example, to 110%) then we cannot regard it as *any* kind of democracy. But a polity that has an ADV score of 100 is still (just) within the liberal democratic fold.[13]

In the 2005 election (as in 2001) the north east achieved the dubious distinction of achieving an 86% ADV score, which makes this result five sixths of the way to not being a liberal democratic outcome at all. With only 47% of the votes capable of being distorted here (since the largest party had 53% of the vote), there was none the less a 41% DV score, with Labour winning all but 2 of the 30 available seats. Yorkshire and Humberside came a fairly close second, followed by two other regions (Wales and the north west) that were more than two thirds of the way to not being a liberal democracy at all. Four other regions were just below the half-way mark. But only in the south west was anywhere near reasonable proportionality attained on the ADV measure. High though the ADV scores are here, they none the less show a slight improvement in around two thirds of the regions compared with 2001, reflecting a lower 'leader's bias' for Labour due to its reduced vote share.

A second approach to estimating the fairness or otherwise of plurality rule voting is to consider what would have happened if other voting systems were in place and had to cope with the precise patterns of voting across the country found in 2005. Our approach here is to use a simulation method, where we move from the constituency data to run specific alternative electoral systems.[14] Some important voting methods count multiple preferences—notably the alternative vote (AV), where voters rank parties in order numerically, used to elect the Australian lower house and sometimes advocated for the UK by Labour loyalists such as Peter Hain; the supplementary vote (SV), a simplified form of AV where voters indicate their top two preferences by X voting, used to elect the Mayor of London and ten other directly elected mayors in England; and the single transferable vote (STV), where voters indicate numerical preferences across candidates in different parties, to be used for the first time in mainland Britain for electing Scottish local councils and already deployed in Northern Ireland for many years. Unfortunately at the time of writing there are no viable data on the regional second and subsequent preferences of voters in 2005, a lamentable state of affairs reflecting the 'system biased', Westminster-orientated view of the ESRC-funded British Election Studies of focusing on voter's top preference alone over many decades.[15] So at this stage we cannot model multi-preference systems, although we hope to do so later on with data collected from the BES self-completion questionnaire.

However, from existing election results we are able to model two other proportional systems which count basically first preferences. The first is List PR, which is used to elect the UK members of the European Parliament in regional constituencies. The second is the additional member system (AMS), which can be set up in a number of ways. 'British AMS' systems used for the Scotland Parliament, the Welsh National Assembly and the London Assembly have a small majority of seats elected by plurality rule in local constituencies and then subregional (or in London, city-wide) top-up seats elected in compensating fashion using List PR so as to give overall proportional results. The Jenkins Commission on voting system reform for the House of Commons recommended a stronger form of British AMS with the proportion of local seats kept very high at 83% and the top-up seats kept to just a sixth. Research we conducted for the Commission suggested that this system would be broadly proportional.[16] However, subsequent experience with British AMS systems has shown that the release from the constraint of plurality rule encourages voters to display a broader range of party preferences and by somewhat increasing the proportion of small party votes raises the DV scores for the existing British AMS systems. We have concluded accordingly that it now seems highly unlikely that a Jenkins solution could deliver broad proportionality and that a larger proportion of top-up seats is almost certain to be required.[17] In Table 4 below we accordingly show data for the original Jenkins solution and a more generous 75% local and 25% top-up seats solution, which we now think is likely to be the minimum top-up seats needed for broad proportionality.

We also show for comparison the seats distributions resulting from a 'pure' AMS system on German or New Zealand lines, with a 50:50 local/top-up seats split. There is an additional methodological reason for showing this, namely that the simulation carried out here is a pretty rough and ready one. We have essentially paired up existing constituencies (with one or two cases of triple constituencies) across the country, so as to create 50% spare seats that can be allocated in regional level top-up areas, unlike the Jenkins Committee recommendations that top-up areas should be localised at the county level.

4. Simulation Results Showing How a List PR systems and Differently Structured Additional Member (AMS) Systems Would Work with the 2005 Voting Patterns in Great Britain

Regions	Lab	Con	Lib D	UKIP	SNP	Plaid Cymru	Green	BNP	Other	Total
Actual result	355	197	62	0	6	3	0	0	4	628
List PR	239	207	140	11	11	7	5	4	3	628
AMS 50% local/50% top-up	234	210	145	13	10	4	2	2	8	628
AMS 75% local, 25% top up	275	203	118	12	8	4	3	1	4	628
AMS Jenkins Commission (83% local,17% top up)	299	197	107	7	7	3	3	1	3	628

We have then essentially interpolated the 75:25 and 83:17 results by assuming a smoothly operating transition from the 50:50 solution we have defined to the 100% local seats general election result, hand-correcting for the inevitable anomalies thrown up by this interpolation process. This is a labour-intensive process and it produces results which need to be interpreted with some caution. But simulation predictions using this approach have modeled the existing British AMS elections relatively well, once we control for changes in voting behaviour under PR, which of course cannot be anticipated in advance.[18]

We should also note two further limitations of the AMS results below. First, British AMS systems all give citizens two votes, one for the local and for the top-up contests. In Scotland and Wales around a quarter of voters split their two votes and in London rather more do so, reflecting the increasingly conditional character of modern voters' party attachments. We cannot reproduce this effect here, but must rely on reaggregating local votes at the top-up level. Second, the Jenkins Commission's recommended system was AV-plus, since it combined a small proportion of top-up seats with a shift towards using the alternative vote in the local seats. So in Table 4 our AMS solution assumes only plurality rule local contests, since we do not have multi-preference data. (However, we can say from past work that the effect of AV in the Jenkins scheme is likely to be fairly predictable, cutting Tory seats by about a dozen and with Labour and the Liberal Democrats roughly equal beneficiaries, as tactical voting between the two parties' supporters is somewhat facilitated.)

The key result from Table 4 is that either List PR or 50:50 AMS would have reduced Labour's seat numbers by at least 120 seats. The main beneficiaries would be the Liberal Democrats, whose MPs would soar by at least 80, and the newer fourth and subsequent parties, whose seats would increase from 13 to 39 in Great Britain. UKIP would have a Parliamentary group of 13, outnumbering the SNP, on this basis. These are interesting results because in our simulation we have employed the de Hondt seats allocation system that discriminates in favour of large parties, which is used in all the British AMS and List PR systems. Even with this factor working against them, all of the top eight parties in terms of regional placings would gain seats under the purer PR systems, along with some independents and perhaps Respect in east London. However, the Conservatives would stand to benefit relatively little from PR, gaining only a baker's dozen of extra seats.

Table 4 also shows that as the mix of local to top-up seats shifts towards a preponderance of local contests then the damage to Labour's number of MPs is cut dramatically. Labour's losses under a Jenkins solution would be half those under more proportional systems and the Liberal Democrats and minor parties would lose half their gains as a result. The Conservatives under a Jenkins ratio of local and top-up seats would be no better off than they were in 2005 under plurality rule. It is little wonder, therefore, that the party continues to be stony-faced rejectionist in its attitudes towards electoral reform.

Finally on simulations the detailed tables, from which Table 4 derives (available from the authors), show that the List PR and 50:50 AMS systems both make a huge difference to the patterns of political representation across Great Britain. They particularly would bring to an end the problem of electoral 'deserts' for main parties that apply under plurality rule and give a balanced regional representation to all three of the main parliamentary parties. This effect is severely attenuated with the 75:25 and 83:17 mixes of local to top-up seats. But while numbers thin down outside the parties' core areas of strength in the less proportional AMS arrangements, the effect of broadening regional presence continues to operate. The smaller parties also have small regional bases from which they could realistically hope to expand their support.

The remaining strengths of plurality rule

In many places in the modern world, except US Congressional elections, plurality rule systems are now under stress. While the American perfect two-party polity can continue unchanged, producing very low disproportionality (DV) scores of around 7% in legislative elections, even in the presidential race plurality rule has been under pressure from third party candidates causing presidents with only minority support to be elected. In Canada the changing party system has produced chaotic party fortunes and a hung Parliament nationally in 2004–05. A slow-moving national committee of Parliament is considering reform options, and change initiatives are under way at provincial level in British Columbia, Ontario and Nova Scotia, with almost three fifths of BC voters backing a proposed change to STV in a May 2005 referendum. In India, the world's largest plurality rule country, the number of parties in Parliament has now passed 150 and plurality rule clearly no longer has much of a 'nationalising politics' effect.

So how strongly embedded is plurality rule in the UK? There are some aspects of the system that tend to prop up its effectiveness, including for instance the fact that national DV scores are significantly below regional ones, as offsetting pro-Labour and pro-Conservative biases cancel each other out. In addition, as Table 5 below shows the electoral system will still confer a degree of influence on representation that spans somewhat beyond the supporters of the largest or governing party alone. Here we examine whether people got the result that they wanted nationally, in terms of the party they voted for controlling government, or locally, in terms of the party they backed successfully electing the local MP. We also include as successful those people who voted for a party that emerged as preponderant in the region where they live, whether or not that party won their local seat. A 'triple winner' in

5. Winners as a Percentage of All Voters, Great Britain 2005

	Lab	Con	LD	Other Parties	Total
Triple winner	21.9	0	0	0	21.9
Double winner					
National/local	3.2	0	0	0	3.2
National/ regional	5.5	0	0	0	5.5
Regional/local	0	10.5	0	0	10.5
Single winner					
National	5.6	0	0	0	5.6
Regional	0	4.2	0	0	4.2
Local	0	6.3	4.9	0.7	11.9
Triple loser	0	12.2	17.8	7.2	37.2
All voters	**36.2**	**33.2**	**22.7**	**7.9**	**100**

Table 5 is someone whose vote proved effective at all three levels in 2005, and just over a fifth of voters fall into this category, all Labour voters by definition. By contrast, 'triple losers' found their votes completely unreflected at any level, and they accounted for over 37% of voters in 2005, all from opposition parties, with Liberal Democrats the biggest component grouping, followed by Conservatives and then other party voters. However, most Conservative voters were either 'double winners' at the regional and local levels or were single winners at their local constituency level. No Liberal Democrat or other party voters were even double winners, but some were single winners at the local constituency level.

Overall 63% of voters in Great Britain got something of what they wanted from the general election result, a very low number compared with (say) PR systems where 90% plus of voters get something of what they want, but still a lot larger proportion than the 36% who backed Labour alone. Comparing the proportion of winners over time also shows that in 1992 it was 73%, and in 1997 only 61%, so the 2005 result is a small improvement on 1997 but still far worse than 1992.[19] The proportion of all voters who were winners at some level but did not support the largest and governing party was less than 17% in 1997. But rose to nearly 27% in 2005, thanks to Labour's falling levels of support. This suggests a broadening out of the base of people who got something of what they wanted from the electoral system.

It may perhaps also suggest that disaffection from the system is unlikely to grow in the sort term, although a lot will depend on how the Prime Minister's evident unpopularity as a political leader in 2005 develops over the remainder of his period in office. A rapid leadership succession and new policies and a different climate of relations with voters from a presumably Gordon Brown-lead government, could compensate for Labour's poor legitimacy in government (with only 35% of the UK vote) so that the voting system fades as a concern. On the other hand, a lingering Blair premiership accompanied by spin and unchanged policies, perhaps with deteriorating foreign policy fortunes in the EU and Iraq, might be the trigger for dissatisfactions with the 2005 electoral race to find expression both in strong anti-government mid-term swings, continued growth of support for parties beyond the main three, and continuing overt dissatisfaction with plurality rule elections.

One dimension of the 2005 election suggested continuing problems for plurality rule. Despite radical measures taken to ease postal voting, and a big growth in postal votes returned, the overall turnout rate in 2005 rose only very marginally from the record low achieved in 2001. Indeed if we screen out the 'artificial' rule-change effects of new postal balloting rules, the *underlying* rate of general election turnout continued to decline by one or 2% in 2005. This compares unfavourably with local elections earlier in the second Blair term and the increase in European election turnout from 24% in 1999 to 36% (after adjusting for all-postal ballot region effects) in 2004. The fundamental way in which plurality rule very actively and obviously seeks to constrain how voters express their preferences in our view lies behind this continuing malaise. It was interesting to see in 2005 also that Labour and Conservative efforts to publicise and play up these constraining effects met with far more sustained media and public criticism than in any previous election, notably the rubbishing of Labour claims that a small fraction of their voters defecting to other parties would 'let the Tories back in'. This effect suggests that the forced constraining of voters' preferences will be a hard act to sustain in 2009, especially for Labour when the party will have been continuously in office for 12 years.

Conclusion

The dialectic of electoral reform in the UK is a subtle and long-run one. A chaining of differently aligned developments contributes an overall momentum towards broader multi-party politics, declining long-run vote shares for the two best established parties, general election turnout that is still falling (behind the masking effects of more generous postal voting arrangements), and many small signs of popular dissatisfaction with the forcing and constraining of choices that is an inevitable concomitant of plurality rule in a multi-party context. The 2005 general election results continue to show levels of distortion of voters' preferences by the electoral system that are very high by international standards. Plurality rule reduced the number of parties represented in the legislature in some regions by more than half and the alternative deviation from proportionality scores show many regional results that are well on the way to not being judged liberal democratic outcomes at all. Although slightly more voters than in 1997 or 2001 got something of what they wanted out of the electoral system, the stagnation of turnout, the dislike of major party campaigning expressed in many quarters and the continuing post-election criticisms of the system all suggest that the trend towards an eventual constitutional adjustment to broader multi-party politics was reinforced rather than counteracted in 2005.

* LSE Public Policy Group, London School of Economics and Political Science.
+ Oxford Internet Institute, Oxford University.
We thank Pippa Norris and Chris Wzielan for their help in providing data and commenting on an earlier version of this paper. All the data here are based on the analysis of the 2005 constituency database prepared by Pippa Norris and available on her website at http://ksghome.harvard.edu/~pnorris/datafiles/Britain%20Votes%202006%20Resources.htm. This paper can usefully be read in conjunction with P. Dunleavy and H. Margetts, 'The Electoral System', *Parliamentary Affairs* 1997/3, pp. 734–49. Special Issue on the 1997 General Election (edited by P. Norris).

1   J. Colomer, 'It's Parties that Choose Electoral Systems (or, Duverger's Laws upside down)', *Political Studies* (2005), 53(1), pp. 1–21.
2   See P. Dunleavy and H. Margetts, 'From Majoritarian to Pluralist Democracy: Electoral Reform in Britain since 1997', 13 *Journal of Theoretical Politics* 3, 2001, pp. 295–319: also part republished as 'United Kingdom: Reforming the Westminster Model' in J. Colomer (ed.), *Handbook of Electoral Choice*, Palgrave, 2004, pp. 294–305. Also see P. Dunleavy, 'Facing up to Multi-Party Politics: How Partisan Dealignment and PR Voting have Fundamentally Changed Britain's Party Systems', *Parliamentary Affairs*, July 2005, forthcoming.
3   See P. Dunleavy, 'Political Behaviour: Institutional and Experiential Approaches' in R.E. Goodin and H.D. Klingemann (eds), *A New Handbook of Political Science*, Oxford University Press, 1996, pp. 276–393.
4   Dunleavy, 'Facing up to Multi-Party Politics', p. xxx.
5   For a discussion of longer-term, historical trends in major party vote shares and governmental dominance, see P. Dunleavy, 'Electoral Representation and Accountability: The Legacy of Empire' in A. Gamble, I. Holliday and G. Parry (eds), *Fundamentals in British Politics,* Macmillan, 1999, pp. 204–30.
6   See H. Margetts, P. John and S. Weir, 'Latent Support fo the Far-Right in British Politics: The BNP and UKIP on the 2004 European and Local Elections', Paper to the PSA Elections, parties and Public Opinion Conference, University of Oxford, 10–12 September, 2004.
7   Dunleavy, 'Facing up to Multi-Party Politics', pp. 3–8.
8   For a fuller exposition of how the index works, see P. Dunleavy and F. Boucek, 'Constructing the Number of Parties', *Party Politics* 3, 2003, 9(3), pp. 291–315.
9   See R. Taagepera and M. Shugart, *Seats and Votes: The Effects and Determinants of Electoral Systems*, Yale University Press, 1989, p. 273.
10 See Taagepera and Shugart, *Seats and Votes*, Chapter 10.
11 See Dunleavy and Margetts, 'The Electoral System' for this effect in 1997; and P. Dunleavy and H. Margetts, 'The Experiential Approach to Electoral System Effects' in D. Beetham (ed.), *Indices of Democratization*, Sage, 1994, pp. 155–81, for cross-national evidence of similar results.
12 Putting this more formally, ADV = $(DV*100)/(100 − V_1)$, where DV is the conventional DV score and V_1 is the vote share of the largest party.
13 A score above 100% is feasible in several ways, for example if all or most of the seats are won by the second largest party.
14 For earlier, more extensive and more sophisticated simulation work on the 1992 and 1997 elections, see P. Dunleavy, H. Margetts and S. Weir, *The Politico's Guide to Electoral Reform in Britain*, Politico's, 1998, and the same authors' *Making Votes Count 2: Mixed Electoral Systems*, Democratic Audit of the UK, 1998, and *Replaying the General Election of 1992: How Britain Would Have Voted Under Alternative Electoral Systems*, LSE Public Policy Group/Joseph Rowntree Reform Trust, 1992; P. Dunleavy, H. Margetts, B. O'Duffy and S. Weir, *Making Votes Count: Replaying the 1990s General Elections Under Alternative Electoral Systems*, Democratic Audit of the UK, 1997.
15 Dunleavy, 'Facing up to multi-party politics', discusses this issue in detail.
16 See Jenkins Commission, *The Report of the Independent Commission on the Voting System*, Cmnd 4090-I, Stationary Office; Dunleavy *et al.*, *Politicos' Guide to Electoral Reform* analyses the proposals in detail.
17 See P. Dunleavy and H. Margetts, 'How Proportional are the British AMS systems?', *Representation*, 2004, 40(4), pp. 317–29.
18 Dunleavy and Margetts, 'How Proportional are the British AMS Systems?'
19 For comparable 1992 and 1997 data see Dunleavy and Margetts, 'The Electoral system', pp. 744–6.

CHRISTOPHER WLEZIEN AND PIPPA NORRIS

Conclusion: Whether the Campaign Mattered and How*

The foregoing chapters tell us a lot about what happened when the voters went to the polls on 5 May 2005. In chapter 11 we saw that voters split along traditional cleavages such as social class. In chapters 10 and 11, we found that voters also responded to shorter-term forces. To begin with, performance mattered. The economy played a big role. The government's record in various areas, such as health and education, did too. This clearly benefited Labour. Put simply, things in the country were going pretty well and most people did not want to change course, at least on these grounds alone. The story has a familiar ring to it and is the one that most accounts for Labour's first reelection.[1] Policy also mattered, just as it did in 2001, though the consequences in 2005 were more mixed. While the government benefited from a moderate tack on fiscal issues—New Labour's pillar of policy strength—it nevertheless suffered from positions on other issues. Despite a clear performance advantage and an apparent leadership advantage too, Labour eked out a small plurality victory in votes. With the seats-votes translation well in its favour, as discussed at some depth in chapters 9 and 13, the government still won a healthy 66-seat Parliamentary majority.

Although we know a good amount about what voters did on Election Day, we know relatively little about how preferences evolved to that point. How did the outcome come into focus as the election campaign unfolded? Did voters' preferences evolve in a patterned and understandable way? Or was the outcome largely already in place when the campaign began? What role did the election campaign actually play? Scholars debate the influence of campaigns and campaign events in electoral decision-making. Few argue that campaigns do not matter at all, but a number of scholars maintain that campaigns mostly serve to steer the vote toward a verdict that can be foreseen in advance.[2] From this point of view, the campaign effectively delivers the effects of fundamental variables, such as economic and policy performance, that are known or

© Oxford University Press 2005
doi: 10.1093/pa/gsi070

knowable before the campaign itself begins. Others argue that the conduct of campaigns determines election outcomes.[3] That is, it has effects that cause the final outcome to differ from what the so-called fundamentals would predict. Election campaigns may have both types of effects, of course. It also may be that the outcome already is in place early on, before the formal campaign begins, and that what happens during the period of the campaign has little ultimate effect.[4]

This concluding chapter considers the effects of the 2005 UK election campaign, focusing on voter preferences for the nation as a whole. We first examine voting intention in the many polls conducted over the course of the election year, especially the period of the official campaign. We want to see whether there was real change in electoral preferences as opposed to mere noise due to survey error. Our analysis suggests that preferences did change during the campaign. We then consider why preferences changed, focusing on issues and other factors. Based on our examination, it appears that the campaign served to *persuade* some voters as to which party was best on the issues and perhaps also to *prime* certain domains for voters. It also served to activate individuals' underlying predispositions. We consider the implications for our understanding of voting behavior and elections in the UK and beyond.

The evolution of preferences

For over half a century, pollsters have been asking samples of the public about their choices in the next election. The practice now is so common that hardly a day passes during the official campaign without encountering results of new polls, often from multiple organisations. In these trial-heat polls, citizens typically are asked about how they would vote 'if the election were held tomorrow', with some differences in question wording. In some polls, respondents are asked how they will vote 'in the general election', also with some differences in wording depending on the survey organisation.

From 1 January 2005 until 5 May 2005, we located results for 67 country-level polls of the Labour-Conservative-Liberal Democrat vote division reported by different survey organisations. The population is Great Britain, not the UK, as none of the organizations poll in Northern Ireland. The data were drawn primarily from the BBC poll tracker website but were supplemented using other sources, including the MORI compilation.[5] The polls are from seven different survey organisations— BPIX, Communicate Research, ICM, MORI, NOP, Populus, and YouGov—two of which (BPIX and YouGov) rely on internet polls. Excluding the internet polls makes almost no difference and does not change any of the results and conclusions that follow. Each of the survey organisations reports results for a sample of 'likely voters'. That is, they attempt to anticipate the Election Day electorate. This is not easy to do.[6] Some organisations rely on 'screens' to classify voters as likely or not likely. Late in the campaign, for example, MORI reports results for those respondents who say they are 'absolutely certain' to vote, those who respond with '10' when asked to place themselves on a one to ten scale of voting likelihood. Other organisations use combinations of variables to weight the probabilities of voting. ICM, for example, uses responses to the subjective likelihood scale as well as past voting behavior itself.[7] Note finally that we have eliminated all overlap in polls conducted by the same house for the same reporting organisation, as with tracking polls. For example, where a survey house runs a daily tracking poll and reports three-day moving averages, we only use poll results for every third day. Thus, our 67 polls provide *separate* readings of electoral preferences.

Figure 1 displays results for the complete set of polls. Specifically, it shows the percentage shares for Labour, the Conservatives, the Liberal Democrats, and all other parties for each poll. Since most polls are conducted over multiple days, each poll is dated by the middle day of the period the survey is in the field.[8] The 67 polls allow readings for 42 separate days during 2005, 24 of which are after the election was called, which permits a virtual day-to-day monitoring of preferences during the 30-day official campaign.[9] Prior to that time, polls are much less frequent. We can see in Figure 1 some patterned movement over time. From day to day, however, the poll results bounce around a lot. For any given date, the results differ. Some of this noise is sampling error. There are other sources of survey error, reflecting the practices of

1.   **Voting Intention by Date During the Election Year, 2005**

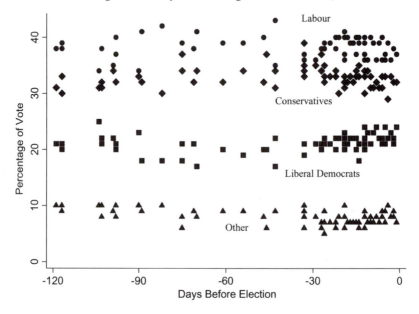

the different survey organisations, or houses. These commonly are referred to as 'house effects'.

The daily *poll-of-polls* in Figure 2 reveals more distinct pattern. The observations in the figure represent vote intention shares for all respondents aggregated by the mid-date of the reported polling period. That is, the numbers for each day register support for the grand N for all polls centered on the particular day. We can see in the figure that we began the year about where we ended up in the polls on Election Day. Labour's percentage share was in the mid-to-high 30s, the Tory share in the low 30s and the Liberal Democrat number in the low 20s. The total for all other parties was 10%. Over the course of the 'long campaign' between New Year's Day and Election Day, the polls do change. Some of the change is survey error, but there also is evidence of real change in preferences.[10] Early on the Liberal Democrat share drifted up but the apparent gains dissipated leading up to the election call on 5 April. During the same period the Conservatives' share edged upward in a fairly secular way, reaching within a percentage point of Labour just before the official campaign began. In contrast to 1997 and 2001, Labour's popular vote victory was not obvious, at least in the polls.

Much of the action was in the final 30 days. Figure 3 focuses on this period and on support for the three major parties, incorporating a 'smoothed' preferences series.[11] Here it is clear that the Conservative share declined from approximately 35% at the beginning of the period to 32% at the end. Meanwhile, the Liberal Democratic share increased

2. **Voting Intention During the Election Year Aggregated by Date, 2005**

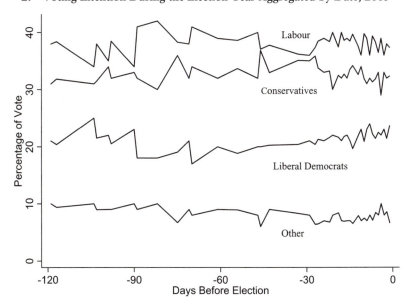

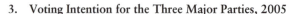

3. Voting Intention for the Three Major Parties, 2005

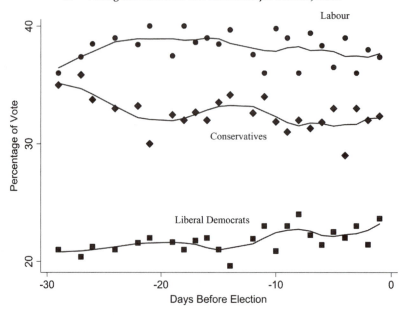

from 20% to 22%. It also appears that Labour's share peaks slightly in mid-April before dropping off, though we cannot be absolutely sure that the change is real. What we are confident about is that the final polls on average exaggerated—by about 1.5 percentage points—the Labour portion of the vote, as we saw in chapter 2. Perhaps there was a last-minute shift away from the government, too late to be detected in the pre-election polls. Perhaps instead the polls were biased and overstated the Labour share from beginning to end, *which would imply that the Conservative Party may really have been ahead when the campaign began*.[12] Regardless of what did happen at the very end, Labour vote preferences did not move very far for very long during the official campaign. This contrasts with what we observed in the previous two elections, in 1997 and 2001. In those years, the leading party at the beginning of the campaign consistently lost ground during the last 30 days. This can be seen in Figures 4 and 5, which displays the daily poll-of-polls for the two elections.[13]

The pattern of polls in 1997 and 2001 is exactly what we observe in US presidential elections. There, polls almost always overstate the margin of victory. Leads on Labor Day, the unofficial start of the general election campaign some two months before Election Day, ultimately are halved.[14] Even final polls from the day before the election do not neatly predict the ultimate vote. The pattern implies a systematic evolution of preferences during the campaign. One possibility is that some portion of old shocks to preferences, which benefit the leader by definition,

4. Voting Intention During the Campaign Aggregated by Date, 1997

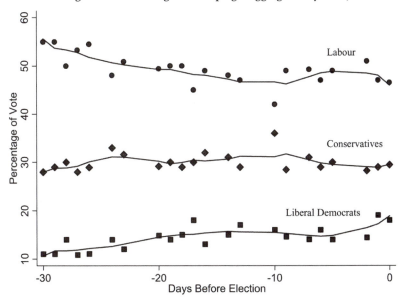

5. Voting Intention During the Campaign Aggregated by Date, 2001

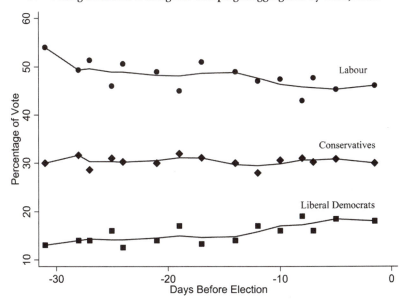

decays as the campaign unfolds. Preexisting leads would thus decline quite naturally. Another possibility is that individuals' underlying preferences actually diverge over time, i.e. preferences become more polarised. It may be that the campaign activates voters' predispositions, causing them to gravitate toward their partisan 'equilibria' or some broader underlying preference, or it just may be that individuals react differently to the events and media coverage of the campaign. Regardless of its particular underpinnings, the polarisation of underlying preferences during the campaign would produce a predictable decline in poll margins.[15]

This did not happen during the 2005 UK campaign, as we have seen. The Labour share did not change much at all; if anything, it increased. What did change are the Conservative and Liberal Democratic shares. The increase for the latter was not surprising, as we also saw such an increase in 1997 and 2001 (see Figures 4 and 5). In those years, however, the Liberal Democrats gained at the expense of Labour. This was not true in 2005. Rather, the Conservative share declined. The change in preferences during the campaign was not fundamental, in that it did not alter party control of Parliament or even the rank ordering of the parties. Yet it did alter the balance of power in meaningful ways. Based on our simulation, it cost the Conservatives 38 seats, 23 of which went to Labour and 14 of which went to the Liberal Democrats.[16] In effect, had preferences not changed, Labour's majority would have been a mere 18 seats or so, more like what John Major had during his term as Prime Minister. The election campaign clearly mattered in 2005. Let us now consider how.

The coordinates of preference change

As we noted at the beginning of this chapter, various factors impacted the Election Day result. We want to see whether and how this structure changed during the campaign. There are two well-known mechanisms.[17] First, the events of the campaign can change people's evaluations of parties. That is, the campaign may have persuaded voters on different policy issues and caused them to change their electoral preferences over time. Second, the events of the campaign can alter the importance of different factors, in effect priming some things in voters' minds at the expense of other things. To the extent that the public perceives differences in the parties on different dimensions of evaluation, priming will tend to produce changes in vote intention over time as one party benefits from the added salience and others lose. Of course, it may be that both processes were at work and that campaigns serve to prime and persuade.

Ideally, to assess the impact of the campaign in 2005, we would have data on individuals' characteristics and their attitudes and perceptions, along with vote intention, at weekly intervals in the cycle. This would allow us to neatly trace changes in attitudes and voting intention over time. As we conducted our analyses in May 2005, however, we did not have such data. We did have access to aggregate results of polls conducted by ICM Research, available on-line.[18] This information allows us to assess changes in the poll aggregates from the beginning of the campaign until the end.

POLITICAL ISSUES.   We begin with the issues. For the analysis, we rely on the results of the four April polls and the final pre-election poll conducted for the *Guardian*. In each of these five polls, ICM interviewed a stratified random sample of slightly more than 1,500 adults and then weighted the data to the profile of all adults 18+ years of age.[19] To be clear, the data are not weighted to take into account individuals' likelihood of voting, either subjective or objective. The respondents were asked various questions relating to the election. Among the items is a battery that asks about which party is best on different issues. The specific question wording is:

Irrespective of how you yourself will vote at the next election, which political party do you think is putting forward the best policies on . . .

Respondents were asked about health, education, law and order, asylum and immigration, Europe, the economy generally, taxation and public services, and the fight against terrorism. Exactly the same question and categorical answers were used in each of the five surveys, providing us with a basic time series. We thus can see whether and how the numbers changed over time. Table 1 summarises the 'best party' responses across the different issues early and late in the campaign. The upper frame is based on responses from the first two April surveys, conducted 1–12 April. The lower frame relies on data from the last April survey and the May pre-election survey which were in the field between 24 April and 3 May. Issues are aligned along the top in order of Labour preference, with Labour's best issue, the economy, on the left and it's worst issue, asylum and immigration, on the right. The numbers in the table are percentages of responses in each survey, e.g. 44% of adults surveyed in early April thought that Labour was the best party on the economy. Vote intention is included in the first column to provide a basis for comparison. It is an important baseline because we know that people's political judgments can color their evaluations of candidates and parties on the issues, in addition to influencing perceptions and issue positions.[20]

In the upper half of Table 1 it is clear that Labour was advantaged on most issues early in the campaign. It was the plurality winner in six of the eight domains, and the differences between the percentages thinking Labour and the Conservatives were the best parties exceeded the difference in vote share in each case. This was true even for Europe. Whether the result of performance judgments or policy evaluations per se, Labour stood in good stead with the public on most issues. Only on law and order and asylum and immigration did the Conservatives have the advantage. The Liberal Democrats, meanwhile, were rated much less favorably across the board. On average, only about 11% thought that they were the best party on issues, less than half of their declared vote share (22%). There were hints of latent strength on education and taxation and public services, though only 13% of the public thought that they were best even on these.

1. Best Party on the Issues Early and Late in the Campaign, 2005 (Percentages of Responses)

Early in the Campaign (April 1–12), Sample size = 3,031

Party	Vote Preference	Economy	Health	Education	Terrorism	Europe	Tax/Services	Law/Order	Immigration	Average
Labour	38	44	38	37	36	32	34	30	25	34.6
Conservatives	34	24	27	24	24	25	29	35	37	28.2
Lib Dems	21	9	12	13	9	11	13	9	10	10.9
Other	7	2	1	1	1	4	2	2	2	1.9
DK	–	17	17	21	23	25	18	20	21	20.3

Late in the Campaign (April 24–May 3), Sample size = 2,991

Party	Vote Preference	Economy	Health	Education	Terrorism	Europe	Tax/Services	Law/Order	Immigration	Average
Labour	39	44	38	35	35	31	33	31	26	34.2
Conservatives	33	22	24*	23	23	23	25*	31*	34*	25.6
Lib Dems	22	10	13	16*	10	12	17*	11	12	13.9
Other	7	2	2	1	2	4	2	2	3	2.0
DK	–	18	19	20	23	26	19	21	21	20.9

Notes: Numbers in bold designate a two-point change from early to late in the campaign (approximate p ≤ .05); Numbers with an asterisk (*) designate a change of greater than two points (approximate p ≤ .01). Source: ICM Research (http://www.icmresearch.co.uk/reviews/pollreviews.asp).

Things changed to a degree as the campaign evolved, which can be seen in the lower half of Table 1. Notice that Labour retained its advantage across most issues while its vote share edged up slightly. There was a small but significant drop-off on education and on taxation and public services, but otherwise things remained essentially the same as at the beginning of the campaign. This was not true for the Conservatives and the Liberal Democrats. During the campaign, evaluations of the former clearly dropped and assessments of the latter rose, changes that even exceeded the shifts in party vote shares in the polls.[21] The changes in issue assessments were mostly concentrated in the four domains where the Conservatives were doing best— immigration, law and order, taxation and public services, and Europe—and the shifts for the Conservatives and Liberal Democrats largely mirrored each other. The pattern implies that in these issue areas Liberal Democrats gained at the expense of the Conservatives. The changes were greatest on taxation and public services, one of the main planks of the Liberal Democratic campaign. Interestingly, gains also were large on one of the Liberal Democrat's other main planks, education, though these looked to be mostly at the expense of Labour. The Conservatives, meanwhile, found themselves losing ground in other areas—health and the economy—but to no one party's evident benefit. Policy really mattered in the 2005 election campaign. Regardless of the details, the campaign helped the Liberal Democrats and hurt the Conservatives on the issues. There was persuasion. This may explain the evolution of electoral preferences visible in Figure 2.

Now let us consider whether there also was priming. This is trickier to detect. How does one tell whether an issue is important to people? Survey organisations do frequently ask, for instance, 'Which of the following issues is most important to you in deciding how you might vote?' But what exactly do the responses to this question reflect? It is hard to tell, at least at particular points in time. The fact that I say that 'health care' is more important than 'the economy' to my vote may not tell us much about their real effects on vote choice. We simply do not know much about what different responses to the question reflect. The change in responses over time may be more meaningful, however. That is, it may tell us something about the changing importance of issues to voters. We examine responses to the question about issue importance included in the five ICM polls used above. They asked:

Which of the following issues will be most important to you in your decision on how to vote in the next general election?

Respondents were provided with a list of issues, including the eight from the 'best party' battery summarised in Table 1 and also 'Iraq'. One response was coded for each respondent. The results for each of the five polls are shown in Table 2.

2. Most Important Issues During the Campaign, 2005 (Percentages of Responses)

	April 1–3	April 10–12	Survey Dates April 17–19	April 24–26	May 1–3
Health	21	21	21	21	21
Tax/Services	16	13	14	14	15
Education	12	15	13	15	15
Law/Order	14	16	13	15	13
Economy	11	13	12	13	12
Immigration	12	8	10	8	9
Terrorism	5	3	3	3	3
Europe	4	3	3	3	3
Iraq	—	3	3	2	2
Sample size	1507	1524	1513	1547	1444

Source: ICM Research.

We can see in Table 2 that responses were quite dispersed, especially just prior to the election call in early-April. At that time, six different issues were named as most important by more than 10% of the respondents. Among these issues, health was the plurality issue winner, considered the most important by 21%, followed by tax and services with 16% and law and order with 14%. Education and immigration were named by 12%. The economy was mentioned by only 11%. The ordering differs from what we saw from the British Election Study (BES) rolling campaign data in chapter 10. In particular, the percentage mentioning immigration is much lower, about half of what we observe in the BES, and the percentages for health and education are both about seven points higher. The numbers from ICM are much more consistent with what we see in surveys prior to the campaign.[22] The different results may be traceable to the differences in methodology, as ICM rely on a close-ended question wording that lists the different issues for respondents, whereas the BES uses an open-ended wording. It is possible that the latter encourages people to name what is top-of-the-head and thus increases the mentions of issues being emphasised in the campaign. It also is possible that the coding of open-ended responses has an effect. Of course, there are other possibilities, including the use of internet polls by BES for the rolling campaign survey.

What we do know is that Labour had the advantage on most of the issues at the top of the most important list in Table 2—all but law and order and asylum and immigration. Things changed little during the course of the campaign. The most notable development is the increase in the importance of education, which rises to 15% and becomes the second most important issue, along with taxation and public services. We also observe an initial drop in the importance of immigration that lasts through Election Day. There is a hint of an increase on the economy, but only that—a hint. On other issues, there was no change whatsoever.[23] Based on this analysis, then, the campaign did not fundamentally alter the salience of issues to voters, at least at the broad aggregate level. It may have primed some issues at the expense of others, and these were

ones on which the Liberal Democrats were making gains in support—
education and immigration. Still, the main impact of issues on electoral
change is the persuasion documented in Table 1.

PARTY LEADERS.   Evaluations of party leaders may also contribute to
changing vote preferences during the campaign. We know from chapter 11
and elsewhere that assessments of leaders influence vote choice.[24] Did
evaluations of the leaders change during the campaign? Does any change
help us account for the evident gains by the Liberal Democrats and the
losses by the Conservatives? To see, we rely on a broad summary judg-
ment of party leaders from the ICM polls. Respondents were asked:

Irrespective of which party you yourself will vote for, which of these three do
you think would make the best prime minister for Britain?

Only Howard, Blair and Kennedy were named, though 'someone else'
and 'none of the above' responses were recorded. The percentages for
each of the five polls are described in Table 3.

Notice first in the table that Blair held a clear lead over Howard
before the campaign began. Fully 38% thought Blair would make the
best prime minister, exactly the same as his vote preference share in the
poll (see Table 1). Only 26% named Howard, which is eight points
below his vote share. Kennedy was well below at 18%, though this is
closer to his vote share in the polls—only four points less. Things do
change when the campaign begins. In particular, Kennedy's evaluations
increase to 21%. Thereafter, we see Howard's evaluations drop and
then Blair's jump up sharply. By the end of the campaign, however, the
numbers were exactly where we began in early-April. Basically, nothing
had changed overall. It may be that true underlying evaluations did
fluctuate and that the effects decayed before Election Day. While this is
an interesting possibility, it ultimately does not explain why aggregate
electoral preferences changed in 2005 from the beginning to the end of
the campaign. To the extent that party leadership influenced the final
outcome, based on our analysis, the effects were already in place when
the official campaign began.

UNDERLYING DYNAMICS.   Priming and persuasion may produce changes
in broad public opinion aggregates, as we have seen. They also may

3. Best Prime Minister During the Campaign, 2005 (Percentages of Responses)

	April 1–3	April 10–12	April 17–19	April 24–26	May 1–3
Blair	38	39	38	44	38
Howard	26	27	23	22	26
Kennedy	18	21	21	19	18
Other	1	0	1	1	0
Sample size	1507	1524	1513	1547	1444

Source: ICM Research.

generate shifts in the underlying distribution of preferences across individuals, ones that may not have any real implications at the aggregate level. For example, as we noted earlier, campaigns can activate political predispositions. This is the gist of Gelman and King's conjecture about 'enlightened preferences'.[25] They argue that campaigns inform individuals about candidates and parties and thus enlighten their electoral preferences over time. To Gelman and King, this means that certain fundamental variables, such as the voter's ideological orientation and party identification, and various demographic variables, such as class and race, better predict the vote as the campaign progresses. The hypothesis has a certain intuitive appeal, and ultimately may reflect priming and/or persuasion. It may be that campaigns prime certain factors, such as ideology, that cause them to increase in importance over time. It alternatively may be that campaigns persuade people, as candidates and parties take positions designed to win votes, for example. The difficulty is sorting among these possibilities.

Let us consider how underlying preferences evolved. For this, we again rely on the ICM polls. Specifically, we assess the evolution of vote intention for different demographics recorded in the surveys, specifically, age, gender, and social class. These are the only demographic variables included in the surveys. Although we might have expectations regarding age and gender, our theoretical expectations are strongest for class. ICM used the Market Research Society's A-E classification of social class based on occupation. In the coding scheme, 'A' designates upper middle class, 'B' middle class, 'C1' lower middle class, 'C2' skilled working class, and 'D' working class. The last category, 'E', designates people at the lowest level of subsistence. For purposes of analysis, ICM combined upper middle and middle class into one category, A/B, and working class and subsistence into a single category, D/E. This is common practice in political surveys. Table 4 summarises 'vote intention' responses across the different demographic categories both early and late in the campaign. As in Figure 1, the upper frame is based on responses from the first two April surveys, and the lower frame relies on data from the last April survey and the May pre-election survey. Once again, overall UK vote intention is included in the first column to provide a basis for comparison.

The top frame of Table 4 shows some demographic structure to vote preferences at the beginning of the campaign. Women were slightly—by two percentage points—more supportive of Labour and the Liberal Democrats than men and equally less supportive of the Conservatives and other parties. Older votes (65+) were almost twice as likely as young voters to support the Conservatives. They were much less likely to vote for the Liberal Democrats, who received most of their support from voters under the age of 35. Young voters also were more supportive of 'other' parties. The effect of age on Labour support was less pronounced, as vote preference ranged between 35% among the 65+ group

4. Vote Preferences by Selected Demographics Early and Late in the Campaign, 2005 (Percentages of Responses)

Early in the Campaign (April 1–12), Sample Size 1,738

Party	All	Gender		Age				Social Class			
		Male	Female	18–24	25–34	35–64	65+	A/B	C1	C2	D/E
Labour	38	37	39	40	39	38	36	33	34	45	43
Conservatives	34	35	33	24	26	34	43	35	38	29	30
Lib Dems	21	20	22	27	29	20	15	26	21	19	19
Other	7	8	6	9	7	8	6	6	7	7	8

Late in the Campaign (April 24–May 3), Sample size 1,514

Party	All	Gender		Age				Social Class			
		Male	Female	18–24	25–34	35–64	65+	A/B	C1	C2	D/E
Labour	39	37	40	44*	42*	39	33*	31	34	46	48*
Conservatives	33	35	30*	22	23*	33	43	38*	34*	29	26*
Lib Dems	22	21	23	24*	27	21	17	26	23	19	18
Other	7	7	7	10	8	7	7	6	9	7	8

Note: Numbers in bold designate a two-point change from early to late in the campaign; Numbers with an asterisk (*) designate a change of greater than two points. Source: ICM Research.

to 40% for the under-25s. The patterns are not surprising. As expected, social class also is important. The middle and upper middle classes (A/B) are more supportive of Conservatives than either of the other two parties. The lower middle class (C1) is as well. Among these groups, the Conservatives received an average of 36% of the vote share in the polls against 34% for Labour and 24% for the Liberal Democrats. Among the working class (C2 and D) and below (E), the portrait is quite different. Here support for Labour is about 44% on average against 30% for the Conservatives and 19% for the Liberal Democrats. Given the parties' positions and previous patterns of voting behavior, the differences come as little surprise.[26]

The underlying structure became even clearer during the campaign. This can be seen in the bottom frame of Table 4. Notice first that gender differences widened. Specifically, women became less supportive of the Conservatives. Preferences among men did not change. The result is a real, if small, gender gap in vote intention leading up to Election Day. The effects of age also changed during the campaign. It clearly became more important for the Labour vote, as support among young people increased and support among the elderly declined. Age became more important for the Conservative vote, as support dropped among young voters in approximate correspondence with Labour gains. For the Liberal Democrats, however, age mattered less late in the campaign than it did early on. That is, the differences across categories declined, particularly for the very young (18–24) and very old (65+), the latter of which actually became more supportive of the Liberal Democrats.[27]

The class structure evolved most of all. Support for both Labour and the Conservatives much more neatly reflected class differences toward the end of the campaign. Indeed, we see clear polarisation. Among middle and upper middle classes, support for Labour declined and for the Conservatives increased;[28] among the working class and those on at subsistence levels, support for Labour increased and for the Conservatives declined. There were no such effects for the Liberal Democrats, and the pattern of class voting remains comparatively modest, as expected given previous research. Indeed, the effect of class on Liberal Democrat support may be more apparent than real, reflecting differences in education.[29] (We cannot explicitly address this possibility given that the ICM data do not contain a measure of education.) It nevertheless is fairly clear that the campaign did in some way activate class interests, with implications for the distribution of Labour and Conservative voters. How exactly it happened, we do not know. The same is true for other demographic variables, the effects of which may not have been foreseen. There is reason to think that the issues emphasised and the strategies adopted by each of the parties, as well as the news media coverage of the election, influenced how preferences evolved. We just cannot be sure given our analysis. The nature of the process remains elusive.

Conclusion: the fundamentals and the campaign

Election outcomes are remarkably predictable.[30] Certain 'fundamental' variables matter. This was true in 2005. Our investigation indicates that the 30-day official campaign played an important role to effectively deliver these fundamentals on Election Day. In particular, we see that social cleavages, especially class, became much more pronounced as the campaign unfolded. We also observe increased gender- and age-related structuring. Although the official campaign mattered, the long campaign set the stage; indeed, electoral preferences at the national level were largely in place when the election was called on 5 April. Presumably, this partly reflects what the parties and candidates did. In 2005, the New Year began with political initiatives by the Conservatives and Liberal Democrats. There were the spring conferences and the party platforms. Candidates were in the field through the winter and spring. The official campaign now is only a part of a much longer campaign.

In one sense, the process begins the day after the last election. The 2009/10 campaign is *effectively* underway. Between now and Election Day, the parties will continually reposition themselves with the political future in mind. Candidates will do the same. The public, meanwhile, will update their evaluations of parties and candidates, especially about the performance and policies of the sitting government. What the opposition parties do also matters, of course. It clearly is not easy to win an election from across the aisle. It nevertheless is easier to win in some positions than in others. Crucially, parties can to a large extent control their locations. They can choose policy positions; they can select new party leaders; they can undertake activities that best exploit their advantages on the issues and their leaders. Candidates can do the same at the constituency level. This is what election campaigns are all about, as we saw in chapters 4–7. To a large extent, these campaigns serve to deliver the fundamentals on Election Day.

Yet campaigns can have less predictable effects. There is evidence of both in the 2005 election cycle. Of course, what we reveal at the national level may conceal more pronounced effects at the constituency level where 646 or so separate (though related) campaigns were waged. There is a strong hint of this in chapter 9, where we see that the swing in the vote between 2001 and 2005 was hardly uniform across constituencies. Given the differences in the balance of party preferences across constituencies and the focus of the campaigns on key marginal seats, this may come as little surprise. Given the advantages the government had, the final result on Election Day also comes as little surprise. It was Labour's election to lose, and they didn't lose it.

* We thank Nick Sparrow and Alan Perry of ICM for sharing data and results relating to the polls they conducted for the Guardian during the 2005 election campaign. We also thank Harold Clarke for helping us access the British Election Study data. For interesting and useful input on content, we thank Steve Fisher, Jane Green, Ron Johnston, James Tilley and especially John Curtice.

1 H. Clarke, D. Sanders, M. Stewart and P. Whiteley, *Political Choice in Britain*, Oxford University Press, 2004.

2 T. Holbrook, *Do Campaigns Matter?*, Sage, 1996; J.E. Campbell, *The American Campaign: US Presidential Campaigns and the National Vote*, Texas A&M University Press, 2000.

3 See, e.g. R. Johnston, A. Blais, H.E. Brady and J. Crete, *Letting the People Decide: Dynamics of a Canadian Election*, McGill-Queen's Press, 1992. Also see R. Johnston, M.G. Hagen and K. Hall Jamieson, *The 2000 Presidential Election and the Foundations of Party Politics*, Cambridge University Press, 2004.

4 For a detailed exposition of different models of campaign effects, see C. Wlezien and R.S. Erikson, 'The Timeline of Presidential Election Campaigns', 64 *Journal of Politics*, 2002, pp. 969–93.

5 The BBC poll tracker site is: http://news.bbc.co.uk/1/shared/vote2005/polltracker/html/polltracker.stm; the MORI compilation is at: http://www.mori.com/polls/trends/voting-allpub.shtml.

6 R.P. Daves, 'Who Will Vote? Ascertaining Likelihood to Vote and Modeling a Probable Electorate in Preelection Polls' in P. Lavrakas and M. Traugott (eds), *Election Polls, the News Media and Democracy*, Chatham House, 2000.

7 For more information on the methodologies employed by the different survey organisations, see the BBC website: http://news.bbc.co.uk/1/hi/uk_politics/vote_2005/basics/4275273.stm.

8 For surveys in the field for an even number of days, the fractional midpoint is rounded up to the following day. There is a good amount of variance in the number of days surveys are in the field: The mean number of days in the field is 3.06; the standard deviation is 1.09 days.

9 Note that polls on successive days are not truly independent. Although they do not share respondents, they do share overlapping *polling periods*—the periods during with surveys are in the field. Thus, poll results reported on neighboring days will, by definition, capture much of the same information.

10 Specifically, the probability that the movement is due to chance is less than one-in-a-hundred.

11 The smoothed series were generated using the 'lowess' (locally weighted scatterplot smoothing) procedure. This procedure creates a new value for each time point based on the results of regressions using a designated number of surrounding data points. To generate the new value, predictions from these regressions are weighted based on their temporal distance from the particular point in question. Lowess tends to follow the data quite well, though the degree to which it does depends on the bandwidth, or share of time points in the full series, one uses to generate the smoothed values. For this exercise, a bandwidth of 0.3, which means that (a rolling) 30% of the cases was used to generate each point. See W. Jacoby, *Statistical Graphics for Univariate and Bivariate Data*, Sage, 1997. For applications to pre-election polls, see R.S. Erikson and C. Wlezien, 'Presidential Polls as a Time Series: The Case of 1996', 63 *Public Opinion Quarterly*, 1999, pp. 163–77.

12 This is what the British Election Studies shows among likely voters, i.e. those scoring a '10' on their likelihood of voting scale: http://www.essex.ac.uk/bes/, though they overstated Labour's share at the end by about 1%. All of the other polls also overstated Labour's share—see http://news.bbc.co.uk/1/shared/vote2005/polltracker/html/polltracker.stm—except for NOP, who were spot on.

13 Data are drawn from the MORI on-line compilation: http://www.mori.com/polls/trends/voting-allpub.shtml. We exactly followed the procedures used with the 2005 polls, described in the text above.

14 Wlezien and Erikson, op. cit.

15 C. Wlezien and R.S. Erikson, 'Campaign Effects in Theory and Practice', 29 *American Politics Research*, 2001, pp. 419–36.

16 To generate these estimates, we simulate the voting day results at the constituency level, using Pippa Norris' *British Parliamentary Constituency Database, 1992–2005* at: http://ksghome.harvard.edu/~pnorris/datafiles/Britain%20Votes%202006%20Resources.htm. Specifically, we assume uniform swing and adjust the results in each constituency based on the changes in preferences from our exercise: (1) we subtracted 1.16% from Labour; (2) added 2.76% to the Conservatives; and (3) subtracted 3.25% from the Liberal Democrats.

17 See E. Gidengil, A. Blais, N. Nevitte and R. Nadeau, 'Priming and Campaign Effects: Evidence from Recent Canadian Elections' in D. Farrell and R. Schmitt-Beck (eds), *Do Political Campaigns Matter? Campaign Effects in Elections and Referendums*, Routledge, 2002. Also see the review in J.N. Druckman and J. W. Holmes, 'Does Presidential Rhetoric Matter? Priming and Presidential Approval', 34 *Presidential Studies Quarterly*, 2004, pp. 755–78.

18 Http://www.icmresearch.co.uk/reviews/pollreviews.asp.

19 For more specifics relating to their sampling and weighting methods, see the results pages for any of the specific polls on the ICM website: http://www.icmresearch.co.uk/reviews/pollreviews.asp.

20 See A. Campbell, P.E. Converse, W.E. Miller and D.E. Stokes, *The American Voter*, Wiley, 1960. Vote intention even appears to influence people's perceptions of the economic future and past. See C. Wlezien, M.N. Franklin and D. Twiggs, 'Economic Perceptions and Vote Choice: Disentangling the Endogeneity', 19 *Political Behavior*, 1997, pp. 7–17. It also appears to structure issue positions as well. See G. Evans

and R. Andersen, 'Do Issues Decide? Partisan Conditioning and Perceptions of Party Issue Positions across the Electoral Cycle', 14 *British Elections & Parties Review*, 2004, pp. 18–39.

21 Note that, due to rounding, the numbers in Table 1 do somewhat understate change in vote intention in the ICM polls.

22 See the MORI website: http://www.mori.com/polls/trends/issues12.shtml.

23 The BES internet rolling campaign data also reveals little change in issue importance during the campaign.

24 See A.F. Heath, R.M. Jowell and J.K. Curtice, *The Rise of New Labour: Party Policies and Voter Choices*, Oxford University Press, 2001, and Clarke, Sanders, Stewart and Whiteley, op. cit.

25 A. Gelman and G. King, 'Why are American Presidential Election Polls so Variable When Votes are so Predictable?', *British Journal of Political Science*, 1993, pp. 409–51. Also see the extensive examination of campaign communication in P. Norris, J. Curtice, D. Sanders, M. Scammell and H. Semetko, *On Message: Communicating the Campaign*, Sage, 1999.

26 See Clarke, Sanders, Stewart and Whiteley, op. cit.

27 Perhaps the party's promises on tax relief for the elderly really paid off.

28 Conservative support among the lower middle class (C1) did drop during the campaign, from a level that actually was above that for the upper middle and middle classes (A/B) to one in between that for A/B and the working classes. In one sense, support early on was 'too high' given the underlying class structure and the national political context.

29 G. Evans (ed.), *The End of Class Politics? Class Voting in Comparative Context*, Oxford University Press, 1999.

30 See D. Sanders, 'The Political Economy of UK Party Support, 1997–2004: Forecasts for the 2005 General Election', 15 *Journal of Elections, Public Opinion and Parties*, 2005, pp. 47–71. For a similar approach to US presidential elections, see J.E. Campbell, 'The Fundamentals in US Presidential Elections: Public Opinion, the Economy and Incumbency in the 2004 Presidential Election', 15 *Journal of Elections, Public Opinion, and Parties*, 2005, pp. 73–83.

INDEX